You're Here for a Reason

Discover and Life Your Purpose

By Marnie L. Pehrson

Highlighting Truth & Talent Through
www.pwgroup.com
www.IAmJoyful.com
www.SheLovesGod.com
www.MarniePehrson.com
www.IdeaMarketers.com

If you enjoy this book, please visit www.IAmJoyful.com
for more lessons, videos and audios.

Published by C.E.S. Business Consultants
Tel: 706-866-2295 * marnie@pwgroup.com
http://www.IAmJoyful.com/purpose/

Cover Design by Tammie Ingram of The Art Pad, Lehi, UT

ISBN 0-9676162-7-1
Library of Congress Control Number: 2008902586

Table of Contents

These 52 lessons were originally created as an online coaching program called "Rejoice in 2007." If you're interested in videos, audios and more lessons to accompany this book, please visit www.IAmJoyful.com.

Marnie L. Pehrson

About This Book

Is your life not going as you'd like it to? Do you struggle in relationships? Do you feel like you're a magnet for ill will or bad circumstances? Did you know that you have more control over these aspects of your life than you think? The people around you don't even need to change for you to get better results. The only person who needs to change is you. Most of this change need only be a shift in your thinking. With the right thoughts and beliefs, God can help you change.

At the core of how other people treat you is how you feel about yourself. I'm talking about more than self-esteem; I'm talking about taking control of who you are. You may believe your mindset is too hard to change or that old habits are too difficult to break; but if you're patient with yourself, it's really not as difficult as you think.

The first step is the most important. Think of the foundation of a home. Everything else rises upon it. If you lay a sturdy foundation, you control the stability of a home. Similarly, if you lay the proper foundation for who you are, then your life falls into place as well.

How do you create this foundation for success, happiness, and harmonious relationships? You might think it will be difficult, but really it's quite simple.

Everything hinges on you getting clear about who you want to be and your core values. Once you get clear on WHO you want to be, you'll write it down in a positive statement and memorize that statement. This action alone will set in motion a chain of events that will draw to you all the knowledge, people, and events to make it happen. It doesn't matter how far you currently are from the ideal. That doesn't matter any more than not having roofing shingles matters when you're laying the foundation of a house.

Once you lay the foundation, the walls will go up and you will start to become the ideal person you envisioned on paper. As you become this person, you change the way people perceive you, and thus the way they treat you. You'll start getting positive results instead of negative ones.

In 1991 my life felt out of control and unbalanced. I was going in a hundred directions – none of which were very effective. I took out some paper and a pen and jotted down 5 headings that represented different roles I filled in life: Daughter of God, Wife, Mother, Friend, and Business Owner.

Then I wrote down the type of person I'd like to be in each area of my life: how I would act and be if I were the ideal wife, mother, friend, etc. Once I had these written, I looked for the commonalities between each area and created one consolidated mission statement for my life.

I wrote it as a positive present-tense statement. I normally don't share this statement publicly, but I will here to show you how a statement can guide and direct your life without you even consciously knowing or realizing it:

> *"I am a daughter of God who gladly and selflessly gives more than she takes. I am a seeker of truth who makes truth an integral part of my life and personality, thus enabling me to share that truth with others. I am a woman who builds others up, helping them be the best they can be as I continue to develop my own mind, body, talents and abilities for the benefit and use of my God, family, country and fellowman."*

Your statement will be different than mine. It will fit you uniquely and it can take different forms. For example, a friend who has a unique gift for reaching out to others, giving them hope and helping them rise to their full potential uses the Prayer of Saint Francis as her mission statement:

Lord, make me an instrument of Thy peace;
where there is hatred, let me sow love;
where there is injury, pardon;
where there is doubt, faith;
where there is despair, hope;
where there is darkness, light;
and where there is sadness, joy.

O Divine Master,
grant that I may not so much seek to be consoled
as to console;
to be understood, as to understand;
to be loved, as to love;
for it is in giving that we receive,
it is in pardoning that we are pardoned,
and it is in dying that we are born to Eternal Life.. Amen.

Sometimes your mission statement might be a sentence or a theme. Phillip Davis, the official naming and branding expert at IdeaMarketers.com, sums up what he does by saying that he "creates environments where people thrive." Nancy Spivey, our real

Marnie L. Pehrson

estate investing expert, is all about "transformation" -- whether it's transforming lives, homes or neighborhoods. If I were to narrow my mission down to a simple theme it would be, "highlighting truth and talent." Look back at my original mission statement on the previous page, and you'll see this theme statement of "highlighting truth and talent" encapsulates all I do.

But I didn't have the simplified version back in 1991. I used the longer one. Once I wrote and polished the mission statement, I committed it to memory. I repeated it daily in the beginning, and compared my decisions against it. If something fit with my mission, I did it. If it was out of alignment, I didn't.

Over time, I honestly forgot about it. Several years passed and then in a conversation with a friend, I mentioned I had a mission statement. She wanted to hear it. As I quoted it from memory, I realized I had made great strides toward becoming the person described in the statement. Even she could see that I fit the description. As more years passed, I've pulled this mission statement to mind and each time I do, I marvel at this joyous journey that continues to shape me into the person I envisioned years ago.

Of all the things I could tell someone that would make lasting effective changes in their life, this is probably the simplest and most powerful. That is why over the next few lessons, I'll have you work on developing your mission statement. **If you have trouble with it, don't let it bog you down... just keep going through the lessons and keep mulling your mission statement in the back of your mind until it takes shape.**

Everyone is in a different place in their lives. Some people may easily formulate a mission statement. Others may have to ponder for many months. Don't force it. It will come in God's perfect time if you really desire to know it.

It is my prayer that by the time you reach the end of this book, you will be well on your way to understanding your purpose and living it. Not only that, but you'll have the tools and resources for demystifying life to a great degree. You'll know God better, and you'll know how He works in your life. You'll also know just how much He loves you and wants you to be all you can be.

Like a bird, you were born to fly in your own unique way. If you will trust God and trust the feelings He plants in your heart, you will come to know who you are at the core and who you were born to be.

Introduction: Would You Like to Leave a Legacy?

Somewhere deep inside each caring human heart is a desire to leave a legacy - to make a difference in the world. We want this planet to be a better place because we were here.

About 446 BC a Jew named Nehemiah wanted to make a difference for his people - just like you want to make a difference in your sphere of influence. His story holds important keys for discovering and living your purpose. Nehemiah was a cupbearer to the king of Persia. This was a trusted position for him to hold because he was to protect the king's food and drink from poisoning. One day while working in the palace a group of men from Judah came to visit him. Nehemiah asked them about the Jews who had left captivity and returned to their homeland of Jerusalem.

The men began to paint a picture for Nehemiah of the affliction and reproach the returning Jews were under. "The wall of Jerusalem is broken down," they said. "And the gates thereof are burned with fire." (Nehemiah 1:3) The Babylonian destruction of Jerusalem in about 586 BC left their homeland in rubble. After being carried off to Babylon for 70 years, the Jews returned under Persian King Cyrus who enabled them to rebuild their temple. They had expended every effort to rebuild the temple of Solomon from the foundation up and succeeded. But it appears the rest of their city still showed signs of captivity and death.

Being constantly surrounded by a visual reminder of their oppression and bondage did little to improve the Jews' spirit. The words used to describe the people were "afflicted" and under "reproach." Imagine how you'd feel in a burned out city, its walls crumbled and buildings still in ruins from a massive attack by a foreign power. Emotions like despair, despondency and hopelessness come to mind. The state of Jerusalem's wall and gate is a vivid illustration of how our external environment affects our internal state of mind and our resulting actions.

Upon hearing this dismal tale, Nehemiah *"sat down and wept, and mourned for days and fasted and prayed before the God of heaven"* (Nehemiah 1:4). His prayer is recorded in the remainder of chapter 1. He prayed for his people, and he acknowledged before God his own sins and the sins of his people which led them to destruction in the first place. They had intermarried with foreigners and forsook God to worship their spouses' false gods.

Have True Concern for Others and a Desire to Help Them

So here Nehemiah sat praying and fasting for days, calling upon God and reminding Him of His promises to gather Israel once more. His heart was completely drawn out toward God and his people. Nehemiah focused on others. He wasn't selfishly thinking of himself. He thought about his countrymen and their needs. This is the first step toward leaving a legacy: feel and sense the pain of others and have a desire to comfort and support them.

Fast, Pray and Repent

Nehemiah fasted and prayed for himself and especially for his people. He repented of his own sins — making himself a pure receptacle for truth and enlightenment and enabling him to be a righteous instrument in God's hands. When we put in that kind of "work" to seek God's face and His will, we clear our channels for revelation. Somewhere between Nehemiah chapters 1 and 2, Nehemiah got the idea to rebuild the wall and gates of Jerusalem. He pictured in his mind the Jewish homeland restored so they could be a nation again. **He gained a vision!**

Identify the Problem and the Possibilities

Notice that Nehemiah was in the unique position of being outside the rubble. He lived in the palace of the king. He knew the possibilities for beauty and order. He knew things didn't have to be chaotic and desolate. From his outside perspective, it was easier for him to have a vision of a restored Israel. Sometimes it takes spending time in a place of beauty and order so that when we come back to our day-to-day lives we can clearly see what we've been tolerating. It's important to step back and take breaks! Other times it takes a friend on the outside to help us see that things don't have to be the way they are.

Share Your Idea

As Nehemiah returned to work in the palace, the king noticed how sad Nehemiah was. He knew he wasn't sick, but he was concerned for his servant's state of mind. At first Nehemiah was afraid of disappointing the king. He was afraid to ask for time off to return to Jerusalem and rebuild the city wall. But the king pressed him to share what was on his mind. So Nehemiah said, *"Why should not my countenance be sad when the city, the place of my fathers' sepulchers lies in waste, and the gates thereof are consumed by fire?"* (Nehemiah 2:3)

The king replied, *"For what dost thou make request?"* This king was a friend to Nehemiah. He was concerned for him and wanted to help. So Nehemiah said a quick prayer to God and made his request to return to Judah and rebuild the land of his fathers. Not only did the king grant him leave, but also gave him letters that enabled Nehemiah to pass by any gatekeepers on his journey. The king even provided timber and supplies for rebuilding the gates and wall!

Had Nehemiah been too scared to share his idea with the king, he never could have accomplished his goal. Many of us break down at this step of the process. We might be afraid someone else will steal our idea and take credit for it. Or maybe we're afraid they'll make fun of us or tell us we can't do it. You have to share your ideas to make them happen. God has structured this world in such a way that we need each other to accomplish great things. You simply must open your mouth and share your big ideas with key people you trust. Otherwise you may never get it done.

Act, Act, and Keep on Acting

Nehemiah set off for the city of Jerusalem, walked into town, and in an inspiring speech enlisted citizens to help him rebuild the city wall and gates: *"Ye see the distress that we are in, how Jerusalem lieth waste, and the gates thereof are burned with fire: come and let us build up the wall of Jerusalem, that we be no more a reproach."* Then he told them how good God had been to him and how the king had helped. *"Let us rise up and build!"* he said. In response, the people *"strengthened their hands for this good work"* (Nehemiah 2:17-18).

Stick to Your Purpose and Your Vision

Almost immediately, people came to laugh at him and accused him of wanting to rebuild the city wall so that he could rebel against the king and set himself up as king.

Nehemiah ignored the scoffers and continued. As things progressed, his enemies did various things to try to stop the work. They claimed the king was on to him and was coming after him to punish him. They brought him false prophesies of people out to kill him and suggested he hide in the temple for protection. Nehemiah refused to listen to them. He would not succumb to fear.

They tried to distract him by sending him letters asking him to leave the wall and come speak with them about what he was doing. For Nehemiah the time for talking had ended. It was time to act and keep on acting. He and his men watched continually against their enemies but kept on working. In the end, Nehemiah finished the wall and gates and served as governor of Judah for twelve years.

Marnie L. Pehrson

If we wish to make a difference in the world — if we wish to live a life of joy, purpose and passion — we too must follow the steps that Nehemiah followed. Nehemiah went down in history as more than a man who built a wall. He was a man who inspired the Jews to rise up from the ashes and live in hope. His wall is a perfect example of how our outward environments affect our inward state of mind. More importantly his wall is a symbol of every broken life, every soul in bondage, who turns to the Savior of the world and through repentance finds life instead of death, freedom instead of captivity, and hope instead of desolation.

Challenge

Look around you for people in need. Pray to God for those you have a heart to help. Ask Him how you can be of service. Repent where necessary and allow yourself to be God's chosen vessel worthy of His enlightenment and guidance. When your inspired idea comes, share it with those you trust and enlist their aid in the journey. Nehemiah couldn't do it alone and neither can you! God has placed within your circle people who can make your vision a reality. Trust Him to provide those people and then walk forward in faith. Stick to your purpose and your vision and act, act, and keep on acting no matter what opposition or potential distractions may come.

If you will do this, I promise you a life of passion, happiness and joy!

Lesson 1: Evaluate the Building Blocks of Your Mission

In preparation for creating your mission statement, this lesson gives you a chance to get to know yourself by taking a little inventory. Please don't skip this worksheet. It will help you evaluate your talents and interests. They are an important part of God's plan for your life and understanding them will help you do a better job of creating your mission statement.

Isaiah 51:1 gives the ingredients for being a righteous servant of the Lord, "Hearken to me, ye that follow after righteousness, ye that seek the Lord: look unto the **rock whence ye are hewn**, and to the **hole of the pit** whence ye are digged." When you are trying to understand your mission, you'll want to look to two important places -- the rock from whence you were hewn (who you are) and the hole of the pit from whence you were dug (where you've been).

The Rock Whence Ye Were Hewn

The rock whence ye were hewn is what you are made of - who you are. You are a child of God, hewn from The Rock - God Himself. You have spiritual gifts which you inherited from Him. In addition, you have unique talents, characteristics, interests, and abilities. This is the rock from whence you are hewn. So when trying to understand your divine destiny, it is important to evaluate your interests and talents. Use the following questions to help you evaluate them.

Take a Talent Inventory   **Date(s):** _____

What do people tell you that you do well? What kind of compliments do you receive from others -- now or in the past?

_____
_____
_____
_____
_____
_____
_____
_____

Marnie L. Pehrson

What kind of activities do you enjoy?

_____
_____
_____
_____
_____

Do you relate better to children, youth, adults, the elderly, animals?

_____
_____
_____
_____
_____
_____

What is your preferred method of communicating? On the phone? Email? Writing? Speaking? Teaching?

_____
_____
_____
_____
_____
_____

Do you enjoy helping a friend with his/her problems? (Explain)

_____
_____
_____
_____
_____
_____

Do you enjoy music? In what ways: listening, playing, performing, leading, writing?

_____

_____

_____

_____

Do you enjoy the arts? What types: painting, drawing, crafts, quilting, building things, sewing, decorating, writing, photography, Web design, scrapbooking etc?

_____

_____

_____

_____

_____

_____

_____

_____

Do you enjoy gardening, landscaping, growing flowers, plants, or vegetables?

_____

_____

_____

_____

Do you enjoy cooking? Entertaining?

_____

_____

_____

_____

_____

Do you enjoy cleaning and organizing?

_____

_____

Do you enjoy reading? Silently? Aloud to others? Do you enjoy sharing what you've learned in books with others?

_____

_____

What else do you enjoy? What motivates you?

_____

_____

_____

_____

Do you have a secret wish? Something you've always wanted to do but were too afraid or felt too inadequate to try?

_____

_____

_____

_____

_____

_____

_____

_____

_____

_____

_____

_____

_____

_____

Combine your interests. For example, let's suppose you enjoy visiting with friends, quilting, and reading. You might gather with a group of women each week or each month and work on quilts and discuss uplifting books that you read with them. In this way you can uplift and inspire others while sharing and developing your God-given gifts.

Or maybe you enjoy young people, creating crafts and painting. You might volunteer to work with youth groups, teaching them how to make crafts or how to paint. In this way you are building and developing your own talent while helping youth do something positive and uplifting as well as helping them develop their own talents.

In the space provided below, brainstorm ways you could combine your interests with your feelings of compassion toward others.

_____

_____

_____

_____

_____

_____

_____

_____

_____

_____

_____

_____

_____

_____

_____

_____

_____

_____

_____

_____

Marnie L. Pehrson

The Hole of the Pit Whence Ye Were Digged

What challenges or trials have you endured and overcome? What lessons have you learned through the school of hard knocks? This is the hole of the pit from whence you were dug. God doesn't want you to berate yourself for past mistakes for which He has forgiven you; neither does He wish you to be bitter or feel He loves you any less because of the hardships you've endured. He wants you to remember how He delivered you. He wants you to remember what you were before He transformed you. Remembering this will keep you grateful and better able to serve others.

God never wastes the pain. When you turn your life over to Him, He can make all your mistakes, poor choices, and unfortunate circumstances work together for your good, and usually for the good of others. Countless individuals are able to, with God's help, overcome difficult trials such as lawsuits, divorce, financial ruin, addictions, and abuse and then use those experiences to better understand and help others who are enduring similar circumstances.

Even though you may feel alone in your challenges, there is no temptation or challenge which is not common to others (1 Corinthians 10:13). The trials that you endure and the lessons you learn in overcoming them build valuable character traits and knowledge that you can use to serve others going through similar troubles.

Examine Your Past   Date(s): _____

What personal or business challenges have you endured and/or overcome? What do you feel like you've learned from them?

_____
_____
_____
_____
_____
_____
_____
_____
_____
_____
_____

_____

_____

_____

_____

_____

_____

_____

_____

_____

_____

_____

_____

_____

_____

_____

_____

_____

_____

_____

_____

_____

_____

_____

_____

_____

Marnie L. Pehrson

Combining the Rock and the Pit

Your mission will involve using your life experiences combined with your unique talents and interests as an instrument in God's hands to selflessly serve others. It's that simple. He gave you everything you need to accomplish your mission. It's what you are ideally suited to do.

Be prayerful. Ask the Lord to help you catch a vision of your mission. Prayerfully consider the following questions. What do you like to do and with whom do you like to spend your time? What lessons have you learned from your journey through life? Combine these three in as many ways as you can think of and then prayerfully select the most appealing combination with which to start.

Here's an example. Let's say you have overcome addictions in your life, enjoy the goal-setting process and working with youth. You could combine these experiences and interests by volunteering as a youth mentor: helping youth to set and achieve worthy goals and to stay away from drugs.

Another example, let's say you're a woman who was once overweight, but have learned to adapt your eating and exercise habits to be healthier and maintain an ideal weight. If you also enjoy the company of other women, you might start a support group for women where you study healthy eating habits, hold each other accountable, and exercise together.

Don't feel as if you have to create a "ministry" to be of service to God. Your employment, your role as a parent, and the everyday things you do in life build His kingdom when you do them with an eye single to His glory. Think of the honey bee. It goes about its work gathering pollen, and in the end it pollinates a world and provides a sweet treasure for mankind. Don't underestimate any of your talents or gifts. Never perceive them as only "temporal." Everything to God is spiritual.

Most of all, enjoy yourself! Heavenly Father created you that you might have joy, and joy is to be found in service. He gave you your innate talents, abilities and interests so that you could build your self worth while serving and edifying others. He never wastes the road you've traveled.

Brainstorm Combinations

Use the journal space below to brainstorm ways that you can combine what you like to do, with whom you like to spend your time, and the lessons you've learned in your journey through life. Don't worry about "how" you'll do these things and don't spend a lot of time worrying about whether you want to do each one that badly. Just brainstorm and let your thoughts flow on ways that you can selflessly serve others by combining these three things.

Note: This isn't your final mission statement. We'll work on that in lesson 2. Just have fun brainstorming here and ponder and pray for the Lord's guidance on knowing how you can best serve Him in joyful ways.

_____

_____

_____

_____

_____

_____

_____

_____

_____

_____

_____

_____

_____

_____

_____

_____

_____

_____

_____

Marnie L. Pehrson

Date(s): _____

_____

_____

_____

_____

_____

_____

_____

_____

_____

_____

_____

_____

_____

_____

_____

_____

_____

_____

_____

_____

_____

_____

_____

_____

_____

_____

_____

Marnie L. Pehrson

Lesson 2: Define Your Mission

Remember, you may not be able to immediately create your mission statement. It may take time - even several months. Just do your best by prayerfully completing the following exercise while keeping in mind what you learned in lesson one about your life experiences, talents and interests. If you have trouble with this lesson, don't let it immobilize you... go on to the next lesson and keep the thoughts of your mission statement percolating in the back of your mind.

1. *Create mini-mission statements for each area of your life (give some thought and time to developing these.)* For each area listed below, write down the characteristics of the person you would like to be - the person that would make you happiest and most fulfilled. Describe the "ideal you" in each area of your life. Use only positive attributes and characteristics. For example, instead of saying, "never scream at my kids" you could say "always respond to others with patience, love and consistency."

Child of God
Friend
Wife/Husband
Mother/Father
Career/Business Person
Citizen

Other roles you fulfill might include: Grandparent, Sunday School Teacher, Physical Development, Athlete, etc. Use the space provided for each of your roles. Use as many of these as needed.

Role:_____

_____

_____

_____

_____

_____

_____

_____

Role:_____

_____

_____

_____

_____

_____

_____

_____

_____

_____

Role:_____

_____

_____

_____

_____

_____

_____

_____

Role:_____

_____

_____

_____

_____

_____

_____

_____

Marnie L. Pehrson

Role:_____

_____

_____

_____

_____

_____

_____

_____

_____

_____

Role:_____

_____

_____

_____

_____

_____

_____

_____

_____

Role:_____

_____

_____

_____

_____

_____

_____

Create a Summary Mission Statement

Next, create a summary mission statement based on the contents and similarities of the mini mission statements. By now you should have completed a paragraph or two under each area. Go back and reread your statements for each of these areas. Look for the similarities and common characteristics found among them all. For example, under your *Mother* heading it may say "Give the necessary time and attention to my children." Under business you may have "Listen to the needs of my customers with respect and a desire to serve them." Both deal with other people and giving them the necessary respect, attention and sincere listening. So, your summary mission statement would include something like this, "Always listen to others with respect and attention and a desire to serve their needs."

Create a Rough Draft of Your Summary Mission Statement

Compose a summary mission statement by analyzing your mini-mission statements for commonalties. Some areas may contain statements that do not cross into other areas. Write these in a broad way in your summary statement so that it can be applicable to other areas of your life.

Once you have all the ideas in your summary mission statement, read over it. Take time to polish it. Rewrite it if necessary until it means something to you and can be a part of your life.

Use the space below to create rough drafts of your mission statement until you have it polished to a succinct statement that you can write on a card and keep with you at all times.

_____

_____

_____

_____

_____

_____

_____

_____

Marnie L. Pehrson

Date(s): _____

_____

_____

_____

_____

_____

_____

_____

_____

_____

_____

_____

_____

_____

_____

_____

_____

_____

_____

_____

_____

_____

_____

_____

_____

_____

_____

_____

_____

Date(s): _____

_____
_____
_____
_____
_____
_____
_____
_____
_____
_____
_____
_____
_____
_____
_____
_____
_____
_____
_____
_____
_____
_____
_____
_____
_____
_____
_____

Marnie L. Pehrson

Look At Your Mission Statement Daily

Now, write your statement on a 3x5 card and put it somewhere you will see it daily or even twice a day. You could use your 3x5 card as a bookmark for your scriptures so that you will be sure to read it every day. Work on memorizing it. Then, when an opportunity develops, run through your mission statement in your mind to see if it is compatible. If it is incompatible with your mission statement, do not do it.

It is amazing how quickly this mission statement becomes a part of you. You will not immediately change your actions and become the person on the card, but you will catch yourself when you are doing something contrary to your mission statement. Your mission statement will direct your actions and the goals you set. It also helps eliminate many last minute decisions. Be patient. No one changes overnight. It took time to develop your current habits and characteristics, and it will take time to change them. Yet, it is amazing how a few weeks of reading this statement daily will lead you, almost subconsciously, toward opportunities that fulfill your mission.

Lesson 3: Walk with God

"And Enoch walked with God: and he was not; for God took him"
(Genesis 5:24).

In the Old Testament we read that both Enoch and Noah "walked with God." Most of the time we think of this as a metaphorical walk, but what if it was a literal one? In the summer of 2006, I started the habit of walking 5-6 days/week. During this walk, I take time to pray, review my mission statement, count my blessings and memorize scripture passages.

It didn't take long before this practice became the highlight of my day. If I wake up in a bad mood, I go for a walk in the morning and by the end I'll be in a cheerful mood and in a grateful state of mind. If I miss a day walking, it is as if I've missed a spiritual feast.

(Note: If you are disabled and can't walk, please keep reading. This lesson can be adapted for your circumstances.)

A Little Preparation

1) **Find your location to walk.** Optimally your walk will take place in a natural outdoor setting where you can appreciate God's creations. This might be a park, a field, your neighborhood. If this isn't possible you could walk around your office complex. In case of inclement weather you can walk inside your house, on a treadmill, or in a mall. Find somewhere you can walk without being interrupted by other people. Even walking in a mall, you can have some level of solitude if no one's stopping you to interrupt your thoughts. It just won't be advisable to pray aloud in a public setting. (If you can't walk, find a peaceful place to go and meditate upon this exercise.)

2) **There are scripture verses at http://www.IAmJoyful.com/verses.php** that you can use. You can put them on index cards or card stock.

3) **Put your scripture cards and a copy of your mission statement in your back pocket or your purse.** I keep my scriptures and mission statement in my back pocket at all times. When I change jeans, I just move them over.

Marnie L. Pehrson

Walking with God

> *"Noah was a just man and perfect in his generations, and Noah walked with God"* (Genesis 6:9).

Here's the format that works for me as I walk. If you can't walk, go through these steps in a quite, peaceful place:

1) **Count your blessings.** Spend the first part of your walk offering a prayer of gratitude for all the good in your life. Really think of the good that surrounds you. On a bad day, it may simply be the sunshine on your back, the birds singing and other beauties of God's world around you. Start looking for the good and thank the Lord for everything – even your trials, for they are your opportunity to learn and grow. Make this a prayer of complete gratitude. Ask for nothing. The only exception might be to ask for His help in memorizing your scripture passages.

2) **Pull out one scripture card and read over it several times.** It helps if you can read it aloud. Then take one line at a time and try to memorize it. Some scriptures may be easier to memorize than others. Some can be memorized in a day, others may take several days. Work on one card until you have it memorized. Really think about the verse and what it means to you.

3) **Review** - As days pass and you've memorized more verses, review each of the previous verses you've memorized and quote them from memory each day – so that they stay with you.

4) **Review your mission statement - read it, commit it to memory.** If you have it memorized, quote it to yourself and really think about it.

5) **Spend the rest of your walk praying and talking to your Father in Heaven** – really talk to Him about your life – your troubles, concerns, your mission, and what He wants you to do for the day. Remember to close all prayers in the name of Jesus Christ so that you're always focusing on Him and evoking Him as your advocate with the Father. Remember, He is on your side! He wants you to experience joy.

6) **Listen** – spend some time in quiet contemplation, listening for God's reply.

As you walk with God each day, you'll start to see a change in your attitude and in your ability to identify and listen to the Spirit.

While I enjoy walking in the morning because it starts my day in a wonderful way, you may need to adapt when and where you walk to fit your own climate, capabilities, and situation.

If your health is such that you cannot walk, then go through these steps without walking. But if you can walk, do it. There is something powerful about engaging both your body and spirit in a conscious effort to communicate with your Father in heaven.

Lesson 4: Make Room for Joy!

Now that you have an idea about "what" you want and "who" you want to be, it's time to make room for it. Most of us have dozens of things that waste our time, drain our energy, or block our paths. They may be little or they may be big, but even if they are tiny, cumulatively they add up and place a heavy burden on our backs.

These "stressors" are things we tolerate. We allow them to exist and put up with them for various reasons. Some examples of stressors are clutter, clothes that don't fit, a car that frequently breaks down, extra weight, a job that makes you miserable, inadequate income, annoying coworkers, demanding bosses, controlling family members, a house that's too small for your needs, self-imposed deadlines, bad habits, unresolved issues with family or friends, or poor diet.

Anything or anyone can be a stressor. If it's not helpful… if it's hindering your progress… it's a stressor.

You might say, well everyone has little things that stress them out. It's just part of life. Everyone has something to put up with. That might be true, but if you can eliminate or reduce the number of things you put up with, you can liberate an immense amount of time and energy to do what brings you joy. It's been said that if Satan can't make you bad, he'll make you busy. Stressors are often the "busy work" Satan makes us believe is necessary. He keep us so busy with these tasks that we never get around to being who we are meant to be. Stressors are the things that distract us, that keep us from growing and moving forward, and from dealing with important issues. They lower the quality of our lives and bring negative thoughts instead of positives ones.

If you reduce the number of things that you tolerate and that bring you stress, then you'll free up the time and energy to live your God-given mission and find true joy!

> Jesus said, *"Come unto me, all ye that labor and are heavy laden, and I will give you rest. Take my yoke upon you, and learn of me; for I am meek and lowly in heart: and ye shall find rest unto your souls. For my yoke is easy, and my burden is light"* (Matthew 11:28-30).

A "yoke" is a tool that animals or humans wear on their backs. It enables them to carry heavier burdens than they normally could. If a yoke isn't fitted properly it can chafe and cause great discomfort. If a yoke is properly fitted to the wearer, it makes his/her burdens light. Christ can fit you with the ideal yoke that will help you feel peace during your greatest challenges. But the thing is, it is counterproductive to keep wearing your old yoke while attempting to take up His.

Each of us has our own ways of dealing with burdens. Some hide from them with drugs, alcohol, food or busyness, but these are not effective yokes. They wear you down and damage your body and spirit. Tacking Christ's yoke on top of your ill-fitted and burdensome yoke is not only foolish but also ineffective. You must first lay down your yoke.

One way you can lay aside your yoke and make room for His is to remove as many of the stressors in your life as you can. By doing so, you'll liberate yourself and make room for Christ's peaceful, easy yoke. Later on in the year, we will talk about other yokes that burden us; but for this exercise, we'll deal with typical stressors.
Before I give you the exercise for identifying and eliminating your stressors, I should mention why you might feel tempted to keep them.

1. First, Satan doesn't want you to eliminate them – especially if you have a goal to use your redeemed time and energy in the service of God. Satan may tempt you to postpone or "wait until conditions are more ideal" to do something about your stressors. I cannot emphasize enough how important it is to ignore him and act now in areas where you can.

2. Second, you may feel you don't have the time or energy to deal with the things that you tolerate. Taking the time to identify your stressors can work wonders. Please don't skip this exercise. It can make or break your success in achieving your dreams. Once you identify them and commit to eliminating them, God will open doors of opportunity to help you do so. Don't let a perceived lack of time or energy hold you back. God is not limited by your time or energy.

3. Third, sometimes we tolerate things because it helps us avoid taking responsibility for our lives. For example, you might put up with the dominating parent because it's easier to say, "She won't let me" than it is to act and do something about your life. Or it may be easier to blame your dilapidated car for not pursuing a better education. Don't let your stressors become excuses for not taking responsibility for your life.

Marnie L. Pehrson

The benefits of removing even your smallest stressors can be immeasurable. Doing so will free up your energy and time and enable you to enjoy a greater quality of life. If you redeem that time and energy and devote it toward your mission, you'll see miracles occur. I can testify to that! So let's get started…

Step 1: Admit that your stressors are not working for you. Stress, drama and crisis are not adding to your spiritual, physical or emotional well-being. Admit that. Some people thrive on drama. Don't be one of them. That's just Satan's way of neutralizing you. The time and energy you waste on drama is time and energy God can't use to bring you joy.

Step 2: Commit to getting rid of your stressors. Make a sincere commitment to the process. It may take weeks, months or even years to completely eliminate them; but if you'll commit, God will open doors for you. A way will be made for you to live a simpler "drama free" life that enables you to find true joy and happiness in what you were born to do.

Step 3: Identify your stressors. Use the space below to identify the things you put up with. Make a **specific** list. For example, don't just say your house is messy, get specific – your closet is cluttered, your kitchen counters have junk piled on them, etc.

Around the House

_____

_____

_____

_____

_____

_____

_____

_____

Your Car

_____

_____

_____

_____

_____

_____

Other material things you own

_____
_____
_____
_____
_____
_____
_____
_____

Your finances

_____
_____
_____
_____
_____
_____
_____
_____

Your health/physical appearance

_____
_____
_____
_____
_____
_____
_____
_____

Your career

_____
_____
_____
_____

Marnie L. Pehrson

_____

_____

_____

_____

Your relationships

_____

_____

_____

_____

_____

_____

_____

_____

_____

_____

_____

_____

Church and community

_____

_____

_____

_____

_____

_____

_____

Miscellaneous

_____

_____

_____

_____

Step 4: Identify what your stressors are costing you. What are you missing out on because you have each of these stressors in your life? As you go through this process, you'll probably see that a few of your stressors are causing the others. They are your root issues. Deal with them, and others will fall into place. For example, a job that doesn't pay well enough could keep you low on funds. Not having enough money can keep you from repairing cars, your house, and other belongings. Find a new job that pays well and the other things would fall into place.

Step 5: Figure out what it would take to fix or eliminate your stressors. I remember several years of my life when I put up with having a house that was painted an ugly yellow green and that had an overgrown back yard. Finally we put it up for sale and fixed the problems. We spent about $600 to have the house fixed up and it was like a new place. It made me sick because I realized I could have been living in a house that made me feel good all that time, but I always assumed it would cost thousands to repair instead of only hundreds.

Make calls, get estimates, and find out exactly what it will cost in time, labor or materials to fix your stressors. It may not be as bad as you think. And if it's a lot, don't worry. One of my stressors was a ½ mile dirt driveway that needed several truckloads of gravel. It would cost thousands to repair, but one day our neighbor (who owns a sod farm and uses our road to work his farm) regraveled it for us! It came totally by surprise.

We had no idea he intended to do it, nor had we ever mentioned it to him. Identify your stressors and commit to removing them and God will provide a way.

Step 6: Commit to invest your time and resources into eliminating your stressors. Everything hinges on commitment. *The moment of decision is the key to your treasure chest of miracles.*

Step 7: Deal with each stressor completely. Don't do the job halfway. For example, don't jimmy rig a repair on your car only to have it break down again in three months. Get it completely repaired or replaced so the problem doesn't return.

Now that you've gone through these steps, act now on the ones you can quickly remedy or remove. Then put your list away. Don't obsess over it. This is not your "to do" list. Don't look at it every day. You might pull it out once every few weeks or once a

Marnie L. Pehrson

month to see how you're doing. But you don't want to focus on negatives and these are negatives. Just having identified your stressors and committed to do something about them will lead you subconsciously toward dealing with them. Opportunities will arise. Act upon inspiration and you'll be surprised at how the Lord will lead you to solutions.

Lesson 5: Drop and Give Me 20

Ever wake up in a bad mood? Ever have to do something you just don't want to do? Ever get stuck in a negative frame of mind where you can't think of anything good? I used to work with a sales team, and some days they just weren't up to making phone calls. There was a little trick I had them use to turn around their frame of mind before they ever picked up the phone. I had them "drop and give me 20." Not 20 pushups, no. I had them drop what they were doing and list on paper 20 things for which they were grateful. It was amazing to watch the results they achieved after this little exercise.

It works for anything – list 20 things you're grateful for in your life and your outlook will change in an instant. It also works when you're dissatisfied with other people.

- List 20 things you love about your spouse (when s/he's not so loveable).

- List 20 things you love about your children when they're driving you nuts.

- List 20 things you're grateful for about your job when it's stressing you.

- List 20 things you appreciate about your coworkers when they're difficult.

So that's your assignment… drop what you're doing and give me 20 things you're grateful for in your life. Don't skip this… really think…

1

2

3

4

5

6

7

8

9

10

Marnie L. Pehrson

11

12

13

14

15

16

17

18

19

20

Don't you feel better now? The next time you're in a bad mood or are having a bad day, drop what you're doing and list 20 things for which you're grateful. Make this a tool in your toolbox.

Lesson 6: Let the Attitude of Gratitude Adjust Your Altitude

Jesus taught, *"Ask, and it shall be given you; seek, and ye shall find; knock, and it shall be opened unto you: For every one that asketh receiveth; and he that seeketh findeth; and to him that knocketh it shall be opened. Or what man is there of you, whom if his son ask bread, will he give him a stone? Or if he ask a fish, will he give him a serpent?"* (Matthew 7:7-10)

God wants to give good things to his children, but nowhere does He say, "gripe and ye shall receive" or "whine and it shall be opened unto you." Nor did he say "pester me and you'll get what you want." He simply said to ask. Once we've asked and we've received an answer or a feeling of peace, we should expect that what we've asked for will arrive in God's good time. James 1:5-6 tells to "ask in faith, nothing wavering."

But sometimes we become discouraged, and we fall back into griping or doubting. It can be difficult to hold the right attitude — an attitude of faith and expectant hope - when circumstances appear as if you're standing still or moving in reverse.

I have performed a series of "experiments" (for lack of a better word) on the principle of gratitude. These "tests" have been very enlightening and quite effective in not only shifting my attitude from doubt to faith but also in unlocking the blessings that God has in store for me.

Whenever I hit a problem or challenge, my initial human reaction is one of the following:

- get angry, upset or pout

- start to lose faith that things are going to work out

- blame myself or others for my misfortune

- give up hope

- assume God is giving me a "serpent" when I asked for a "fish."

None of these are productive or healthy. Each of these reactions slackens my hope, weakens my faith, and distances me from God and my worthwhile goals. For you see, all the promises are unto them that believe. None of these human reactions foster faith — none of them persuades one to believe. Without faith, nothing happens.

Marnie L. Pehrson

STEP 1: Decide "what" you want and "when" you want it.

I have made it a practice of turning myself around when I catch myself reacting to a disappointment in a negative way. Instead of entertaining myself with a pity party, I force myself to examine the situation and ask: what would have to happen in this situation to make me feel better about it? What do I want?

For example, when my refrigerator and car broke down in the same week, I asked myself what would resolve the situation to my satisfaction. I wanted them both fixed and I wanted it done in a specific time and within a certain budget.

When the car I'd purchased with my savings only 3 months before blew a gasket, I asked myself what solution would satisfy me. What I really wanted was to stop driving 10-year-old vehicles. I was spending more on repairs and replacing them than I would with a car payment on a newer vehicle. I wanted a van that was still under warranty, that ran well and that I could rely on to take our six children where they needed to go. Instead of settling for what I could "get by on," I decided what would make me feel satisfied and secure in our mode of transportation.

STEP 2: Pray and get a confirmation that your desires are in harmony with God's will for you.

The next step is to pray about your desires and ask for a confirmation that what you want is what God wants for you. For example, in the case of the desire for a new van, I prayed for a couple weeks about whether it was what God wanted for our family before the answer finally came — literally within a few hours before the decision had to be made.

STEP 3: Write a gratitude statement and repeat it.

I am about to explain how I use a gratitude statement to shift my thinking. Please note that there is nothing magical or mystical about a gratitude statement other than that it shifts your own mind from fear to faith and from doubt to belief. Remember that faith is the "substance of things hoped for and the evidence of things not seen" (Hebrews 11:1). Your ability to muster faith is critical in your ability to take possession of blessings. Thus, a gratitude statement is simply a tool to help you achieve a level of faith that God can use to bring about your "miracle."

A gratitude statement should be written in the present tense and start with something like, "I am so happy and grateful now that . . . ." It should end with a statement that ensures that everything happens in the best way. For example, I use, "I am so excited, thrilled and amazed to see these things happening in ways that are for the highest good for us and all concerned. Thank you!"

Here's an example of a gratitude statement at work. One time, because of some unexpected expenditures, I didn't have the money to meet some important obligations. My initial reaction was to get upset and begin to doubt. But then I remembered that on so many occasions the Lord had pulled us through in a pinch. He has confirmed to me time and again that He will care for us if we will put our trust in Him. So, pulling myself up by my bootstraps, I took a break from my pity party and decided to use gratitude to change my attitude.

Instead of giving up hope and assuming the worst, I forced myself to take a hard look at my finances and make a list of what was due by a specific date. I totaled it and decided on the dollar value that would satisfy my obligations and would meet our family's needs for a given period of time. In this case it was a 3-day period. I decided on the dollar amount needed within that period to meet our obligations.

It was a rather large amount and while my husband and I each had paychecks coming in over the next 3 days, they would only cover two-thirds of the amount needed. The rest would have to come from somewhere else. Instead of worrying about "how" this would happen, I crafted a gratitude statement which I began to repeat to myself. It went something like this:

> "I am so happy and grateful that at least $X in funds are flowing into my bank accounts by [Specific Date] enabling us to meet all our needs and obligations for this period of time. I am excited, thrilled and amazed to see this happening in ways that are for the highest good for us and all concerned. Thank you!"

After offering a prayer of thanks that what I needed was on its way, I began repeating the statement in my mind and aloud. Remember it's not God I was trying to convince — it was myself! The first day — when I was most discouraged — I repeated it nearly a hundred times. I'd say it out loud as I was driving down the road, or in my mind as I was cleaning my house. It was amazing how quickly my negative attitude shifted to one of hope and positive expectation. I began to get excited to see how the Lord would make that money flow into my bank accounts. The following days I started my day by repeating the gratitude statement several times or whenever a discouraging doubt crept into my mind.

At the end of the "deadline" I was still about 10% short of the amount specified, but things had happened over those days to allow me more time to meet certain obligations. In the end, we had what we needed when we needed it. The Lord provided.

I have used gratitude to activate blessings time and again and while my deadlines are not always met, my needs are. In the activation of blessings, you specify the "what" and let God take care of the "when" and "how." It's an exercise in faith and patience, but it is amazing how gratitude can turn around your attitude and give you faith when you don't think you can muster another ounce of it.

So now it's your turn to use gratitude to shift your attitude so God can adjust your altitude:

Step 1: Decide "what" you want and "when" you want it.

Hint: reflect on your "stressors" from Lesson 4. Select something from your list that you'd like to improve/change. Select something that doesn't seem impossible, but is still a stretch. Write down what you would like to have happen, by when, and how much you're willing to invest, spend or devote to make it happen. What would make you feel like the situation is resolved to your complete satisfaction?

Step 2: Pray and get a confirmation that your desires are in harmony with God's will for you. If you felt a feeling of peace and assurance after your prayer, document it here. If you felt uncertainty, confusion, or like you were going to forget the thing you decided to ask for, then either tweak what you're asking for until it feels right or ask for something else.

Step 3: Write a gratitude statement and repeat it as much as you can. The objective here is to bolster your faith and your belief. Remember to write it in all positive words and phrases. Don't use the word "not" or "isn't." Use all positive phrases and write it as if it's present tense. You can use words like "at least" to set lower limits on what you want and still leave room for something better. For example, "I am so happy and grateful for an enjoyable job that pays at least $75,000 per year where I work 45 hours per week or less."

Marnie L. Pehrson

I am so happy and grateful now that…

… I am excited and grateful to see all this or something even better happening in ways that are for the highest good for me and all concerned. Thank you!

Step 4: Repeat your gratitude statement. Read it or recite it 100 times. If what you've selected seems difficult, then write it 100 times. Listen to your heart and your body. Headaches, irritation, and unease that develop as you read or write your statement are signals that you need to tweak the wording of your statement. Change the wording as necessary until it feels right and you have no physical "side effects."

As you read or write your statement, jot down any ideas or insights that come to your mind here:

Marnie L. Pehrson

Step 5: Continue to express gratitude to God even if things do not develop exactly when or how you specified.

As we cultivate a continual spirit of gratitude, we draw nearer to God from whom all blessings flow. Try the power of gratitude each time life throws you a lemon and see if God won't help you turn it into some sweet lemonade. Use this worksheet over and over again. Make it a part of your life until the steps are second nature to you. As you do so, you'll see your faith muscles grow in wonderful ways.

Lesson 7: Overcoming Your Self-Defeating Behaviors

Have you ever set goals about your weight, money, or overcoming bad habits, but no matter how hard you try you still fail? You may be telling yourself you want to lose weight but deep inside your subconscious mind believes something opposite like:

·   It's too hard to lose weight.
·   I'm huge.
·   I'm just going to be big like my father.
·   I have no willpower.
·   If I lose weight I'll just gain it back.

No matter what you tell yourself or how many diets you go on, if you really believe that you're huge, that you have no willpower, or that you'll just gain it back, then your subconscious mind will do things to sabotage your efforts. Until you take care of your limiting beliefs that are blocking your progress, you'll never see much success in that area.

So what is your goal? State it in a positive way and then ask yourself if there is a natural "yeah but…" that follows in your mind.

For example, with money it might be:

·   I want to save money, but no matter how much I make something comes up to take it away (bills, expenses, etc).
·   I want to save money, but it's too difficult and would require too much sacrifice to make it.
·   I want to save money, but isn't money the root of all evil?

No matter how many positive uses you have for money, as long as you hold beliefs like these, your subconscious mind will continue to sabotage your efforts toward earning it. How do you change these beliefs? I'll show you how, but before I do…

> **A brief disclaimer:** I'm assuming you want something moral and in harmony with God's laws. For example, you wouldn't use this exercise to justify stealing your neighbor's car or cheating on your spouse!

Marnie L. Pehrson

Step 1: Identify your self-defeating beliefs. Just acknowledging them reduces their hold on you. Write down your worthwhile goals. Then write down the "yeah buts" that come to mind. (Reprint the following page as necessary.)

1. I want_____

_____
_____
_____
_____

But…

_____
_____
_____
_____
_____

2. I want_____

_____
_____
_____
_____

But…

_____
_____
_____
_____
_____

3. I want_____

_____
_____
_____
_____

But...

_____
_____
_____
_____
_____

4. I want_____

_____
_____
_____
_____

But...

_____
_____
_____
_____
_____

Step 2: Ask yourself four important questions. Now that you've identified the beliefs that hold you back from your worthy desires, ask yourself the following questions about each belief[1]:

1. Is what I believe factually accurate? Is it logical? (99.9% of the time it's not!)
2. Is the thought/belief in my best interest? (obviously it's not)
3. Does it make my life easier or more difficult? (more difficult)
4. Does it get me what I want? (again, evidently not)

As you thoroughly examine your subconscious beliefs you'll easily see that they aren't working for you.

Step 3: Rewrite your limiting beliefs in such a way that they are addressed in a positive way and become a positive gratitude statement.

Let's go back to our example about money:

- I want to save money, but no matter how much I earn, something comes up to take it away (bills, expenses, etc).

- I want to save money, but it's too difficult and would require too much sacrifice to earn it.

- I want to save money, but isn't money the root of all evil?

You could address each of these concerns in a positive gratitude statement that might go something like this:

> *"I am so happy and grateful now that money comes to me frequently and easily and from multiple sources. It arrives naturally because I flow positive energy, ideas and creativity into the world and thus it has to come back to me. I am able to save 10% of what I make every day. I am a wise steward of the money God gives me and am able to bless others with it. I meet all my financial obligations easily and ahead of time. I enjoy peace of mind in all my financial matters and rejoice in a home that is beautifully furnished, clean, orderly and harmonious. The Spirit of the Lord dwells here. I am excited and grateful to see this all happening in ways that are for the highest good for me and all concerned."*

Notice how we've combined the elements of a gratitude statement - the "I am so happy and grateful now that" beginning and the "highest good" clause at the end.

And each self-defeating belief is addressed:

- **I want to save money, but no matter how much I make something comes up to take it away (bills, expenses, etc).**

  I am able to save 10% of what I make every day…. I meet all my financial obligations easily and ahead of time. I enjoy peace of mind in all my financial matters

- **I want to save money, but it's too difficult and would require too much sacrifice to make that kind of money.**

  …money comes to me frequently and easily and from multiple sources. It arrives naturally because I flow positive energy, ideas and creativity into the world and thus it has to come back to me.

- **I want to save money, but isn't money the root of all evil?**

I am a wise steward of the money God gives me and am able to bless others with it. I meet all my financial obligations easily and ahead of time. I enjoy peace of mind in all my financial matters and rejoice in a home that is beautifully furnished, clean, orderly and harmonious. The Spirit of the Lord dwells here.

Okay, now it's your turn ...

Self-Defeating Belief:_____

_____
_____
_____
_____

Now, how will you turn it around? How will you address it in your gratitude statement?

_____
_____
_____
_____
_____
_____
_____
_____
_____

Self-Defeating Belief:_____

_____
_____
_____
_____

Now, how will you turn it around? How will you address it in your gratitude statement?

_____
_____
_____
_____
_____

Marnie L. Pehrson

Use this process as many times as you need to in order to address each of your self-defeating beliefs.

Now, combine your statements into one gratitude statement about your worthy desire:

I am so happy and grateful now that...

_____
_____
_____
_____
_____
_____
_____
_____
_____
_____
_____
_____
_____
_____
_____
_____
_____
_____

I am excited and grateful to see all this happening in ways that are for the highest good for me and all concerned.

Make this gratitude statement a part of your daily routine. Read it whenever you begin to doubt. Carry it with you and read it in your "Walks with God" and throughout the day. The more you can work on replacing your old limiting beliefs, the faster you will see results.

Resources

[1] These questions came from Dr. Robert Anthony's *Secret of Deliberate Creation* program. http://www.thesecretofdeliberatecreation.com/

Lesson 8: The Music of My Heart

There's a delightful story in 2 Chronicles 20 that illustrates the power of both gratitude and music to influence our faith. Jehoshaphat, the fourth great grandson of Solomon was king of Judah. He was a good, honorable man who served the Lord - a novelty among a long line of wicked kings. Jehoshaphat and his people were surrounded by the Ammonites and Moabites who were ready to make war against Judah.

Jehoshaphat feared because his people were greatly outnumbered, but he didn't let fear get the better of him. He turned to the Lord, gathering his people together and proclaiming a fast throughout all of Judah (2 Chronicles 20:3). He cried to the Lord, "we have no might against this great company that cometh against us; neither know we what to do; but our eyes are upon thee." And all of Judah stood before the Lord, with their little ones, their wives and their children (2 Chronicles 12-13).

Then the Lord spoke to the people through the prophet, *"Be not afraid nor dismayed by reason of this great multitude; for the battle is not yours, but God's. Tomorrow go ye down against them... Ye shall not need to fight in this battle: set yourselves, stand ye still, and see the salvation of the Lord with you, O Judah and Jerusalem: fear not, nor be dismayed; tomorrow go out against them; for the Lord will be with you"* (2 Chronicles 20:16-17).

Jehoshaphat and all of Judah bowed themselves before the Lord and worshipped Him. The Levite priests praised the Lord with a loud voice, and Jehoshaphat stood before the people and said, *"Believe in the Lord your God, so shall ye be established; believe in his prophets, so shall ye prosper"* (2 Chronicles 20:19-20).

Then Jehoshaphat appointed singers who went before the army and praised the Lord through song. He didn't send out the military. He sent out praise singers! They exhibited their faith and gratitude to the Lord through song, and as they sang the Ammonites and Moabites annihilated each other. Jehoshaphat and his people literally watched their enemies fall before them.

Music has a powerful impact on our minds and emotions. The right music can make us feel gratitude when we might otherwise feel fear. Jehoshaphat knew this. He had his people sing praises to God so that they could maintain their faith when all around them was chaos and destruction.

You can have this powerful tool in your life. Today, more than ever, it's easy to obtain wonderful uplifting music. It can be downloaded one song at a time from the Internet or you can order it online from a myriad of sources. I've made it an active pursuit to

Marnie L. Pehrson

collect music that uplifts and inspires. If I'm feeling down or life becomes overwhelming, I put on one of my inspirational collections and feel renewed in minutes.

This week, I'd like to encourage you to start building your own collection of inspiring, faith-building music. It doesn't have to all be religious or choir music. Anything that is positive, beautiful and uplifting will have a corresponding impact on your mind.

To get started, here's a few of my personal favorites. You're welcome to select from these or look for your own:

Jana Stanfield's *Brave Faith* **2-CD set** is a *must* for anyone trying to bolster their faith and find the courage to live their God-given mission. I purchased this CD set several years ago and I never tire of it. I've given it away to others and they've found it every bit as inspiring. http://www.janastanfield.com

Phillips, Craig and Dean have some excellent songs including *Will You Love Jesus More, How Great You Are, Your Grace Still Amazes Me, and Freedom's Never Free.* http://www.phillipscraiganddean.com/

William Joseph is fantastic if you love piano music. You can listen to much of his music on his Web site at http://www.william-joseph.com

Sheldon Pickering is another one of my all-time favorite pianists. He has a unique style that is both soothing and inspiring. http://www.shelovesgod.com/sheldon/

Stefanie Kelly - if you like a soulful style, you'll enjoy Stefanie Kelly. I particularly love her song *"I Know He Knows."* http://www.stefaniekelly.com

Jessie Clark has a wonderful voice. Some of my personal favorites of hers include *Clay in His Hands, Hold On the Light Will Come, The Station,* and *How Do You Move a Mountain.* http://deseretbook.com/store/search?search=jessie+clark&x=0&y=0

Steven Curtis Chapman - I love his *Be Still and Know, I'll Take Care of You, I Will Be Here, and What I Really Want to Say.* http://www.stevencurtischapman.com/

Mercy Me has some great songs like *Here Am I, How Great Is Your Love, In You, I Can Only Imagine.* http://www.mercyme.org

Most of these artists and songs you can also find on Walmart.com under their music download section, or via www.MusicMatch.com

Lesson 9: Prove Me Now Herewith

Do you struggle with making ends meet? Do you wrestle with debt or need help with managing your money wisely? The Lord has a solution!

Most of the time when we read Malachi 3:8-11 we think of the law of tithing and how the Lord promises to open the windows of heaven for our sake when we are honest with Him and give Him ten percent of our increase. Tithing is a principle I've been taught and practiced since childhood. I've found that paying tithing has blessed me with the things I need when I needed them. There have been times when we've scraped by financially but somehow the money we needed appeared when we needed it most; or we were given the wisdom to get by on what we had. The windows of heaven have opened for me spiritually and physically in knowledge, wisdom and understanding.

But I'll be honest with you, I'm not the best money manager in the world and monetarily-speaking I don't know that you could say that the windows of heaven have poured out more money than I could receive! Over 22 years of marriage we've struggled with debt. Perhaps you know what it's like when it feels like every dollar you earn is already earmarked by the interest monster. Or maybe you know what it's like when no matter how much you make, you still manage to spend it all. Getting out of debt and managing our money wisely has been a heightened concern for me in recent years. I've felt an urgency to get out of debt and have made it a matter of prayer and fasting. The Lord has repeatedly opened the windows of heaven and given me insights and hope.

Then, a couple years ago while listening to a lesson at church I heard a powerful principle taught which I'd either never heard or never paid attention to before. Perhaps I wasn't ready to receive it until that particular Sunday morning when it hit me with such force that I decided to test it. Before I tell you this principle, let's take a look at Malachi 3:8-11 because it's in here... I just never noticed it before.

> *"Will a man rob God? Yet ye have robbed me. But ye say, Wherein have we robbed thee? In tithes and offerings. Ye are cursed with a curse: for ye have robbed me, even this whole nation.*
>
> *"Bring ye all the tithes into the storehouse, that there may be meat in mine house, and prove me now herewith, saith the LORD of hosts, if I will not open you the*

Marnie L. Pehrson

windows of heaven, and pour you out a blessing, that there shall not be room enough to receive it.

"And I will rebuke the devourer for your sakes, and he shall not destroy the fruits of your ground; neither shall your vine cast her fruit before the time in the field, saith the LORD of hosts" (Malachi 3:8-11).

Most of the time when we read this passage we think of tithing ten percent. But He says we rob God when we do not give tithes AND offerings. Offerings are over and above the 10 percent. While tithing is generally what we give to our church to help it function and provide the building, facilities, utilities, etc to operate, our offerings are over and above the ten percent and would go toward other charitable causes like feeding the hungry, clothing the naked, healing the sick, supporting missionaries, helping the needy obtain education, etc.

I believe that the windows of heaven are not fully opened until we address both tithes AND offerings. If we really want to have showered upon us so much that we cannot receive it, then we must be generous in our offerings as well. I realize this can be hard to do when you're still struggling with the tithing principle, but it is one of those tests of faith that Jesus spoke of when he said, *"If any man will do his will, he shall know of the doctrine"* (John 7:17).

Malachi 3 is one of the few places in scripture where the Lord says "prove me." In other words, *test me, try me, and see if I don't do it.* When I heard this, I decided to put the principle to the test and I've seen amazing results. My husband has been able to retire (almost unheard of for a man in his mid-forties) and start his own part-time chef business (a long-time dream). And my business revenues have quadrupled to a level that it can entirely support a family of 8 (which includes a daughter at a private university).

I've also corroborated these results with a friend who has faithfully paid generous tithes and offerings for years. It has been our experience that whatever we give over and above tithing comes back to us ten-fold – if not more. We looked at what we normally make and compared our increase to the amount we gave in offerings and it was ten times the offerings. For example, if you give a dollar, you get back ten. If you give ten, you get back one-hundred.

It's almost as if the Lord is saying, if you'll give me ten percent of your increase, I'll see that you're taken care of. If you'll give me more, I'll repay you ten-fold. I searched for a scriptural reference to back up this ten-factor, and found this verse in Matthew 19:29:

"And every one that hath forsaken houses, or brethren, or sisters, or father, or mother, or wife, or children, or lands, for my name's sake, shall receive an hundredfold, and shall inherit everlasting life."

While most of us aren't asked to forsake homes, family or land for Christ's sake, we can give back to Him in the form of tithes and offerings. Doing so is like planting a seed. The Law of the Harvest is then activated in our behalf. Plant a bean and you get a lot more beans back than a single one. The same works for this principle. As you give to the Lord, I promise you that the windows of heaven will open in more than just monetary ways. Your family will be blessed and protected. God will rebuke the devourer for your sake. You will be blessed with wisdom, understanding and treasures of knowledge.

As someone once said, you can't give the Lord a piece of crust without recieving a loaf in return. I challenge you to put this principle to the test. Let the Lord prove His faithfulness in your life.

Marnie L. Pehrson

Lesson 10: Activating the Creation Process in Your Life

Have you ever known someone who seemed to have everything going for them? Maybe you thought they were lucky or that God must love them better than He loves you. I've heard some people suggest that if a person is rich they must have done something crooked to obtain their wealth.

Why do some people prosper while others barely exist? Does righteousness mean poverty? Or does it mean prosperity? I'm here to tell you that it doesn't necessarily mean either one. There are very good people who are poorer than a church mouse and there are wonderful Christians who flourish.

You may be doing your best to follow God, but your finances are a mess or your relationships are out of harmony, or you still aren't happy. While trials are inevitable in life, there are certain universal laws that bring happiness even during our trials.

In reality, there really is no such thing as luck. Luck is merely **L**iving **U**nder **C**orrect **K**nowledge - knowledge of the universal laws by which God operates. Some people live in harmony with these laws without even realizing it. They may have been raised by parents who modeled these principles. Others have sought out, learned, and intentionally tried to live by these laws.

In John 10:10 Jesus says, *"I am come that they might have life and that they might have it more abundantly."* He also said that God sends rain on the just and the unjust. Whether one believes in God or not, He does have laws. When you abide by His laws you reap the corresponding blessings. When you don't, you reap negative consequences.

Universal laws are not like traffic laws that we can violate and sometimes get away with. Universal laws are immutable and operate like gravity. It doesn't matter how righteous you are or how much positive thinking you exhibit, if you fall off a skyscraper, you will be at the mercy of the law of gravity. The laws that we'll be discussing this month are like that. They're as vital to your happiness and well-being as understanding gravity.

Jesus promised an abundant life to those who follow His teachings. Abundance can be defined as a great plentiful amount, fullness to overflowing, or affluence and wealth. Thus far you've learned that you are a child of God and that He has a divine plan for your life - a mission for you to fulfill. You may or may not have discovered it yet. But in order to learn and live it, you need certain things. You need God's abundance in your life. You may need an abundance of knowledge, education, time, energy, resources, connections, or even money to fulfill your divine mission.

In my life, I've been blessed with an abundance of children, friends, family, land, and ideas. I'm also surprised at the abundance of knowledge, answers and talents that the Lord is more than willing to share with us when we're seeking first to build the kingdom of God and promote righteousness on the earth. Your abundance could be in different areas than mine, but when you are on the Lord's path for your life you can expect an abundance of everything you need to accomplish your righteous desires.

The earth is full and there is plenty to spare. There is no scarcity. There is only abundance. Christ is about abundance and Satan pushes the false belief that scarcity rules – that only a privileged few may be saved or only a privileged few may be blessed with the abundance of the earth. He knows that this false belief makes us fearful, competitive, covetous, and selfish. It stalls our progression.

Too many people never fulfill their divine destinies to their fullest degree because they do not understand the principles and laws surrounding abundance. They do not understand that the Lord fully intends and WANTS to give you everything you need to fulfill your divine mission. They believe that God wants you to suffer privation and lack in order that you may remain humble, when in reality nothing could be further from the truth. God wants you to choose to be humble - not be compelled to humility. The Lord wants you to have all the resources, talents, knowledge, experience, energy, associations, and time that you need to build His kingdom in the unique way that only you can.

The Law of Creation

And so that is why this month we're focusing on 7 principles of abundant living. In this lesson, I'm going to share with you a law which I like to refer to as the Law of Creation or in scientific circles it's called the "Law of Perpetual Transmutation."

This law simply states that nothing stands still. Everything is either growing or disintegrating. It's either increasing or it's self-destructing.

As a writer, I'm fascinated with the creative process. The more I study and try to develop my creative talents, the more I come to believe that the part of our minds that creates things is a piece of divinity within us. Whether it be a book, artwork, a piece of furniture, a scientific discovery, a poem, or a musical piece, we tune into a creative channel (if you will) that enables us to do it. Some tune into the Light of Christ and produce positive works. Others tune into the master of darkness and formulate that which destroys. If you'll notice, Satan never creates anything productive. He only devastates. He takes inventions such as TV, music, radio, the internet and uses them to create despair, despondency and darkness in the world. God, on the other hand, inspires men and women to produce beautiful, positive things and to uplift and enlighten the world.

John 1:5 tells us that *"Jesus is the light that shineth in darkness and the darkness comprehendeth it not."* Only those who have a light within them tune into that light, see it, feel it and channel it to brighten a darkened world.

Whether you think you're creative or not, you were born to be a creator. Why do I say that? Because you are made in the image of God. In Genesis 1:26 we read, *"And God said, Let us make man in our own image, after our likeness: and let them have dominion over the fish of the sea, and over the fowl of the air, and over the cattle, and over all the earth and over every creeping thing that creepeth upon the earth."*

There are two things that stand out to me in that verse and the first is that we are made in the image and likeness of God. We have attributes and characteristics that are like Him. The second is that we are made to have dominion over our world. We are free to act for ourselves and not be acted upon. Do you think the Lord was saying, "You have dominion over everything but your finances"? Or "You have dominion over everything but your weight." Or "You have dominion over everything but your happiness." Certainly not!

Exercise: Name 1-3 areas of your life that you feel are outside your control. Now consider that with God's help you really can have "dominion over" these areas:

_____
_____
_____
_____
_____

The Power of Words

We are endowed by our Creator with similar creative abilities as He has. Granted they aren't as powerful, but I believe they are more powerful than we realize. To understand our own creative abilities, let's take a look at those of our Creator.

God "spoke" the world into existence. He said, *"Let there be light and there was light."* In John we learn that the Savior was with our Heavenly Father in the beginning – during this creation process. In John 1:1-14 we read about his role, *"In the beginning was the Word; and the Word was with God; and the Word was God. The same was in the beginning with God. All things were made by Him; and without Him was not anything made that was made…. And the Word was made flesh and dwelt among us, (and we beheld his glory, the glory as of the only begotten of the Father,) full of grace and truth."*

God's Word is so powerful that Jesus Christ is referred to as the Word. The Word was "made flesh" or went from a spiritual to a physical form. By God's words the worlds were created. God thought of something and then literally spoke it into existence.

Hebrews 11: 3, 6 says

3) Through faith we understand that the worlds were framed by the word of God, so that things which are seen were not made of things which do appear.

God created the worlds with FAITH. Faith is the substance of things hoped for and the evidence of things not seen.

6) But without faith it is impossible to please him: for he that cometh to God must believe that he is, and that he is a rewarder of them that diligently seek him.

We too must have faith – not only that He exists, but also that he rewards those who diligently seek after Him. Faith is the literal substance from which God creates our miracles. Without it, nothing happens! Nothing is created! We must not only believe in Him, but also we must believe Him when he says that He will heal our broken hearts and lives. We have to believe Him when he tells us to *"ask in order to receive and to knock in order to have blessings opened to us."*

Just like our Father in Heaven, we have the ability within us to direct our thoughts, channel our desires, and to create them in our physical world. We can't do it on as grand a scale as He, but we still have the ability nonetheless. Our words have the ability to create our own world.

If we're praying for financial healing, but our words say, "I never have any money." Or "Every time I make a little extra money, something comes along to take it away." Then we are nullifying our prayers. Whatever faith we exercised to start the creative process in motion has just been reversed by our doubting words.

Marnie L. Pehrson

Challenge: Examine your words. What statements are you making that are contrary to the goals and mission statement which you've set for yourself?

_____

_____

_____

_____

_____

Make a conscious effort to stop yourself when you speak contrary to your goals and mission. Use positive statements instead.

Spiritual to Physical Creation

In 1 Chronicles Chapter 28 we learn about David and how the Spirit of the Lord gave him a wonderful plan for a temple. David had a great desire to build a temple to God and he gathered all the things needed – down to the gold for the meat hooks and candlesticks to the laborers to build it. But when it came time to build the temple, the Lord took the privilege away from David because he had not lived worthy of it. He had Uriah killed in battle. His murder of an innocent man kept him from fulfilling his dream. And so he gave the plans and supplies to his son Solomon and Solomon built the temple instead.

The building of the temple is symbolic of any righteous desire we may have. It starts out in a spiritual way. It's simply an idea or a desire planted by God in us through the Spirit. Then we start gathering the things we need – the materials, supplies and people we need to accomplish it. When all is ready, the righteous desire becomes a physical reality.

In addition to materials, you need patience to work your plan. Allow it to come to pass in its appointed time. While you're being patient, be faithful. We must never be so arrogant as to think the righteous desires God has given us cannot be fulfilled by another if we do not hold out faithful. David lost the privilege of being the builder of the temple because he did not remain faithful. We must be faithful to God and to the nourishment of our divine destiny in order to bring it to pass.

God has a special plan for each of us – a special mission to fulfill – just like David had a mission to build the temple. Whether we're allowed to fill that mission is entirely up to us. Will we proceed in faith? Will we remain faithful? Or will we give up in fear or doubt?

> Like Solomon's temple, every great thing starts as a thought in someone's mind as an idea. Gradually it starts accumulating what it needs to become a physical reality. That's what Creation is – organizing matter and energy into something new. You are a creator!

There is a law of nature that states that "Energy moves into physical form." The image you hold in your mind most often materializes into results in your life.

Whatever you give energy to grows. Whatever you give your focus, faith and feeling to grows. Whether it's what you want or what you don't want. Worrying is focus and feeling. When you feed worry, you feed what you DON'T want! Don't worry, be grateful instead. Be grateful for what you have and for what is on its way to you.

Nothing stands still. Everything is either growing or disintegrating

- Pregnant mother – is her baby coming or going?

- 70 year old man – is he coming or going? His eyesight may be going and his hearing may already be gone.

- You can't stand still – you're either growing or disintegrating in any area of your life.

Think of how steam condenses into water and then can become ice. Your ideas crystallize in a similar fashion. The level of doubt or faith you have determines whether this happens.

Vapor	Ideas/Inspiration	Doubt/Fear
Water	Spiritual Form	Diligence/Purpose
Ice	Physical/Natural Form	Faith, Confidence, Patience

It takes time for this process to take place. We do not sow and reap at the same time – at least not the same seeds anyway. After we receive an initial burst of inspiration or righteous desire, many of us proceed a little ways and then reality sets in. We start looking at our surroundings and say, "This is impossible. There's no way." For example, if you have a feeling of peace that the Lord will deliver you from your financial challenges, but then the bill collectors start calling and your bank account is low, the natural thing to do is doubt. But doubt and fear are the worst things you can do because they send your idea back into the nothing. They reverse the creative process.

Paul warned the Hebrews against losing confidence in Hebrews 10:35-38:

Cast not away therefore your confidence, which hath great recompense of reward. For ye have need of patience, that, after ye have done the will of God, ye might receive the promise. Now the just shall live by faith: but if any man draws back, my soul shall have no pleasure in him.

In 2 Timothy 1:7 we also read: *"For God hath not given us the spirit of fear; but of power, and of love, and of a sound mind."*

In Philippians 4:8 we learn that thoughts Are THINGS: *"whatsoever things are true, whatsoever things are honest, whatsoever things are just, whatsoever things are pure, whatsoever things are lovely, whatsoever things are of good report; if there be any virtue, and if there be any praise, think on these things."*

Think about an acorn. Within it lies the plan for a full grown oak tree. But it isn't an oak yet. It's just the plan. It must be planted in the right type of soil and nourished so it can grow and develop into its ultimate creation.

Notice that the acorn only gathers what it needs as it needs it. It doesn't collect bark while it's sprouting from a seed and it doesn't worry about going out and finding leaf elements while it's small. It has the vision or blueprint for its ultimate objective – an oak tree – but it doesn't know when or how the things it needs will come to it. It doesn't go out and fight and claw to get what it wants. Everything it needs comes to it. We need to be like the acorn and trust the vision and take action on our current environment.

Wallace D. Wattles said, "It is not your part to guide or supervise the creative process. All you have to do with that is to retain your vision, stick to your purpose, and maintain your faith and gratitude."

He also said, "By thought, the thing you want is brought to you. By action you receive it." We must do more than just think positively and envision our goal. We must take efficient action. We must work for what we want. A worthy desire we hold in faith naturally propels us to positive action.

James Allen, said the following in his book, *As a Man Thinketh*:

"Men imagine that thought can be kept secret, but it cannot. It rapidly crystallizes into habit… Thoughts of fear, doubt, and indecision crystallize into weak, unmanly, and irresolute habits, which solidify into circumstances of failure, indigence, and slavish dependence.

Loving and unselfish thoughts crystallize into habits of self-forgetfulness for others, which solidify into circumstances of sure and abiding prosperity and true riches.

A particular train of thought persisted in, be it good or bad, cannot fail to produce its results on the character and circumstances. A man cannot *directly* choose his circumstances, but he can choose his thoughts, and so indirectly, yet surely, shape his circumstances." (James Allen, As A Man Thinketh)

One of my favorite parables of the Savior's is the parable of the talents. I'm sure you know it well. There were three servants and each was given a varying number of talents (or coins). The first was given five talents, the next two and the third one. The servant who had one hid his in the earth because he was afraid. The servants with five and two talents doubled theirs to ten and four respectively. When the master of the servants came, he punished the person who hid his in the ground and took away his one talent and gave it to the servant who had ten. Then he praised those with ten and four saying, "well done thou good and faithful servant. Thou hast been faithful over a few things, I will make you ruler over many things."

The reason I love this parable is that each time I study it I learn something new from it. In the context of our discussion here, let's change those "talents or coins" to righteous desires. The people who had five and two righteous desires set to work to fulfill those desires. They didn't bury them. They worked toward them with faith and purpose and in the process, they acquired new desires, talents and resources. They became better. They increased – just like everything that God creates is intended to do. But the person who had one (and in fear hid his desires and did not seek after them) lost His ability to create. He did not increase. He did not grow, learn or develop. He was in essence "damned" and by that I mean "blocked or stalled in his progression." He couldn't have an increase.

If we're seeking material things so that we may consume them upon our own lusts, for vanity, praise or power, then we are not seeking the kingdom of God.

But too many Christians are afraid to dream. They are too afraid to believe that God wants more for them. They think that God wants them to barely get by or be content with the bare minimum. Nothing could be further from the truth. God wants you to not only be grateful for what you have, but also to develop all of your talents and skills. It may take money, connections and resources for you to do that. It is not wrong for you to accept those things or even ask for those things when they are part of a righteous desire. When we seek to build up the kingdom of God, He adds everything we need to get there.

We, like the lilies of the field, don't have to toil or worry about where it's going to come from. We simply hold the faith that it will arrive and in its perfect time, it will.

I talk to so many people who have a desire to do wonderful things. They want to help others, lift each other's burdens, and make the world a better place. If you are one of these people, then God gave you that desire. And where there is desire, there is power. Your Heavenly Father isn't cruel. He doesn't give you a desire for something and then not provide a way to accomplish it. Learn God's laws. Learn how He works and together with Him, make those righteous desires a reality.

As Galatians 6:9 says, *"And let us not be weary in well doing for in due season we shall reap, if we faint not."* Faint not, fear not and doubt not, but be believing for you are laying the foundation of a great work and out of small and simple things are great things brought to pass.

Lesson 11: To Everything There Is a Season

"To every thing there is a season, and a time to every purpose under the heaven" (Ecclesiastes 3:1).

Are you like me? Do you get frustrated waiting for the things you want? Most of us despise waiting and it's primarily because we have some goal out in front of us that we want to reach and we want to reach it **right now**.

Something that happened to our family a couple years ago is a good illustration. My husband Greg and I took our six children up to Gatlinburg, Tennessee in the Smokey Mountains for the day. It's about a 2.5 hour drive there and a 2.5 hour drive back. We got up around 4am, loaded up the kids and were off by 4:45. We arrived at our favorite pancake house around 7:30. My husband always likes to be early. In fact, we were so early, that when we finished eating, none of the shops were open and it was drizzling outside. So we went into a little Mountain Mall to wait. Maybe two shops in the entire mall were open then, so we passed the time letting the kids ride up and down the elevator or the escalators or having races to see who could beat the elevator down the stairs.

Finally the stores opened and we window shopped until about noon. Then, my husband informed us that it was time to go to Cades Cove – a scenic drive up into the mountains to a primitive little village. I've been to Gatlinburg and Cades Cove so many times, it really didn't matter to me where we went or what we did.

So we set off on an hour drive to Cades Cove through the beautiful Smokey Mountains. It hadn't been cold enough for the leaves to change much, but it was still beautiful to see the subtle yellows, oranges and greens and the rocky river winding along either side of us as we listened to inspiring music.

Cades Cove is a park with a six-mile loop that passes through a few cabins, but mainly it's forest and meadows. There's also a mill at about the half-way point where you can park and walk around. It took us literally 2 hours to creep along bumper-to-bumper through this six-mile loop. After about an hour or so of this, my husband started to lose his temper. Couldn't people read the signs that say: "Be polite, no stopping, keep the traffic moving?" Evidently not. They stopped for every squirrel or deer. Drivers hung out their car windows taking pictures.

My husband and I have an unspoken system, if he loses it, I must remain calm. If I lose it, he remains calm. So as he began to lose it, I rallied the children into a series of games to keep them occupied – everybody names a place that starts with A, then B, then C and so on. We invented imaginary worlds – each person describing some element of it. And the time passed rather painlessly - for us anyway. But because the traffic was so bad, my husband didn't even stop at the mill. We just kept on driving so we could get back in time for dinner.

Finally, we were out of the cove, traffic moving at a good clip until we hit another bottleneck and spent 30 minutes going 8/10ths of a mile. This time, even I became impatient, because when the traffic started rolling, having had no lunch, we had all begun to anticipate dinner. It was after five before we reached the restaurant and nearly six before we sat down to our delicious meal.

But you know what, those children didn't complain once. Ten hours total in the car all day and they didn't gripe or complain one time about it. You see, with six kids, you don't go a lot of places and they were grateful just to be taken somewhere. It was all new to at least four of the children who'd never spent any time in Gatlinburg. Even riding in the car couldn't put a damper on that for them.

The only person who didn't enjoy the trip was Greg. He was too irritated to join in the games. For him the trip was a disappointment, but for the rest of us who used the waiting time to bond and enjoy the scenery and listen to music, we had an enjoyable time. Now, I'm not saying I'm better than my husband in this regard. We just have that unspoken rule and he claimed "irritated" first and tenaciously hung onto it so I had to claim "make the best of it." Maybe someday we'll learn to "make the best of it" simultaneously.

So why do I share this story with you in a lesson about "To Everything There Is a Season?" Because we spend much of our lives waiting for what we want to happen. When we're a kid, we can't wait until we're sixteen to drive and then eighteen to graduate and then we can't wait until we get married or can't wait until we have our first child. Then we can't wait until that child starts school or until he or she graduates.

We spend our lives rushing the seasons past. It's as if we can't enjoy anything but the harvest – the times when all the fruit comes in. We need to enjoy every season of life.

> *"Don't be afraid of the space between your dreams and reality.*
> *If you can dream it, you can make it so."*
>
> *- Belva Davis*

This brings us to another law: The Law of Gestation

This law states that every seed has a gestation or incubation period. If you look at a packet of bean seeds, you'll see they take a few months to grow. A baby takes about 40 weeks inside its mother. A fruit tree takes about three years to bear fruit. God has placed around us in nature constant reminders of the fact that everything has a set period of time to grow and bear fruit.

He's trying to tell us that just as natural seeds have germination periods, so do spiritual seeds. Ideas are spiritual seeds and will move into form or physical results, provided they are given the nourishment they need. Your goals will materialize in their perfect time. Just as it takes time for water to crystallize into ice, and just as it takes some time for an acorn to become a tree or a bean seed to become a bean plant and grow more beans, so it takes time for your ideas to germinate and become physical realities.

Every idea seed has its own gestation period… the time it takes to grow. Unfortunately, there's no packet to read to find out how long it's going to take. But just as physical seeds grow faster with proper nourishment and rich soil, so do spiritual seeds. Your level of faith and diligence can speed up or slow down the process. But, generally there's going to be a certain time frame that has to take place before it will become a reality.

Give your idea seeds time to grow. Don't rip them out of the ground in doubt or unbelief. Remember, you don't sow and reap at the same time.

The nourishment you give your idea seeds is diligence, purpose, faith and patience. If you want to kill your ideas, feed them doubt, fear and negativity.

When I learned this principle, it was like a light bulb went on inside me. I could look back at any achievement and see that it took time to grow and that it eventually did take shape – even if it took months or even years.

"There is a time for every purpose and for every work."
Ecclesiastes 3:17

I'm an idea person and have more ideas than I know what to do with. I used to become overwhelmed and run around like a chicken with its head cut off trying to do too many things at once. One of my friends encouraged me to create a master list of ideas so that they were recorded for later reference. I've kept up this practice off-and-on over the years and when the opportunity and knowledge presented itself to turn those old ideas into a reality, I learned an important lesson.

Sometimes God gives us ideas whose time has not yet come. For example, many times ideas come to me with such force and in such a burst of light and knowledge that I know they didn't come from within me. There's no doubt that they came from God. I recognize these ideas because they fill me with joy. They are filled with light. But often, I become so frustrated because at the time they come, I may not have the means or the knowledge to make them a reality. So reluctantly, I file the idea back into a corner of my mind and eventually the time, season and purpose for that work presents itself.

I remember one time in particularly when almost effortlessly, ideas I had two years prior quickly became a reality. There was a major programming problem on one of my Web sites that required me to act quickly, research a solution and repair the problem. In my moment of need, the Lord led me to a piece of programming code that not only fixed the current problem, but also gave me the knowledge to quickly and easily implement the ideas He gave me two years prior. Within a week's time those ideas became a reality. They were there waiting for their time and their purpose.

What I learned from this experience is that we need not question the inspiration or answers we receive because the way or means to accomplish them are not readily available. Sometimes the Lord gives us this insight so we

1. Have a direction to pursue,

2. Accumulate the knowledge and experience the idea requires,

3. Can be on the lookout for the opportunity when the perfect time arises ,

4. Realize that many times the opportunity we need is hidden within a crisis.

We need not be discouraged because we can't do everything we want to do right now. We can take comfort in knowing that the Lord has a time and a purpose for every righteous desire that He puts within our hearts.

The hard part for us as humans is having the patience to wait for God's perfect timing. We often try to force the issue. But our own efforts to manipulate a situation to change the foreordained timing of events will only lead to frustration. In God's timing, events just flow. I can always recognize when the timing is off by when I'm working too hard to make things happen. That's a sure sign that God's telling me to wait for the right moment. Most people interpret this as God telling them that the idea is bad. And this probably isn't the case – especially if you received a confirmation that this idea was good. It's just not the right timing yet – you don't have all the pieces you need.

Constantly remind yourself that the timing of inspiration and fruition don't always coincide. You can console yourself in knowing that the inspiration and vision He showers your way today will eventually become a reality - even if it's in a distant tomorrow. Document enlightenment as it comes, and praise Him when its season arrives.

Exercise: Look back over your life and reflect on God's perfect timing in bringing to pass events. Record your thoughts in your gratitude journal. Also record any insights you receive about the timing of your current goals and mission.

Lesson 12: The Law of the Harvest

I have come to love the wisdom of Ecclesiastes. Chapter 11, in particular, is a rich tutorial on the principle of sowing and reaping, otherwise known as the Law of the Harvest or "Cause and Effect" or in the vernacular, "What goes around comes around." My closest friends embody this principle in their lives. They generously give. In business, they are "team players" and realize that if we expect to receive, we must first give. We have to make room for the things we seek *before* we can receive the new we desire.

Ecclesiastes 11:1 explains, *"Cast thy bread upon the waters: for thou shalt find it after many days. Give a portion to seven, and also to eight; for thou knowest not what evil shall be upon the earth."* In other words, put out good, help others, and it will return to you in your hour of need. If you have sown good seeds, then in your moment of crisis, it will return to your rescue in the exact moment that you need it. If you don't cast your bread upon the waters, it can't come back to you when you need it most.

Whatever you put out, by eternal law, has to come back to you. Ecclesiastes emphasizes the certainty of this principle with two comparisons, *"If the clouds be full of rain, they empty themselves upon the earth: and if the tree fall toward the south, or toward the north, in the place where the tree fell, there it shall be."* As surely as heavy clouds send forth rain and as surely as you'll find the tree where it fell, so assuredly will you reap what you have sown.

Paul taught the Corinthians *"He which sows sparingly shall reap also sparingly; and he which sows bountifully shall reap also bountifully"* (2 Corinthians 9: 6).

There is a time to sow and there is a time to reap, but you don't do both at the same time. You can't be certain when or from where you'll reap, but reap you shall. Most likely the person to whom you gave, will not be the one to return your kindness. This is where most people trip up. They think they have to get back from the exact person to whom they gave, and that simply isn't the way this law works.

Ecclesiastes 11:4 says, *"He that observes the wind shall not sow; and he that regards the clouds shall not reap."* In other words, those who are so preoccupied with only what they can see – their current circumstances – will not put forth the effort to sow or to reap. The fact that they can't see how they're going to benefit will discourage them. So they'll do nothing. Because they will not sow, they cannot reap. Your job is to send out good, and God will take care of the rest. Verse 5 compares the mystery of this principle to a child growing inside a mother's womb: *"As thou knowest not what is the way of the spirit, nor how the bones do grow in the womb of her that is with child: even so thou knowest not the works of God who maketh all."*

God takes what we sow and transforms it into abundance. Just as a tiny pea yields a plant laden with peas, so the Lord takes our efforts and multiplies them in our behalf. We can never be certain when, where or what seeds we sow will yield a harvest. But verse 6 admonishes us, *"In the morning sow thy seed, and in the evening withhold not thine hand: for thou knowest not whether shall prosper, either this or that, or whether they both shall be alike good."* In other words, cheerfully do all within your power to lift, to build, to help and to serve from morning until evening, because you never know when or how your blessings will return.

Have you ever spent ten minutes arguing with a friend about who was going to pay the tip at a restaurant? If we understood the principle that one cannot give without receiving, we wouldn't quibble over a few dollars. We'd graciously accept what someone wanted to do for us or give us because we'd know that our friend would be blessed over and above what s/he gave. I'm not saying to be a free-loader, nor to let other people pay your way all the time, but if someone insists upon giving you something, then don't deny them the blessing of giving!

When you have something you don't need anymore, give it away, don't sell it. If you sell it, the money will be all you receive in exchange. But if you give it away, it will come back to you in a far greater way. Jesus taught, *"Give, and it shall be given unto you; good measure, pressed down, and shaken together, and running over, shall men give into your bosom. For with the same measure that ye mete, it shall be measured to you again"* (Luke 6:38).

If you want a new couch, call Salvation Army to pick up the one you have. If you want new clothes, clean out your closet and give the ones you don't wear or that don't fit to a charity. Make room for the things you desire by giving away the old and making room for the new. Don't be afraid that you won't receive. By law you have to. I challenge you to try an experiment. Pick something around your house that you would like to have replaced. Give it away and see what God brings you in its place. I think you'll be pleasantly surprised.

There's even a Web site that helps you do this. You can find discussion lists in your local area where people give away what they don't want anymore so that it can be put to good use by others. It's called FreeCycle.com – http://www.freecycle.org .

Marnie L. Pehrson

When we think about all our Heavenly Father has done for us – all our Savior has done for us – we naturally want to give something to God in return, don't we? We want to grow closer to Him, to know his will, to know God's thoughts.

James 4: 8 says *"Draw nigh to God, and He will draw nigh to you."*

There are at least four things that you can give to the Lord – ways you can draw close to him so that He will in turn draw close to you. When we do these things, He immediately blesses us, and thus we are forever in His debt. But it is a blessed debt.

1. **Tithes and Offerings.** (See Lesson 9)

2. **Deep and Heart-felt Gratitude.** (See Lessons 6 and 7)

3. **Offer an Obedient and Humble Heart**

Jesus said, *"If ye love me, keep my commandments"* (John 14:15). He also explained how we can tell whether a principle is true, *"If any man will do his will, he shall know of the doctrine whether it be of God or whether I speak of myself"* (John 7:17).

When we obey the commandments of God we are blessed. The Lord is bound when we do what He says. When we don't do what He says, we have no promise. Look at it this way: There are laws in place and these laws have consequences whenever you break them or whenever you keep them. If you break a law, you incur the negative consequences. If you obey a law, you reap the rewards associated with that law. When we receive any blessing from the Lord it is by obedience to that law upon which it is predicated.

The Lord hasn't given us commandments just as a suggestion. They aren't ways for Him to control us or have power over is. He gave them to us because He loves us and wants us to be happy. And He knows that happiness comes when we obey these laws. When we humble ourselves and realize that our Father in Heaven knows best about what's going to make us happy, we submit to his commandments. As a result, we gain a witness that they are from God by the blessing we receive for our obedience.

4. **Offer Selfless Service**

When you are in the service of your fellow beings, you are only in the service of your God. "Do unto others as you'd have them do unto you." Jesus taught us to go the extra mile, give to him that asks, love our neighbors and love our enemies, bless those that curse us, do good to those who hate us and pray for them who despitefully use us and persecute us (Matthew 5:41-44).

Look for ways to use your talents to serve others. There is no greater joy than in using the talents the Lord gave you to bless the lives of those around you. That's why he gave them to you in the first place.

Bottom line, whatever you put out will return to you. Life isn't compartmentalized. If you're dishonest in your business dealings, it won't just be your business that will suffer. It will affect your entire life. If you're cruel to your family members, it won't just be your family relationships that suffer. It will affect all aspects of your life.

If you want to be blessed, then bless others. If you want to be treated with respect, treat others with respect. If you want to receive, you must give. And give generously for whatever you give will come back multiplied. That is the law of the harvest - one seed produces much fruit.

Marnie L. Pehrson

Lesson 13: Count it All Joy

We've talked a lot about gratitude and looking for the good. But if there's one question I hear more than any other, it's "why do bad things happen to good people?" It is my prayer that this lesson which covers two important "laws" will help heal the hurting and give clarity to those in crisis.

The first law is called "The Law of Polarity" or "The Law of Opposition." It states that everything is a compound in one. In order for a book to have a front, it must also have a back. You can't have an up without a down, or an "in" without an "out." If you fall down a three foot hole, you won't be required to climb five feet to get out of it – only three. Within everything bad there is an equal and opposite good. The trick is looking for it and realizing it's there.

A while back, a lady who had gone through a miscarriage wrote me. She was suffering a great deal of pain and confusion about why the Lord would let this "evil" come upon her. Why didn't He protect her and her baby? Why had He let her down? Having suffered a miscarriage myself, I can understand the emptiness she went through, but knowledge of our Heavenly Father and His plan for us gave me peace not only in that particularly painful situation, but also in every trial I've ever endured.

What is our Heavenly Father's plan? And how does it bring peace in trying situations? If we go back to Adam and Eve in the Garden of Eden and read in Genesis 2 and 3, we see that Adam and Eve made a choice. They could have stayed in a perfect environment, never knowing good from evil, pleasure from pain, nor joy from suffering. In the very day that God placed Adam and Eve in the Garden, He presented them with a choice – to stay in the garden in a state of innocence or to eat from the Tree of the Knowledge of Good and Evil and leave. If they stayed in the garden they would never learn compassion because there would be no suffering, never learn patience because there would be no want, never learn faith because they would walk by sight. They were free to choose, but He warned them that if they ate of that tree, they would experience death – both spiritual death (separation from God) and physical death (separation of the spirit from the body).

We do not know how long Adam and Eve were in the Garden or how thoroughly they weighed the choice presented to them, but a choice was made and that choice was a "transgression" or going across from one plain of existence to another. Their choice brought spiritual and physical death into the world. Life became a schoolroom – a place to learn, grow and experience a full range of emotions, challenges, adversities, pleasures and joys. They would have to deal with the pains and sorrow of childbirth, and the frustrations of thorns and thistles. The earth would no longer bring forth fruits and vegetables spontaneously (Genesis 3:16-19). They would learn the satisfaction of a hard day's work and the exhilaration of sowing a seed in faith that one day it would yield its fruit.

Upon entering this schoolroom of mortality they learned about this Law of Polarity - that there is an opposition in all things. Everything is a compound in one – within every bad situation, there is an equal and opposite good. To truly understand pleasure, we must endure pain. To value virtue, one must be exposed to vice. To bask in the light of faith, we must have traversed the darkness of doubt. Even the Savior Himself was required to endure a wilderness experience and temptation before He embarked on His earthly ministry (Mark 1). The son of God was no exception to this requirement.

The choice made in the Garden affects all of us to this day. We live in a fallen world. This schoolroom is a place for us to learn, grow, and develop in ways we never could in a heavenly or Eden atmosphere. It is a temporary state. It's only a single act of a play that goes on for eternity. Birth is the entrance to this schoolroom and death is merely the exit. All is not lost upon walking through the portal we call death. It is simply a transition. Death is not the end, because our Heavenly Father in His infinite wisdom prepared a Savior for us. The Bible tells us that Jesus Christ was *"foreordained before the foundation of the world"* (1 Peter 1:20) as the *"Lamb slain from the foundation of the world"* (Revelation 13:8). His sacrifice for us was planned from the beginning. God knew the choice that Adam and Eve would make in the Garden. He knew we would enter mortality where we would be given the opportunity to make choices and learn to walk by faith.

If every time we were to stub our toe, make a mistake or experience pain, an angel came to stop the event, what would we learn from this life? If only the wicked were punished and the good were always blessed, how much freedom of choice would be necessary to choose righteously? Jesus taught that our Father in heaven *"maketh the sun to rise on the evil and on the good, and sendeth rain on the just and the unjust"* (Matthew 5:45).

In James 1:2-4 we read, *"My brethren, count it all joy when ye fall into divers temptations; knowing this, that the trying of your faith worketh patience. But let patience have her perfect work, that ye may be perfect and entire, wanting nothing."*

Marnie L. Pehrson

If life were nothing but a cushy ride, we would never learn what we came here to learn. Our trials and the temptations we overcome make us stronger. They make us patient which works on us. It perfects us or matures us into the person God knows we can become.

When Job's wife told him to just "curse God and die" he replied, *"You speak as the foolish women speak. What? Shall we receive good at the hand of God, and shall we not receive evil?"* The Bible tells us that in all his afflictions Job did not *"sin with his lips"* (Job 2:9-10).

Even in his worst pain, Job trusted the Lord and prophesied, *"For I know that my redeemer liveth, and that he shall stand at the latter day upon the earth: and though after my skin worms destroy this body, yet in the flesh shall I see God"* (Job 19:25-26). Job knew that *"For as in Adam all die, even so in Christ shall all be made alive"* (1 Corinthians 15:22).

Death is not the end nor is it evil, it is simply a door. Pain and suffering are the flipside of a coin shared by joy and happiness. It is when we realize that our adversities are our blessings that we begin to look for the treasure hidden within every trial. Pain, troubles and distress lead to spiritual growth and progress when we turn to the Lord. This is why James told us to *"count it all joy when we fall into divers temptations (problems, challenges)"* (James 1:2).

If something is a little bad, there's a little good laced within it. If it's catastrophic, then something phenomenal will come as a result. Never doubt that God will make *"all things work together for your good"* (Romans 8:28). But you must look for it. If you concentrate on the lowly, squalid, and mean, that is all you will find. But if you look for whatsoever is lovely, virtuous, praiseworthy or of good report, you will find those as well (Philippians 4:8).

This Law of Polarity not only helps us look for the good in any situation, but it also gives us the faith to forgive.

Have you ever been betrayed by someone you trusted? Someone you loved and counted on? Maybe that person intentionally hurt you or maybe they just made a poor choice that wreaked havoc on your life. At times we may feel as if we've forgiven and moved on, but when we bump up against the ramifications of another's actions old feelings can re-emerge — indicating that we have not completely forgiven after all.

Think of Joseph who was sold into slavery by his brothers. They hated him, threw him into a pit, wanted to kill him, but then enterprising Judah decided that they should sell him to slave traders and turn a profit instead. When Joseph's brothers finally caught up with him many years later, his travels had brought him to the second highest position in all of Egypt. Only Pharaoh held more power and authority than Joseph. But when Joseph revealed his identity to his brothers, it was evident that he had forgiven them and saw the good in the events of his life.

He said, *"Be not grieved, nor angry with yourselves, that ye sold me hither: for God did send me before you to preserve life. For these two years hath the famine been in the land: and yet there are five years, in the which there shall neither be earing nor harvest. And God sent me before you to preserve you posterity in the earth, and to save your lives by a great deliverance. So now it was not you that sent me hither, but God: and he hath made me a father to Pharaoh, and lord of all his house and a ruler throughout all the land of Egypt"* (Genesis 45:8).

What perspective and faith Joseph had! He wasn't bitter in the least. Everything in his life up to that point indicates that he never held a grudge – even when he was thrown into prison and stayed there for years. He always found the good and rose to the top in whatever circumstance he was placed. We can learn a great lesson from Joseph that we can apply to our own hardships. We can look for the good and see how God can use us in our current circumstances.

The following are some questions that we can ask ourselves when enduring adversity caused by others' poor choices:

- What would I choose to do now, in this given set of circumstances, that I may not have had the courage or willingness to do had I not come to this place?

- What have I learned from this experience? How is it making me a better person?

- How can knowing that God will make lemonade from this lemon, help me be more forgiving of the person whose choices have brought me here?

- What new people are a part of my life due to this path that I am traveling? How are these people improving my life? What can I learn from them?

- How is this experience enabling me to serve others with greater love and compassion?

- What options are now open to me that were not available before?

- How has my faith in God grown as a result of this?

- How is God using my adversity to bless others?

Having faith that God will make even your worst experiences work together for your good gives you the ability to forgive those who have harmed you. After all, it is the garden gate of our own little Gethsemanes that leads us to influential people, trains us, and gives us the opportunity to develop the skills we need to become all that God knows we can be. Have you ever considered that the person who has harmed you was put in your life *because* God knew that person would betray you and lead you on the path you needed to travel? Perhaps Joseph's brothers were chosen to be his siblings *because* God knew they could be counted on to betray him and thus set him on the path to save all of Egypt and future Israel! That's quite a thought to consider, isn't it!?

The Law of Relativity

This law states that things just are. We make them big, small, easy or difficult by how we look at them. If I were to draw a circle on a piece of paper the size of a quarter and asked you if it was a large or small circle, you might look at me funny, unsure of how to answer. But if I drew a circle the size of a dime next it and then asked you if the quarter-size circle was large or small, then you would say it was large. But if I then proceeded to show you a circle the size of an entire sheet of notebook paper, you'd say, "oh, that quarter-size circle is small."

You can't tell if anything is large or small until you compare it to something else. It's the comparison that gives it its characteristics. Rich is relative. You may think someone who makes $200,000 per year is rich. But if you compare him to someone who makes $5 million a year, he doesn't look so rich anymore.

Most of us use this law against ourselves. We take our weaknesses and compare ourselves to other people's strengths. We say, "I'll never be able to make as much money as John." Or "My house would never stay as organized and as clean as Jane's." Or we may try to puff ourselves up by saying, "Look at Mary, her house is a wreck. She needs to be more like me."

That's sort of what Martha was doing with Mary in the Bible when she went to Jesus, *"cumbered about by much serving"* and asked him to make Mary help her. Jesus reminded her that Mary had *"chosen that good part"* (Luke 10:40-42).

We don't need to use this law against ourselves – we don't need to be comparing our worst with another's best. Nor do we need to be puffing ourselves up with pride by comparing our bests with another's worst.

The way we can use this law to our benefit is to realize that other people can look at the same situation and see it totally differently than we do. They come from a different frame of reference. It can help us understand other people better. If I tell you something is "expensive" – well compared to what? Don't limit yourself by your perspective on things. What you think may be "hard or difficult" would be a piece of cake for the Lord.

Have you ever felt assured in those sweet hours of prayer that the Lord has promised you a blessing? Perhaps you've felt the comforting peace that you would receive deliverance from a challenge or that a loved one will one day return to God? But then time passes and nothing happens and you begin to wonder and doubt. So much time may even pass that it now seems impossible that you could receive the promise. It seems too late, perhaps you feel too old, too inadequate, or the problem has magnified with the waiting. Notice all of these are relative terms – too late, too old, too inadequate compared to what?

This reminds me of an account in Genesis, when the Lord promised Abraham that he would make him a great nation and that his children would be as numerous as the sands of the sea and the stars in the sky. God promised Abraham this at a time when it certainly seemed possible. He was a young man in love with his wife Sarah. But years passed and Abraham and Sarah tried with no success to have a child. By the time the Lord and three messengers came to visit them, Genesis 18:11 says that Sarah had become *"old and well stricken in age, and it ceased to be with Sarah after the manner of women."* If anyone had a reason to use the law of relativity against themselves, it was Abraham and Sarah!

Upon this visit the Lord assured Abraham once more, *"I will certainly return unto thee according to the time of life; and, lo, Sarah thy wife shall have a son."*

Sarah, who was standing by the tent door as Abraham sat with the messengers, overheard their conversation and laughed within herself, saying *"After I am waxed old shall I have pleasure, my lord being old also?"*

And the Lord said to Abraham, *"Wherefore did Sarah laugh saying, 'Shall I of a surety bear a child, which am old?' Is any thing too hard for the Lord? At the time appointed I will return unto thee, according to the time of life, and Sarah shall have a son."*

According to the word of the Lord, *"Sarah conceived, and bare Abraham a son in his old age, **at the set time** of which God had spoken to him"* (Genesis 21:2). Abraham was 100 years old when Isaac was born to Sarah.

The poignant question, "Is anything too hard for the Lord?" was answered with a resplendent and eternal "NO!" Nothing is too hard for the Lord! A large majority of people who walk this earth are the descendants of father Abraham and mother Sarah. Their grandson Jacob had twelve sons who became the twelve tribes of Israel and those tribes are scattered about the world. Most of us could probably claim lineage through one of them. Abraham's children did become as numerous as the stars of the sky and the sands of the seashore!

This story is a wonderful recap of the laws we've learned. It's filled with lessons we can apply to our lives.

First, When the Lord Makes a Promise, He Keeps It.

It doesn't matter how impossible or challenging it may seem to us, we may rest assured that the Lord can make anything happen.

> "For with God, nothing shall be impossible" (Luke 1:37).

When we compare our situation to the Lord's perspective, there's nothing too deep, too hard, too overwhelming, or too difficult that He can't fix. Problems, challenges, talents, and abilities will vary from person to person. You can always find someone who is better or worse than you at any given thing, but God is better than us all at everything. There is nothing "bad" in Him. There is only the "good." God is bigger than it all.

When we ask in faith according to God's will, he has promised to grant our petitions. In 1 John 5:14-15 we read, *"And this is the confidence that we have in him, that, if we ask any thing **according to his will**, he hears us: And if we know that he hears us, whatsoever we ask, we know that **we have** the petitions that we desired of him."*

Notice that we *have them*! It doesn't say *we might have them* or we *will have them* it says we already have them! They are ours, already promised and now it's just a matter of time for them to be delivered. It's like ordering some products from your favorite mail order company. They're yours, you've bought them. They're on their way. It's just a matter of time to receive the delivery. We can trust that God is infinitely more reliable than any mail order company or postal carrier! He delivers even on weekends, national holidays and during rain, sleet, snow and hail!

Second, God Has Appointed Times

Notice that the account says that Sarah conceived and bore Abraham a son "at the set time." This is a great illustration of the Law of Gestation. God has appointed times for the delivery of our promised blessings. To attempt to change that time will only lead to frustration and unnecessary worry and doubt. In reality, if we comprehended all that the Lord comprehends, we would not wish to alter His perfect timing. To do so may result in an incomplete blessing or missing out on some portion of it that makes it truly wondrous and full. In God's perfect timing and perfect way, He usually helps others while He fulfills your blessing. He never helps only one when he can help two, three or a multitude more!

Third, Appearances Are Not Truth.

We must admit that we do not comprehend all that the Lord comprehends. Just because appearances suggest that the promise will not be delivered, it matters very little. The Lord is the champion of lost causes. He loves to produce miracles in the lives of His followers. Faith is to think truth regardless of appearances. FEAR is False Evidence Appearing Real.

Fear is looking at things through distorted eyes. Faith, on the other hand, knows the truth - that the seed lies beneath the soil swelling and sprouting, even if the plant with the fruit isn't visible yet. No matter how bad things get or impossible they appear, if the Lord has promised, then He has promised. Whether it is delivered in this life or in the eternities, it will be delivered.

Trust in the Lord. Believe in His promises to you, and gratefully thank Him for those blessings even before they arrive. Believe Him when He tells you that "all things work together for good to those who love God and are called according to His purpose." Look for the good in every challenge. When you expect good in any negative situation, it becomes exciting to see how the Lord will turn it around and make it work for you. He always does, but remember you have to expect it and look for it, or you may never see it. If you're so busy looking at the negative, you won't see the positive even though it's right under your nose!

Lesson 14: Take My Yoke Upon You

Jesus said, *"Take my yoke upon you and learn of me; for I am meek and lowly of heart and ye shall find rest to your souls"* (Matthew 11:29).

A "yoke" is used on animals or people to make it easier to carry a load. An ill-fitted yoke can chafe or strain the wearer. But a custom-made, well-fitted yoke can enable the wearer to carry burdens far beyond their normal capacity. In life, we are called upon to carry burdens. Some we pick up on our own - through poor choices or sin. Others are just part of life on earth. All of us carry one type of yoke or another on our backs. This yoke is what we use to deal with life's challenges.

The yoke we bear is either one we've made ourselves through time and experience, or it is Christ's perfectly fitted and perfectly balanced yoke that makes our burdens light. When Christ told us to take His yoke upon us, He did not mean for us to keep our old, unbalanced and ill-fitted yoke plus add His as well. He meant for us to lay aside our old yoke and take His new and better one upon us. This month, we'll be learning techniques that will help you lay down your yoke so you have room for Christ's.

The Analogy of the Onion

When we start out on this earth, we are pure and innocent little children. Jesus often used children as role models. Jesus explains in Matthew 18 that little children are the ones who shall enter the kingdom of heaven, and if we as adults wish to enter there, we must become as our little children – humble and submissive. Whosoever will humble himself/herself as a little child, the same is greatest in the kingdom of heaven. Whoever offends one of these "little ones" – these little children or His humble followers – it would be better for him that a millstone were hanged about his neck and that he were drowned in the depth of the sea.

But over the course of our lives, other people do offend us. Our environment and the poor choices we make start to build up walls that keep us from realizing who we are, and fulfilling our divine mission that we were sent here to perform.

Let's use an analogy here of the layers of an onion. You and Jesus Christ are at the center of the onion. You're there with all your talents, abilities, and potential for greatness that God has given you or ever will give you. But as you were born into this world, your environment and your choices gradually added layers around your soul – layers to the onion, which formed your own burdensome yoke.

How do these layers accumulate? Our first layers are often unwittingly added by our own parents. When a child is born into a family and she is raised, her parents make mistakes. Whether they mean to or not, parents make mistakes – some more than others. The expectations of our parents and their outward directed hopes and dreams for us can often leave a lingering layer that we carry with us through life. It's like packing burdens on our backs. Their poor examples teach us bad habits that later need to be eliminated. Other more malicious parental layers include abuse, neglect, criticism, and false philosophies or ideas. Some layers linger with us and affect us for the rest of our lives until we can recognize and deal with them.

As we start to grow up, go to school, make friends, and become teenagers, we can pick up more bad habits or false ideas that add more layers. These layers can include the following:

- **Insecurities.** Maybe you were the ugly duckling. Maybe you weren't as smart in school and felt dumb; maybe you were made to feel guilty over things that you didn't need to feel guilty over.

- **Vanity.** Concern with vain things of the world – physical vanity, wealth, materialism, popularity.

- **Pride** - self-centeredness, worrying about what other people think, impressing others.

- **Dishonesty** – with self or others

- **Immorality**

- **Chemical Dependencies** (alcohol, cigarettes, drugs, etc.)

- **False philosophies, false belief systems**

Our layers are added in two different ways – from our environment and from our own choices. So when you become an adult, you must deal with a combination of both the things that have influenced you environmentally along with the results of your own choices.

Layers can be added in any order and not everyone has the same layers. Some layers are serious sins while others are merely mislaid priorities or motives. If you had good parents and never became enslaved to worldly habits or addictions, your onion could have fewer layers, or at least the ones you have might be more subtle than your friend with a drug problem. Whatever beliefs, fears, attitudes and habits you develop to help you deal with life's challenges is the yoke you create over time. This yoke often leaves you feeling uncomfortable, fearful, and unbalanced. When you're feeling discontent or hurting in some way, most likely there is a layer in your life that needs to be addressed.

5 Tools for Peeling the Onion

(Removing the Yoke)

To get down to who you are – to reach your full God-given potential and have a clean, pure communication with God, you must peel the onion or remove your yoke. Applying and re-applying the following tools can do this.

Tool 1: Humble Prayer

Sincere, heartfelt prayer is the first tool. This is not ordinary ritualistic prayer. This is sincere, heartfelt, broken-hearted, wrestling, crying, pleading and hungering prayer. This kind of prayer is work and it happens when we really have a need, really want answers with all our heart and soul. Many times this type of prayer is prompted when we are at the end of our rope, have hit rock bottom, or have been humbled enough to realize we can't handle a situation on our own and need Divine assistance. Recognizing a layer often induces this kind of prayer. For example, recognizing you are enslaved to an addiction and don't know how to beat it can cause you to humble yourself in effective, humble prayer.

When we have bad things happen in our lives, it's often God's way of leading us to the point where we will have this kind of prayer that yields results. Think about it, how often do we have this type of sincere heartfelt prayer when everything is going well in our lives? Not very often for most of us.

Prayer might actually be the hardest work we will ever do. Perhaps that is only fitting since it is our greatest protection against becoming so involved with the worldly accolades and honors that we neglect the nourishment for our soul.

Tool 2: Scripture Study

Prayer is just the beginning. There reaches a point where simply praying is not enough. We must begin to learn more about the Lord, and the best way to do that is through the words that He has spoken. These are found in the scriptures – in the words of His prophets.

Just as ritualistic prayer was not enough for tool number one, casual scripture reading is not enough here. Studying and feasting upon the Word of God is crucial. In order to uncover our buried talents and gifts and overcome the layers, we must learn more about what God has to teach us about who we are and about our souls. In the scriptures Jesus uses many metaphors for divine influence, such as *"living water"* (John 4:10) and *"the bread of life"* (John 6:35).

We eat and we drink to nourish our bodies, but we often forget that our spirits need to be fed as well. Symptoms of spiritual malnutrition include depression, despondency, fear and floundering. When we genuinely study and learn as we read the scriptures, we are feeding our spirits. Studying our scriptures is like a nutritional injection straight into the center of the onion. Sincere, heart-felt prayer followed by scripture study often leads to the exact answers we needed to hear.

Tool 3: Loving Service

Tool 3 is where things start to get rough. Satan doesn't want us to uncover our soul. He doesn't want us to fulfill or even know what our divine mission is. So as we approach tool 3, he doubles his efforts to stop us, to distract us. He knows that the most important principle of all is coming. He knows that his efforts will be seriously jeopardized if we truly understand and implement Christ's teaching that to find ourselves, we must lose ourselves. So he begins to block our increased efforts to love God, to love our neighbor, and to love ourselves.

Jesus taught that the great commandment was to love the Lord our God with all our might mind and strength and to love our neighbor as ourselves. If we could master this one commandment, we would discover that we simultaneously unlocked the ability to succeed in all things.

This is not ordinary love like loving our family members or people who are nice to us, it involves loving everyone – even our enemies. This is an action-oriented love that does more than say, "I love you" but puts those words and feelings into action through selfless service. This type of love only comes when we put the Lord first. It often comes when we freely share the gifts and the talents with which the Lord has blessed us. Grudging or reluctant service does not engender this type of love. But selfless, willing service does.

A sure sign of conversion to Jesus Christ is in how we treat other people. Jesus repeatedly taught to turn the other cheek (Matthew 5:39), to be reconciled to each other (Matthew 5:24), to love our enemies and pray for those who despitefully use us (Matthew 5:44). He taught us to serve each other and avoid contention.

With the Savior's help, we must strip away each ineffective layer we've laid throughout our lives. We actually accumulate these layers because we're afraid. Some layers are added in our vain attempts to protect our souls. We numb ourselves from pain or stress with addictive substances, busyness, by seeking worldly pleasures and practices, or by shutting ourselves off from others. But these methods of trying to protect oneself only serve to block the beauty of the soul that lies at the center of the onion.

What we want to do is learn to trust. This is part of what love does for us. It builds our trust in God and helps us believe that no matter how painful it gets as we peel this onion (peeling onions makes you cry, you know) that it's going to be for our good.

Tool 4: Do All You Can Do

The scriptures tell us to *"Remember without ceasing your **work** of faith, and **labor** of love, and **patience** of hope in our Lord Jesus Christ, in the sight of God and our Father"* (1 Thessalonians 1:3). *"For as the body without the spirit is dead, so faith without works is dead also"* (James 2:26). Our ability to hear spiritually is linked to our willingness to work at it and wait patiently for it.

With each layer you peel, the more your trust in the Lord grows. One young woman I know saw her entire onion, like someone slit it in half. It totally overwhelmed her. She lamented, "I can't do it, I can't even begin to become who I need to become. There are just too many changes I need to make in my life." It's better to just take one layer at a time. If you want to become a body builder, you don't start off trying to lift 500 pounds. You start small and work your way up. Similarly you don't try to peel your onion in one sitting. You don't try to change your entire life, and overcome all your bad habits at once. You take them one at a time. You peel each layer. As you do this, you will gain more strength, and you'll know that God helpd you through it. You'll look back and realize it was painful, but it was worth it. A few months later you might discover that you have something else to work on. Because He helped you before, you have more courage to believe that He'll help you again, and it gradually builds your spiritual muscles. Remember the Lord teaches us *"line upon line, precept on precept, here a little, there a little"* (Isaiah 28:10). It is not necessary for us to run faster than we have strength.

Tool 5: Let Go and Let the Lord Do the Rest

It is common when we have done all we know how to do, that we will still fall short of our goals and dreams. It is at this point we must be willing to let go and let the Lord take over, as He says, "be still and know that I am God" (Psalms 46:10). It is common when we have done all we know how to do, that we will still fall short of our goals and dreams. It is at this point we must be willing to let go and let the Lord take over, as He says, be still and know that I am God (Psalms 46:10).

There are many occasions in our lives when answers must come in their own due time – in God's time. Often God does not immediately deliver us from financial bondage, from illness, or tough challenges. Sometimes God's delays are a result of our past rejection of Him. Sometimes He delays answers so that He can bring us to a point where we will be humble enough to listen, to repent and to come unto Him with all we have. Sometimes we have to hit rock bottom so that we'll know that there's nowhere to go but up and so we'll know that God is our only hope. Other times, God makes us wait simply to show forth His power through our deliverance or our example – "that the works of God should be made manifest in [us]" (John 9:1-3). Other times God delays or says "no" to our request because it's not the right thing for us to have in our lives at the moment. Perhaps the struggle will strengthen our faith and shape us into the person we need to become. Or perhaps He knows something we do not about the road that lies ahead.

Using the Tools to Peel the Onion

We must humble ourselves, come unto Christ and allow Him to show us our weaknesses and help us overcome them one by one. This is really a lifelong process. In order to peel the onion (or lay aside our yoke), we must come to a point where we pay less attention to praise from others so that we are not sidetracked from our path when others disapprove. It's definitely not easy or popular to peel the onion.

As we begin to implement the five tools, the process of peeling the onion flows like this:

- First we recognize that this layer exists and needs to be removed.

- We become keenly aware of our weaknesses. Our understanding increases, we become humbled and we begin to develop a "why" for removing the offending layer. We begin to be motivated to change.

- We gain a desire to remove this bad habit or this false belief.

- We commit to change.

- We go through a painful process of removing the layer of the onion. Although painful, it is always worth it.

- After the layer is removed, we gain an increased level of self-worth and joy. Our love for the Lord increases, as does our faith in Him, and our desire to serve others and to teach them what we have learned.

Once this layer is removed, we discover new layers that should be removed and repeat this process as needed throughout our lifetime. Step by step our lives become more joyous. Bit by bit our faith grows until we know to trust the Lord, to allow Him to clean up our lives and make them even better. We learn from experience that He will never allow us to go through anything that will not make us better in the end. We learn to go ahead and submit to His will sooner because we know that it will be much easier if we will, and the joy will come more quickly.

Peeling Clue

The onion analogy gives a wonderful clue to how we should work on our weaknesses. Think about it. How do you peel an onion? You start with the top layer – in this analogy the layer that went on last, then work backward in time through your weaknesses. For as Jesus said, "the last shall be first and the first shall be last." (Matthew 20:16).

You'll often find that your deepest and most challenging weaknesses to remove are those that were laid in childhood. Things your parents did or didn't do, or choices that you made in youth often are the most difficult and tender to remove. Patience is critical in peeling the onion – give yourself time to overcome your weaknesses. God is patient and long-suffering and will give you time to heal and change.

Throughout the next few lessons, we'll discuss common onion layers or yoke-bound burdens that many of us carry, and how to remove them.

Lesson 15: Fear: The Root of Most Burdens

As children of God, we have unlimited potential for making the world a better place. In a world escalating in depravity and humanistic ideals, the influence of righteous men and women can turn the tide. Yet, collectively speaking, we are much like Dorothy and her little party in the Wizard of Oz who were put to sleep in a field of poppies just before reaching their final destination. Today a vast army of spiritual giants slumber and sleep. It is as if Satan couldn't get us to join him, so he cons us into burdening our shoulders with ill-fitted yokes full of spiritual poppies. These spiritual poppies lull us away into a dream world where reality fades, nightmares take hold and false fantasies consume our precious lives. These spiritual "poppies" of which I speak include fear, guilt, self-pity, busyness and feelings of inadequacy.

Fear is the mother of the family of spiritual poppies. It is the root from which the others spring. Fear keeps us from trying, from doing our best, from loving, from giving. We might be afraid of being hurt, being vulnerable, being abandoned, being a failure, or even being a success. Fear is often rooted in very real experiences that we have had sometime in our lives. The things that happen or don't happen to us in childhood and our youth have a profound impact on the fears we hold today.

While studying what the scriptures have to say about fear, I noticed that the words *fear* and *love* are used as antonyms. Particularly, Luke 12 is a rich tutorial in overcoming fear. What causes fear or worry? Sometimes fear is a valuable asset. If our children are in danger, then it is proper to have fight or flight reactions. Parents have performed superhuman feats and gone to great risks to protect their children in danger. But often, we let fear rule our lives. Fear is caused when something that is important to us feels threatened. This causes us to kick into a fight or flight mode. We'll do anything we can to try to protect what is important to us – no matter how rational or irrational it may be.

Others can often see the irrationality of our fears, but to us they are very real and controlling. Often we don't even know the root of our fears, until we delve down into where the fear is coming from. Many times, we must dig back into our childhood to discover the causes of fears that hold us back today.

One example of this is clearly demonstrated in the life of a woman I know. Maureen grew up in a home where her biological father died in a tragic accident. Her mother was left alone to raise several small children, but soon remarried. The man she married

---

Marnie L. Pehrson

was an alcoholic. The mother, in order to dull her own fears and anxiety, turned to prescription drugs. As a small child, Maureen was traumatized by the loss of her father and lived in fear of losing her mother as well. She was so afraid of being abandoned by the key people in her life, that her nickname in kindergarten was "glue" because she clung to her mother's skirt every day when she was dropped off at school.

When Maureen grew up, she had such an intense need to belong to someone that she married poorly at the tender age of 17. She developed addictions to drugs to dull her senses the way she had seen her parents do. For over twenty years she stuck with a marriage to a man who wallowed in the same addictive lifestyle, crushed her self-esteem with his use of pornography, refused to support her and her children, resented any ambition she had, and stifled any desires she had to rise above her situation. Her fear of abandonment kept her stuck, until after 10 years of consistently working to change her thinking, she found freedom with God's help.

As callous as it may sound, fear occurs when our priorities are out of order. When we put anything in a higher place than God, we block His ability to free us from our burdens and fears. Our priorities may be out of order because no one ever taught us correct principles (as in Maureen's case) or because we have willfully chosen to misalign our priorities. Jesus taught, "For where your treasure is, there will your heart be also." So if your treasure is something that can be stolen by thieves or taken by men or damaged or destroyed, then fear, doubt and worry are going to be a very real part of your life.

Some typical priorities that we often put before God are outlined below.

Family

Families are a divine institution. God instituted marriage in the Garden of Eden. But Christ on several occasions warned us against letting even family stand in our way. In Luke 12:51-53 He explains how His message will divide households. "The father shall be divided against the son, and the son against the father; the mother against the daughter, and the daughter against the mother; the mother in law against her daughter in law, and the daughter in law against her mother in law." The gospel of Jesus Christ can cause divisions within households between those who choose to embrace it and those who reject it.

Being overly concerned with what family members think can cause fear and worry because we will be afraid to progress in our growth in the gospel for fear of alienating others. As Jesus said in Matthew 10:37, "He that loveth father or mother more than me is not worthy of me: and he that loveth son or daughter more than me is not worthy of me."

In Maureen's case, her fear of abandonment from childhood made her cling to family members and eventually her spouse for support in place of God. Each of the people in her life proved incapable of giving her the support and strength that she needed. Only God could help her rise above and conquer her fears, and He did. Although we should cherish our family members and spouse, they must not take such a high place in our hearts that they lead us to defy God and live contrary to His commands. If we do, we will find ourselves selling our souls to satisfy others.

Power

If your treasure is in having positions of power and social standing, these can be lost when someone else comes along who is more popular than you and topples you from your position. Depending upon how bad you want power, you might lie, steal, or cheat to gain those positions. And as Christ said, "There is nothing covered, that shall not be revealed; neither hid, that shall not be known. Whatsoever ye have spoken in darkness shall be heard in the light; and that which ye have spoken in the ear in closets shall be proclaimed upon the housetops." (Luke 12:2-3) Fear of losing power and a desire to do anything for it will eventually cause one's demise, because one's sins will always catch up with them.

Materialism

If your treasure or love in life is material possessions, then you are building your foundation on something that can be lost. Economies change, industries collapse, thieves and embezzlers can steal. When we are unduly concerned with material things, when they are our love in life, it is natural to experience fear and worry because these things cannot last forever.

Popularity

If you treasure what others think of you, then you are in a precarious position, because no matter how hard we try, we cannot please everyone all of the time. We cannot force people to love us or to care about us. It seems the harder we try to be popular with others, the more we sway and bend until we no longer stand for anything and end up hating ourselves for our lack of integrity. Fear and worry are continual companions to one who worries about what others think of him because this is something we can never fully control.

The Lord gives the following promise and warning about popularity, "Whosoever shall confess me before men, him shall the Son of man also confess before the angels of God. But he that denieth me before men shall be denied before the angels of God." (Luke 12:8-9)

Life

If your treasure is the longevity of your own life, fear and worry are inevitable. Everyone has to die sometime. Undue concern over death and disease can actually cause so much worry and stress that we induce illness upon ourselves. When we spend all our energies focusing on what we don't want, we end up attracting it into our life. As Jesus said, "Be not afraid of them that kill the body, and after that have no more that they can do." The soul's destination is what matters, not the time or method of our mortal end.

Fear, the Antithesis of Love

Fear is misdirected or imperfect love. There is only one love that does not induce fear. As a matter of fact, it eradicates fear. It is the love of God, the pure love of Christ. "There is no fear in love; but perfect love casteth out fear: because fear hath torment. He that feareth is not made perfect in love." (1 John 4:18)

As followers of Christ, we should not experience ongoing fear. Sure, we might have a burst of fear in a dangerous situation. This is only normal and is a safety mechanism. But fear that keeps us from progressing in life and from being all that we can be is merely a symptom of priorities that are not in order.

Jesus taught His disciples that life is more than meat, and the body is more than raiment. He taught them to consider the lilies of the field and the birds in the sky. The Lord clothes and feeds the lilies and the birds, how much more the Lord will clothe us if we have faith. He admonished the disciples to have faith, to "be not of a doubtful mind." All these things that the world seeks, the Father already knows that we need. "But rather seek ye the kingdom of God; and all these things shall be added unto you." (Luke 12:22-32).

Jesus also said, "Fear not, little flock; for it is your Father's good pleasure to give you the kingdom." (Luke 12:32). God wants to bless us! He is waiting and willing to bless us, but often we tie His hands because we focus on things that don't last.

When we truly put God first and love Him first, the Lord changes our hearts so that we begin to become perfected in love. This love casts out fear. We no longer worry about money or power or prestige or popularity. We no longer care what family or friends may think of us, because we care more about what God thinks of us. The only cure for fear and worry is to put God first. There is no other answer.

Fear, Faith and Opportunities Lost

In Matthew chapter 14, Jesus sent His disciples away on a ship by themselves while He took some time to go into the mountains to pray and rejuvenate after a long day of teaching the multitude. When evening came, He descended from the mountain and observed His disciples on a ship in the midst of the wind-tossed sea. Between 3:00 and 6:00 in the morning (the fourth watch), Jesus went out to them walking on the sea.

When the disciples saw Him, they were afraid and said "It is a spirit." And they cried out with fear. But immediately Jesus spoke to them, saying, "Be of good cheer; it is I; be not afraid." When Jesus called out, Peter answered, "Lord, if it be thou, bid me come unto thee on the water." And Jesus said, "Come." Peter stepped out of the ship and onto the water to go to Jesus. After only a few steps Peter looked around to see the wind boisterously chopping at the sea, became afraid and began to sink. He cried out, "Lord, save me!" Immediately Jesus stretched forth His hand, caught him and said to him, "O thou of little faith, wherefore didst thou doubt?" They went into the ship and the wind ceased. Those who were in the ship came and worshipped Jesus saying, "Of a truth thou art the son of God."

We've touched on this account before, but it bears examining again. It is rich with lessons that we can apply to our lives today.

Many times in our lives, the things that are coming toward us that cause us the most grief and worry are really the best things for us. Just as Jesus coming toward the disciples would bring them peace, knowledge and insight, so our trials and challenges will eventually bring us the same if we choose to look for what can be learned instead of continually crying, "Why me? Why now?" Rather we should ask, "What can I learn from this? What is the Lord trying to teach me from this? What decision will this event cause me to make that I wouldn't have made had not this event occurred? Where is the Lord trying to direct my life?"

Marnie L. Pehrson

We have to make the first move. Often we have to step out of our comfort zone into choppy waters in order to grow spiritually. Jesus was there for Peter, but Peter was the one who had to take that leap of faith from a safe secure ship into the swirling sea. Jesus will never force or compel us. He always beckons, "Come unto me." It is always our choice. We can choose to step out and reap the promised blessings or we can stay in our old, safe way of doing things thereby losing opportunities for amazing spiritual growth.

Keep your eye on the Master. Peter did just fine until he started looking around at what was going on with the wind and the sea. As long as he had his eye on Jesus, he didn't sink. But as soon as he let his earthly environment preoccupy his thoughts, he began to fear. For as soon as Peter began to fear, he lost faith and began to sink. Fear and faith cannot occupy our minds at the same time. We, too, should keep our eyes on the Master. No matter how scary the surroundings, how bleak the future, or how dangerous and unsupportive our environment may appear, we can walk on the water if we keep our eyes on the Master and have no fear.

Jesus identifies Himself. When the disciples were afraid as Jesus approached the ship on the water, the scriptures tell us that He *straightway* spoke to them to calm them, letting them know that it was He. We too can be comforted if we will call upon the Lord during our trials and challenges. If we listen and watch, the Lord will comfort us even in the midst of trials so that we can know that everything that is happening will work together for our good. We can be calm amidst even the most fear-inducing circumstances.

If we do not hear His comforting voice calling out to us, "Be of good cheer; it is I; be not afraid" it is often because our frantic state does not allow us to see with spiritual eyes or hear with spiritual ears.

Jesus is always there to pull us up. He will never leave us nor forsake us. Just as He was there to lift Peter when he feared and sank, so Jesus will be there to lift us up when we sink with fear.

Fear leads to lost opportunities. Peter was lovingly lifted by the Savior out of the water and carried to the ship, but his fear lost him the opportunity to walk on water. We do not know whether or not Peter ever had the chance to walk on water again, but we do know that he lost this opportunity as a result of taking his eye off the Master. When we fear, take our focus off Jesus Christ and sink in loss of faith, we can still be lifted by His loving arms, but we do lose precious opportunities – spiritual highs, growth and precious memories that may never come again.

Let us keep our eye on our Lord Jesus Christ and trust His loving arms, never fearing, never doubting so that we can obtain all the rich blessings He has to give us. Keep your eye on the Master and walk on, walk on.

Exercise: Rate Your Priorities

Be completely honest with yourself. Where do you spend your time? What do you worry about the most? What is most important to you? Rate your priorities below:

1. _____

2. _____

3. _____

4. _____

5. _____

Identify Your Fears

If God isn't #1, what would happen if you moved Him to that spot? Why haven't you before now? What are you afraid of? Sometimes if we just identify what we are afraid of, we can diffuse the fear.

Even if God is in your #1 spot, are there things you'd like to be or do, but fears stand in your way? Name your fears below and then resolve to face them with your eyes on the Master:

_____

_____

_____

_____

_____

This lesson is an excerpt from *10 Steps to Fulfilling Your Divine Destiny*. More details are at http://www.SheLovesGod.com/book/

Marnie L. Pehrson

Lesson 16: Conquering Self-Pity

In the last lesson I compared the poppies in the Wizard of Oz to the tools Satan uses to keep us from reaching our God-given potential and experiencing joy. Continuing with that theme, we'll move on to another costly spiritual poppy.

The self-pity poppy is one that lulls us away into focusing on the negative aspects of our lives. The trap of focusing on the negative is that you can't focus on the positive. Everybody has bad things happen in their lives. There are no exceptions to that. Some may occur because of poor choices, our own disobedience or the disobedience of others, but many times, it's just part of life that bad things happen. No one is immune to the effects of living in a fallen world where disease, death, poverty, natural disasters, disappointment and sin occur.

It sometimes seems that certain people receive more than their fair share of disappointments. One such person is my sister Lisa. Lisa is severely nearsighted, has Crohns Disease, a sponge kidney that perpetually makes kidney stones, has had thyroid cancer, and has lived most of her young adult and adult life in one form of pain or another. Yet, she doesn't go around complaining or wallowing in it. Instead she keeps her sense of humor, focuses on serving in her church, putting her energy into her home, and serving her husband and children. Instead of focusing on all the things she could be sorry for, she uses her energy in positive ways by developing her exceptional art and teaching abilities to enrich the lives of her family and community.

The seductiveness of the self-pity poppy is that it feels so justified most of the time. There's always someone in your life who will tell you "Poor you, you have it so bad! How can you do anything with such horrible things happening in your life?" Listen to this type of self-talk or statements from others long enough, and you begin to believe it. You start to believe, "I can't do this, I'm disabled." Or "If I didn't come from such a poor family, I could have made something of my life." But the truth is, we may not be able to control what happens to us, but we can choose how we will react to it. We can choose to let these things make us bitter or we can use them as stepping stones to become better.

The first question we tend to ask when something bad happens is "Why me? Why now?" Although we can't always know the exact reason, or at least not until some time later, there are some basic reasons why God allows us to endure hardship.

It's a Test

Remember Abraham when he was asked to offer his only son Isaac as a sacrifice? Genesis 22:12-13. Abraham prepared Isaac and placed him on the altar and raised his knife to slay him, when he heard a voice from above saying, *"Lay not thine hand upon the lad, neither do thou any thing unto him: for now I know that thou fearest God, seeing thou hast not withheld thy son, thine only son from me. And Abraham lifted up his eyes, and looked, and behold behind him a ram caught in a thicket by his horns: and Abraham went and took the ram, and offered him up for a burnt offering in the stead of his son."*

Sometimes the Lord is testing our devotion so that we will know just how far we are willing to go to follow Him. Often, we like Abraham, will be given a "ram in the thicket" at the last minute, but sometimes there is no ram. We must not lose confidence or doubt our faith if no miracle occurs to deliver us. Sometimes the test is simply a test of endurance. Life is a test of faith, a test of our ability to take the long eternal look instead of dwelling on the here and now.

It's Shaping Us

In Malachi 3:3 the Lord says He will *"sit as a refiner and purifier of silver."* He purges those who follow Him as gold and silver. There are a few interesting facts about the silver purification process. First, the refiner must sit patiently and watch steadily while the refining process takes place. If the silver is allowed to stay in the furnace too long, it will be damaged. Similarly, Christ monitors our purification process to ensure that we are not tested more than we are able to bear. A second interesting point about the silver refining process is that the silversmith knows that the purifying process is complete when He can see His own image reflected in the silver. This is the end result of the Lord's refining process… to shape us in His image.

Jesus told us to *"Be ye therefore perfect even as your Father in Heaven is perfect."* In Hebrew, the word used for "perfect" means complete, finished, or mature. Much of this polishing and completeness comes through the refiner's fire.

> As C.S. Lewis explained, "Imagine yourself as a living house. God comes in to rebuild that house. At first, perhaps, you can understand what He is doing. He is getting the drains right and stopping the leaks in the roof and so on: you knew that those jobs needed doing and so you are not surprised. But presently He starts knocking

the house about in a way that hurts abominably and does not make sense. What on earth is He up to? The explanation is that He is building quite a different house from the one you thought of – throwing out a new wing here, putting on an extra floor there, running up towers, making courtyards. You thought you were going to be made into a decent little cottage: but He is building a palace. He intends to come and live in it Himself." [1]

It Builds Faith

While Jesus was on His way to raise a ruler's daughter from the dead, a woman, who was diseased with an issue of blood for twelve years, came behind Him and touched the hem of His garment. She had said to herself, *"If I could just touch His garment, I shall be made whole."* When she touched His clothing, Jesus turned around and said to her, *"Daughter, be of good comfort; thy faith hath made thee whole."* And she was healed that very hour. (Matthew 9:20-22)

When we read this story, we marvel at the faith that this woman had – to only touch Jesus' garment and be healed. We often wonder at Jesus himself who was so sensitive that He could tell when a portion of His power was being used by another's faith. But something we rarely think about is the life of this woman. She had spent the last twelve years hemorrhaging. And not only would this have been a total aggravation and weakened her into a state of anemia, but also she would have been an outcast from society.

The Law of Moses required a woman with an issue of blood to be separated. Everything she touched or sat on was considered unclean. Anyone she touched or touched her was considered unclean. Even when a woman's "issue of blood" ceased, she would have been considered unclean for seven more days and then on the eighth day she was to go and make an offering to the priests (Leviticus 15:19-28). This poor woman had been considered unclean and separated from others for twelve years! Everyone and everything she came in contact with would have been considered unclean.

Can you imagine the heartache and the pain this woman must have experienced for twelve long years? Can you imagine the pleading and the cries she must have raised in prayer to her Father in Heaven for healing and comfort? For twelve long years no answer came. No healing occurred. Yet she never lost her faith. If anything her faith appears to have increased with her trial for she knew that all she had to do was touch Jesus' garment and she would be healed.

Did Jesus shun her as unclean? The Law of Moses would have required Him to. But He did not. Instead He recognized her great faith, had compassion on her and healed her according to her faith.

Many times we must suffer for extended lengths of time – pleading for answers, for relief, for healing. Yet the answer appears to be "No." This does not mean that God does not hear our cries or that He loves us any less. It simply isn't the right time yet. Perhaps we haven't learned all we needed to learn yet. Perhaps our faith has not been refined to the extent that God knows it should be.

In three short verses, this woman sets a powerful example of enduring in faithfulness through trials that seem to go on and on. She teaches us that we should never blame God or give up hope. Her story is one of hope – that Jesus loves us and that eventually, in God's time, through our faith (whether in this life or the hereafter) we will be healed and the light will come.

It Teaches Us about Ourselves

In the Garden of Eden, the Lord asked Adam where he was. Of course, the Lord who knows everything already knew where Adam was. It was Adam who needed to think about and evaluate where he was (Genesis 3:9). The Lord knows what we are made of. It is we who need to learn our capacity.

After losing his wife, the love of his life, C.S. Lewis wrote, "God has not been trying to experiment upon my faith or love in order to find out their quality. He knew it already. It was I who didn't."[2]

7 Lifelines for Staying Positive Amidst Adversity

The following is an expansion on some thoughts that were shared with me by Vickey Pahnke, a religious educator, singer, and songwriter. Vickey's friends fondly refer to her as the "poster child for adversity" because of her many health problems over the years. She gave me a list of "lifelines" she uses to help her stay positive amidst adversity.

#1 Remember We Have a Choice in How We React in Any Given Situation

Viktor Frankl, a psychiatrist who suffered years in Nazi concentration camps explained, "Everything can be taken from a man but one thing: the last of the human freedoms — to choose one's attitude in any given set of circumstances, to choose one's own way. And there were always choices to make. . . . Fundamentally . . . any [one] can, even under such circumstances, decide what shall become of him — mentally and spiritually."[3]

We cannot choose many of our circumstances, but we can choose how we will react to them. This is a conscious decision. Our freedom to choose whether to act or simply react is always ours.

#2 Grab Hold of the Positive

"One thing I absolutely believe in the validity of is actively seeking something spiritual every single day because usually, we wallow in misery. That's a very base, worldly thing to do. The Savior had some miserable conditions but He never wallowed. He always looked up. The symbolism there is looking up – where we're focused. It's all a matter of focus. Some people say to take comfort in the fact that there's always someone worse off than you are. But when you're in the middle of something bad, that doesn't help you. What does help is to figure out something to do for someone else. I believe that no matter what we're going through, it doesn't give us license to treat anybody else poorly."[4]

#3 Use Your Resources

What are some resources we have available to lean on in our times of trial?

- Family
- Friends
- Scriptures
- Prayer
- Church members
- Ecclesiastical leaders

"This is really hard to do for a lot of us. We're afraid to ask for help for fear of rejection. We have to become as little children to go back home (Matthew 18:3). Little children are not saddled with pride. Little children aren't working an angle. Little children don't have ulterior motives. They have absolute trust in their parents – if their parents are good.

Our quest is to return to that state – to have absolute trust in Heavenly Father, to get rid of the pride, and to see the wonder in the things that really matter, just like the children do. Sometimes it's the refiner's fire that melts all the junk that we don't need on us and in us. "[5]

#4 Really Look and Listen

"That still small voice is still and it's small so you really have to take time in the midst of all the craziness to really listen to make sure you're hearing so that the Spirit can tell you what you need to help you. Look very carefully. There is more to be seen with our spiritual eyes. Sometimes someone will look at a mother and a daughter and say they look just alike. Another will say 'You don't look a thing like your mother' because people see things differently. Sometimes we see spiritual things, and sometimes we do not. We have to try to use our spiritual eyes.

"Here's an example: You frantically look for your keys and can't find them anywhere. Then you take a deep breath, relax and there they are right there within plain sight. That's how it is in our lives. There are means to alleviate our grief right in front of us. But we're so frantic we're not seeing clearly. It's that same principle with all our spirituality. There are things right in front of us, but if we don't have eyes to see it, we'll miss it. Listen with spiritual ears and look with spiritual eyes for the things Heavenly Father would teach you. "[6]

#5 Pray

"James 5:16 says, '*The effectual fervent prayer of a righteous man (or woman) availeth much.*' In Luke 11:1 one of Jesus' disciples asked, "*Lord teach us to pray.*" Remember that the Lord did teach us how to pray in the Garden of Gethsemane. That was a very personal communication between Him and His Father. The thing He taught us is, 'Please, please take this off me, but not my will but thine.' He did what His Father needed Him to do. That took an amazing level of faith. None of us will have to endure a Gethsemane, but our own little Gethsemanes seem awfully huge sometimes. There is a difference in saying your prayers and praying. We're talking about really praying here – hungering, thirsting, pleading, and communicating."[7]

#6 Have a Sense of Humor

"When you're going through a hard time, it is wonderful relief and release to be able to laugh. Sometimes I will say, 'Ok, it's time for a funny movie' so that I'll be able to laugh. Children laugh a lot more than adults do – they've studied this statistically. Laughter is good.

Laughter is so important that it's spoken of right off the bat in Genesis. Both Abraham and Sarah, when they found out they were going to have a baby, they both reacted the

---

Marnie L. Pehrson

same way. Genesis 17:17 tells us that *'Abraham fell upon his face and laughed.''* Sarah said, *'God hath made me to laugh, so that all that hear will laugh with me'* (Genesis 21:6).

"The Hebrew translation of the word that has been translated 'to laugh' makes this much clearer so we understand. The Hebrew word which means 'to laugh' means 'to rejoice.' In Hebrew laughing is a synonym for rejoicing. Our laughter should be a rejoicing. That does away with all laughter that is crude, course, is hurtful or is at the expense of someone else. We're adding a rejoicing factor to our lives when we have the kind of humor that would lift us."[8]

#7 Wait

"Just have patience. Sometimes we have to wait. To wait on God, no time is lost… wait on. On His timetable things are answered. There is sometimes a war between our human nature and our divine nature. We need to work on our divine nature because there is a spark of divinity within us. *'We are the children of God'* (Romans 8:16). We need to wait patiently on the Lord. "[9]

Waiting is the hard part. The following are two different accounts that express the range of feelings we often experience when waiting on the Lord.

C.S. Lewis wrote in *A Grief Observed*: "Where is God? This is one of the most disquieting symptoms. When you are happy, so happy that you have no sense of needing Him, so happy that you are tempted to feel His claims upon you as an interruption, if you remember yourself and turn to Him with gratitude and praise, you will be – or so it feels – welcomed with open arms. But go to Him when your need is desperate, when all other help is vain, and what do you find? A door slammed in your face, and a sound of bolting and double bolting on the inside. After that, silence. You may as well turn away. The longer you wait, the more emphatic the silence will become. There are no lights in the windows. It might be an empty house. Was it ever inhabited? It seemed so once. And that seeming was as strong as this. What can this mean? Why is He so present a commander in our time of prosperity and so very absent a help in time of trouble?

"You never know how much you really believe anything until its truth or falsehood becomes a matter of life and death to you. It is easy to say you believe a rope to be strong and sound as long as you are merely using it to cord a box. But suppose you had to hang by that rope over a precipice. Wouldn't you then first discover how much you really trusted it? Only a real risk tests the reality of a belief...

Bridge players tell me that there must be some money on the game, or else people won't take it seriously. Apparently it's like that. Your bid – for God or no God, for a good God or the Cosmic Sadist, for eternal life or nonentity – will not be serious if nothing is staked on it. And you will never discover how serious it was until the stakes are raised horribly high; until you find that you are playing not for counters or for sixpencees but for every penny you have in the world. Nothing less will shake a man – or at any rate a man like me – out of his verbal and his merely notional beliefs. He has to be knocked silly before he comes to his senses...

But of course one must take the 'set to try us' the right way. God has not been trying an experiment upon my faith or love in order to find out their quality. He knew it already. It was I who didn't. In this trial He makes us occupy the dock, the witness box, and the bench all at once. He always knew that my temple was a house of cards. His only way of making me realize the fact was to knock it down....

You can't see anything properly while your eyes are blurred with tears." he wrote as he began his journey out of the darkness of doubt. "You can't in most things get what you want if you want it too desperately: anyway you can't get the best out of it... And so perhaps with God. I have gradually been coming to feel that the door is no longer shut and bolted. Was it my own frantic need that slammed it in my face? The time when there is nothing at all in your soul except a cry for help may be just the time when God can't give it to you: you are like the drowning man who can't be helped because he clutches and grabs. Perhaps your own reiterated cries deafen you to the voice you hoped to hear."[10]

As I said earlier, it does little good to cry, "Why did this have to happen to me? Why now? Why this?" There is really nothing we can do to change the reason why things happen. What we need to do instead is ask ourselves, "What does the Lord want me to learn from this? What does He want me to do next? What would I do or learn now that I wouldn't have had this situation not occurred?" These questions can help us tap into the opportunities that lie within adversity and grow further toward the person the Lord knows we can become.

In summary, as we go through trials and troubles, let us remember their purpose and take the long eternal look toward the rewards of our faith and endurance. This is eloquently summarized in Revelations 7:14-17, *"These are they which came out of great tribulation, and have washed their robes, and made them white in the blood of the Lamb. Therefore are they before the throne of God, and serve Him day and night in His temple: and He that sitteth on the throne shall dwell among them. They shall hunger no more, neither thirst any more;*

neither shall the sun light on them, nor any heat. For the Lamb which is in the midst of the throne shall feed them, and shall lead them unto living fountains of waters: and God shall wipe away all tears from their eyes."

Resources

[1] C.S. Lewis, Mere Christianity, page 176

[2] C.S. Lewis, A Grief Observed, p21-22

[3] Viktor E. Frankl, Man's Search for Meaning (New York: Washington Square Press, 1984), 87.

[4] Vickey Pahnke, SheLovesGod.com Interview, September 2000

[5] Vickey Pahnke, SheLovesGod.com Interview, September 2000

[6] Ibid

[7] Ibid.

[8] Ibid.

[9] Ibid.

[10] C.S. Lewis as quoted by Brent L. Top, *God's Megaphone to a Deaf World*, C.S. Lewis: The Man and His Message, p. 137-139)

Lesson 17: Choose That Good Part

Christians are called upon to fill many roles in their lives: wives and husbands, mothers and fathers, professionals, entrepreneurs, students, teachers, citizens and the list goes on. If one word could be used to describe modern civilization more than any other, I would think "busy" would be the most universal descriptor.

With few exceptions, modern men and women are busy. Through this busyness something is lost, something of value. Now I'm not advocating indolence. Too much time on one's hands leads to too self-indulgence and self-pity which can lead to low self-worth and feelings of inferiority. But there should be some balance in between.

It is this sense of balance that we usually ever-elusively try to claim. I'm not sure that it is ever completely achievable in mortality, but it is a worthy goal. Most of us turn to self-help books, organizing resources, time management tools, and mini-classes to help us juggle our busy lives. But, shouldn't we turn to the ultimate source of Truth to discover the answers? Surely there ought to be an answer to this modern dilemma. Or is it really so modern? It's evidently timeless.

Remember the account found in Luke 10:38-42 when Jesus goes to eat dinner at Martha's house. Martha was working hard around the house, preparing the meal, while her sister Mary sat at His feet listening to Him speak. But Martha was *"cumbered about much serving, and came to him, and said, Lord, dost thou not care that my sister hath left me to serve alone? Bid her therefore that she help me. And Jesus answered and said unto her, Martha, Martha, thou art careful and troubled about many things: But one thing is needful: and Mary hath chosen that good part, which shall not be taken away from her."*

What is He saying to Martha? Is He saying, "Stop whining, Martha, you worry too much?" Should we all stop working and cleaning our houses and sit and read our scriptures all day long? No, that's that "all or nothing" mentality we fall into… that it's an "either/or" situation. It is true that work must be done. Earthly cares and needs should be addressed, but not to the exclusion of spiritual nourishment. When all is said and done, the only thing you can take with you is the knowledge and wisdom you gain in this life and the relationships you forge. These are the only things that "shall not be taken away" from you.

If this is true, and I believe virtually everyone who believes in an afterlife would agree this is true, then why do we spend so little time collecting that which "shall not be taken away" from us? Why do we get caught up in continual busyness and starve our souls? One of my friends says, "If Satan can't make you bad, he'll make you busy." I believe there is truth in that statement. He makes Christians so busy, they don't even know they have a divine purpose for being here, much less do they take the time to discover it and fulfill it. Thus, in essence he neutralizes a great force for good on this earth. Collectively speaking, righteous men and women are a great sleeping giant ready to awake. But Satan does not want us to awake! There is too much we could do to thwart his plans.

The destination of future generations lies in the hands of today's mothers, fathers, teachers and leaders. We each shape and mold the future. Yet, most of us go through life with blinders on, like workhorses oblivious to the value of the precious cargo we pull behind us.

Waking Up

The first step to changing behavior is recognizing that there is a problem – awaking that sleeping giant. Several years ago, a friend who used to live on a neighboring farm, but through circumstances beyond her control now lives in the suburbs, was lamenting the loss of her outdoor view. Her son was staying at my house several days a week and when she picked him up; she wistfully longed to have a front porch view like mine and vowed that one day she would again. I reminded her that she was welcome to come by and sit on my front porch anytime. Of course, did I ever sit on my front porch and enjoy the view? Hardly! I was too busy chasing toddlers, studying, writing or building Web communities to make time to relax and enjoy the view 10 steps away from my computer desk.

Then one afternoon she stopped by my house at 4:30 when I was busy at my computer. She urged me out onto my front porch to chat. "Come on, come on, get away from that computer for a few minutes and enjoy this porch! It's gorgeous out here!" she coaxed. Reluctantly, I left my email box to join her on the front porch. I had no clue how unseasonably warm it was outside. As we sat and talked, it struck me how blessed we were. We had so much abundance that we didn't even have the time to enjoy it all. As we spoke, I began to see my blessings through new eyes – through the eyes of my friend who could truly appreciate them. Upon watching her drive away, I was left with a sense of gratitude, but also a sense of sadness for my friend who had lost something so precious to her. This was a gentle reminder for me to not only count my blessings but also to take time to enjoy them.

I believe that life is about learning lessons. And one of the biggest lessons we're here to learn is to appreciate what we have, take care of it, and enjoy it. Life has a way of seeing that we do this through three progressive phases: gentle reminders, warning signals and the whirlwind (calamity). It's like your automobile. You know those little stickers that gently remind you when your oil was last changed and when it needs to be changed again? If you ignore that gentle reminder, the warning light will come on in your car. If you ignore the oil light, then get ready for calamity to strike – serious damage to your car.

Our bodies work similarly. Loss of energy or weight gain act as gentle reminders. Excessive colds and flu, low blood sugar, or anemia can act as warning signals. Then, if we ignore our bodies long enough, they'll use serious illnesses to get our attention. Not only does this principle work for our bodies and automobiles, but it also works in every aspect of our lives and even in societies as a whole.

The older I get, the more I realize that I should be listening to the gentle reminders before they get to warning signals and whirlwinds. But this wasn't something at which I naturally excelled. In fact, it was a motif for my life – ignore it until it gets to the crisis point then scrounge in a panic to repair the damage. I've learned the hard way that an ounce of prevention is worth a pound of cure.

As I was thinking about this, I thought, "I don't think I had gentle reminders in the past. I think my life went straight to warning signals and whirlwinds." But you know what? I'm convinced there were gentle reminders, but I was just too busy or hard headed to see them. I didn't recognize them for what they were. Over time, I've noticed more gentle reminders and have discovered that they come in many forms:

- My small son peeking around a corner with flirty eyes and coy grin is a reminder of how precious these days in his life are and how blessed I am to have happy, healthy beautiful children. This reminder is saying, "Take time to enjoy them!"

- Seeing my friends and family members struggle with illness or loss, are gentle reminders to appreciate my blessings while I have them.

- A friend pointing out my blessings is a gentle reminder to be grateful for what I have instead of continually running on a treadmill for "more and better" things that I'll just eventually ignore and take for granted too.

- My husband coaxing me out onto the front porch to see a stunning sunset is a gentle reminder to enjoy nature and take time for those I love.

Marnie L. Pehrson

- My weary eyes at the end of the day are a gentle reminder to stop burning the candle at both ends and get more rest.

The list could go on and on. What are your gentle reminders? Take the time to notice them, and then act upon their messages before they progress to warning signals and heaven-forbid, the whirlwind.

This awareness that you've been moving through life with workhorse blinders on (and that you've been missing out on the things that really matter) is only the beginning. Just because you become aware that you have a problem, does not mean that you know how to correct it or even that you will correct it. It takes time to change old habits, and rarely does that happen overnight unless some life-impacting event comes along to jolt us into line. Such events might be illness, the death of a loved one, or a business failure. Sometimes God has to burn our bridges so that we will turn to Him for Him to pick us up and put us back on the track that He intends for our lives.

Sometimes It Takes an Angel

At other times, God sends angels to help us make these course corrections. "Angels?" you might ask. Yes, angels in the form of other people who help us find the way, who snatch us up from the trenches and put us on a higher path. The people who are in our lives are there for a reason, and many times God leads us on seeming detours en route to our goals in order to meet people who can help us reach our ultimate destination.

Too many of us try to muddle through life on our own. We refuse to reach out to others or let others reach out to us. We let ourselves drown in a sea of cares, worries and preoccupations and never grasp the life preserver that is thrown out to save us. I am reminded of a hot Chicago summer in the late 80's. My oldest sister, Karen, her children, my mother and I had driven up from Tennessee to visit my second oldest sister Lisa and her husband. One day we were at a large water park. Karen, who is twelve years my senior but nine inches shorter than my 5'10" frame, stood next to me in the wave pool. As a large wave passed us, Karen was caught in an undertow where she stayed for much too long. Finally, I reached over with my right arm, grabbed her by the scruff of her T-shirt and snatched her up in one effortless swoop.

"Thanks, I thought I was a goner there for a minute!" she exclaimed when she finally caught her breath. "How did you do that? There I was under the water one second and the next I'm flying up into the air!" We've laughed about that moment several times over the years – about how almost with superhuman strength I was able to swoop her straight out of the water to a standing position without the least bit of stress or strain.

This moment has taken on new meaning for me as I felt one of those arms snatching me from behavior patterns that had engulfed me in a sea of work. For 10 years in business I let the waves of projects, creative ideas and floods of day-to-day business details engulf my life. Ever so subtly, work became my life. There was no "me" apart from my work. I programmed Web sites in my sleep, solved business challenges while I did housework, and talked business with everyone I knew. It consumed me. In 1999, I was reaching serious burnout but when I thought about selling my business a wave of panic hit, "But who would I be if I wasn't this businesswoman? What would I do with myself?"

Now mind you, I was a wife and mother of 5 children at the time, so you'd think I'd know what I'd be doing if I wasn't working. But somehow being a housewife and a doting mother never seemed quite challenging enough for me. "After all," I told myself, "I'd go insane if I didn't have my work." So I plugged along struggling for air amidst a sea of business responsibilities.

In April 1999, I began working with a coach / strategist. Not that I thought I needed a coach, but thought it might be fun to give it a try since many of my clients are coaches and I thought it would be intriguing to learn more about what they do. For the first three months, she helped me streamline my business and create new bells and whistles for my Web sites. I was amazed at what I was able to accomplish with her help.

Then in August of 1999, my life hit one of those points where I felt totally out of balance. I decided to talk to my coach about it. Before this point everything had been business, but this meant delving into my personal life – which I had kept carefully guarded. She began helping me locate the source of this feeling of imbalance. We worked on spending more time with my family, discussed taking my business to a grander level, and set a schedule for finding more balance and relaxation time. Nothing seemed to shake the feeling. Then, finally after reading an article in a church magazine, it hit me what was missing – my spirit was starving. Sure, I went to church every Sunday. I was even actively involved as a leader in the women's organization of my church. I said those prayers that we all say when we're just going through the motions. But I wasn't really thinking about them. I wasn't studying the scriptures as I should. Basically, my work had swallowed up my spiritual life. I was drowning and didn't even know it.

Marnie L. Pehrson

I took a leap of faith and opened up to my coach about what I had discovered. She was very supportive and started helping me set goals for improving my connection with God. In fact, she was undergoing a spiritual search of her own. As she encouraged me to share my beliefs, she found the answers she needed. There is nothing like seeing your blessings through another person's eyes. As a result, my faith, gratitude and spiritual insight transformed. Through this pivotal friendship, God led me to the mission He had for my life.

I no longer define myself by my work, by the Web sites I own, by how much traffic they get, or by the revenue they produce. My business and I are no longer the same entity. What freedom to breathe again! I've been snatched, pulled up by the scruff of the neck from the claws of an undertow, into the light of day. The interesting thing is that as I began putting God as my number one priority instead of work, my other priorities started to naturally realign. My family floated their way up toward the top of the heap. Now I actually *want* to be a better mother. It's no longer a "should;" it's an increased desire.

As recording artist, Jana Stanfield sings in her *Brave Faith* album, "I believe in this world there is nothing that happens by chance." God puts people into our lives to snatch us from the waves that engulf us. These people who "like a magnet are drawn into our lives"[1]are His angels, His arms to lift us to safety and peace.

Challenge

As you say your morning prayers, ask God to reveal one thing to you that He would like you to do that day. Ask Him how you can better serve Him and His kingdom. How can you reach out to others and be His angel to those in need? Listen for an answer as you go throughout your day and act courageously upon what He tells you to do. I promise you as you do this, as you put first the kingdom of God, blessings will be added upon your head. You'll have more time for the important things, and the unimportant things will fall away.

Resources

[1] Jana Stanfield, "That's the Way I Feel About You," Brave Faith 1999 Jana StanTunes Music, www.janastanfield.com

.

Lesson 18: Take Up Christ's Yoke

Jesus said that His yoke is easy and His burden is light. In Greek the word *easy* means *kindly*. A kindly yoke, molded and shaped by the Master Carpenter is sanded smooth and does not chafe or cause sore spots. It is perfectly balanced so that it does not knock you off balance. It is a custom fit, designed by the Master to form to your exact build – both your spiritual and your physical stature and abilities. But it is our choice to take His yoke upon us. He will not force us to wear it. The irony is, if we refuse to wear His yoke, then we will wear one of our own inept and clumsy making.

Choose to Commit

God will never force us to follow Him. We must use our freedom of choice to choose God. Only we can make the decision to give our whole souls to Him and sacrifice our old life for a new and better one. This requires a leap of faith that many never have the courage to take. Perhaps this is why the Savior referred to it as the "straight and narrow path."

We're often like the young man who came to Christ and asked what he should do to have eternal life. Jesus said that he should keep the commandments and the young man said he had done so since his youth. So Jesus told him, *"Go and sell that thou hast and give to the poor, and thou shalt have treasure in heaven and come and follow me."* And the young man went away sorrowing for he had great possessions (Matthew 19:16-22). It's not that Jesus had anything against owning possessions. He picked the one thing that He knew would be most difficult for this man to give up. He required the sacrifice of his most prized treasure before he could come and follow Him. Why is this? Because where your treasure is, there will your heart be also. Anything that has a higher place in our hearts than God blocks our ability to receive the fullness of His blessings. What do you love most in your life? What do you treasure the most? If it came down to God versus that one thing, would you choose God? Are you willing to lay it on the sacrificial altar in order to give your whole soul to Him?

That's quite a sacrifice He asks, isn't it? But until and unless we are willing to seek heavenly treasures over earthly ones, we cannot fully come unto Him and receive the fullness of His blessings. No wonder God is ever patient with us! No wonder He sends people and events into our lives to teach us, shape us and build our faith until we are ready to give everything we have to follow Him. He knows this transformation is difficult and rarely happens overnight.

Marnie L. Pehrson

In Matthew 23:37 Jesus cried, "O Jerusalem, Jerusalem… how often would I have gathered thy children together, even as a hen gathereth her chickens under her wings and ye would not!" "And ye would not" – what a sad indictment those four words convey. God in His infinite mercy is ready and willing to help us at any time to come unto Him, to shelter us under His protective wing, and give us His ultimate blessings. But it is up to us to choose Him. It is our choice. We are free to choose God now or to take our chances and procrastinate the day of our repentance. It is a surety that the Lord will never send legions of angels to force or compel us. The Lord wants conversion without coercion.

A mind that is not committed is an open invitation to spiritual weaknesses and sin. "Commit thy works unto the Lord, and thy thoughts shall be established." (Proverbs 16:3) Full and complete commitment to do what the Lord wants us to do is a protection. When we commit to act in the way the Lord wants, our thoughts naturally fall into line and become firm and steadfast in the cause of truth and righteousness. Things that used to tempt us will eventually have no claim upon our souls.

Mighty Change of Heart

You might think that forsaking your sins and giving your whole soul to Jesus Christ is the same thing as having a mighty change of heart, but it isn't. The mighty change of heart can only happen when the Savior transforms our hearts, so that we have no more desire to do evil, but to do good continually. Only Jesus Christ can change hearts. Not to say that we won't still make mistakes. We will, but we will desire to do better. Spiritual change is not merely a cosmetic alteration.

> "The Lord works from the inside out. The world works from the outside in. The world would take people out of the slums. Christ takes the slums out of people, and then they take themselves out of the slums. The world would mold men by changing their environment. Christ changes men, who then change their environment. The world would shape human behavior, but Christ can change human nature."
>
> - Ezra Taft Benson, "Born of God," *Ensign*, July 1989

Perhaps you and I have been inadequate in making changes in the past because we have tried to work from the outside in – we have tried to wait for our environments or circumstances to change so that then it would be easier for us to change. Maybe we have tried to do it on sheer will and haven't leaned enough on the Savior?

True transformations from the natural man do not come by sheer willpower on our part. Although, we have to work to "take ourselves out of the slums." We will not be successful until we allow Christ to take the slums out of us.

Obtaining the Pure Love of Christ

Evidence of a mighty change of heart or conversion is the presence of the pure love of Christ in our lives and actions. This pure love of Christ enables us to unconditionally love others even though they may not do what we want them to do, even though they may not believe what we believe or even if they treat us unfairly and cruelly. Showing charity to others is a hallmark of conversion to Jesus Christ.

"None of us needs one more person bashing or pointing out where we have failed or fallen short. Most of us are already well aware of the areas in which we are weak. What each of us does need are family, friends, employers, and brothers and sisters who support us, who have the patience to teach us, who believe in us, and who believe we're trying to do the best we can, in spite of our weaknesses. What ever happened to giving each other the benefit of the doubt? What ever happened to hoping that another person would succeed or achieve? What ever happened to rooting for each other?

It should come as no surprise that one of the adversary's tactics in the latter days is stirring up hatred among the children of men. He loves to see us criticize each other, make fun or take advantage of our neighbor's known flaws, and generally pick on each other." (Marvin J. Ashton, "The Tongue Can Be A Sharp Sword," *Ensign*, May 1992.)

What is Love or Charity?

Love can be many things to many people, but it may be classified into three basic types.

The first type is expressed in the terms "I will love you if." People give this kind of love if others meet certain requirements. It is conditional and always has strings attached. Some examples of this type of love include:

- I will love you if you are popular.
- I will love you if you have a nice car.
- I will love you if you attend church.
- I will love you if you are nice to me.
- I will love you if you do your chores, or if you do what I say.

The second type of love uses the word *because* and emphasizes selfish or worldly aspects. It, too, is conditional love. People love others only because of their attractive qualities or characteristics. Some examples of this type of love include:

- I love you because you are handsome.
- I love you because you help me around the house.
- I love you because you buy me nice things.
- I love you because you do things for me, or because you put me first.

Neither of these types of love is true love. They are conditional and based upon our own self-interests.

The third type of love is unselfish and unconditional. We do not have to earn or deserve this kind of love by acting a certain way or having certain qualities. This kind of love can use the phrase "even though." Some examples include the following:

- I love you even though I disagree with what you do.
- I love you even though you have weaknesses and problems.
- I love you even though you made a mistake.
- I love you even though you don't always do exactly what I want.
- I love you even though we believe in different things.

This is the kind of love that Heavenly Father and Jesus Christ give each of us. They love and accept us no matter what we do or who we are. This kind of love is called charity.

Why Is This Love So Important?

Charity is the measuring stick that determines our eternal destiny. Charity is the pure love of Christ, and it endures forever. Whoever is found possessed of it at the last day, will have a place on the right hand of God.

In Matthew 25: 31-45 Jesus taught this truth using the Parable of the Sheep and the Goats.

"When the Son of man shall come in His glory, and all the holy angels with him, then shall He sit upon the throne of His glory: And before Him shall be gathered all nations: and He shall separate them one from another, as a shepherd divideth His sheep from the goats: And He shall set the sheep on His right hand, but the goats on the left.

Then shall the King say unto them on His right hand, Come, ye blessed of my Father, inherit the kingdom prepared for you from the foundation of the world: For I was an hungered, and ye gave me meat: I was thirsty, and ye gave me drink: I was a stranger, and ye took me in: Naked, and ye clothed me: I was sick, and ye visited me: I was in prison, and ye came unto me.

Then shall the righteous answer him, saying, Lord, when saw we thee an hungered, and fed thee? or thirsty, and gave thee drink? When saw we thee a stranger, and took thee in? or naked, and clothed thee? Or when saw we thee sick, or in prison, and came unto thee?

And the King shall answer and say unto them, Verily I say unto you, Inasmuch as ye have done it unto one of the least of these my brethren, ye have done it unto me.

Then shall He say also unto them on the left hand, Depart from me, ye cursed, into everlasting fire, prepared for the devil and his angels: For I was an hungered, and ye gave me no meat: I was thirsty, and ye gave me no drink: I was a stranger, and ye took me not in: naked, and ye clothed me not: sick, and in prison, and ye visited me not.

Then shall they also answer him, saying, Lord, when saw we thee an hungered, or athirst, or a stranger, or naked, or sick, or in prison, and did not minister unto thee?

Then shall He answer them, saying, Verily I say unto you, Inasmuch as ye did it not to one of the least of these, ye did it not to me."

Love for others and demonstrating that love in our actions is clearly a determining factor in measuring conversion.

True charity is a gift of the Spirit. It is not something we can gain only by our own efforts. Charity is a spiritual gift we should seek to develop. Although charity is a gift of the Spirit, and it's rather hard to define exactly how to get it, there are some steps we can take to obtain it. As we become truly converted to Jesus Christ, his pure love will naturally become a part of us.

We are challenged to move through a process of conversion toward that status and condition called eternal life. This is achieved not just by doing what is right, but by doing it for the right reason–for the pure love of Christ. When we serve others without thought for compensation, acclaim or reward, we express the type of love that Christ has for us.

In *The Bridge Builder*, William Allen Dromgoole describes the typical actions of those who possess this perfect Christ-like love that asks nothing in return.

> *An old man, going a lone highway,*
> *Came at the evening, cold and gray,*
> *To a chasm vast and deep and wide*
> *The old man crossed in the twilight dim,*
> *The sullen stream had no fear for him;*
> *But he turned when safe on the other side,*
> *And built a bridge to span the tide,*
> *"Old Man", said a fellow pilgrim near,*
> *"You are wasting your strength with building here;*
> *Your journey will end with the ending day,*
> *You never again will pass this way,*
> *You've crossed the chasm deep and wide;*
> *Why build you this bridge at evening tide?"*
> *The builder lifted his old gray head-*
> *"Good friend, in the path I have come", he said,*
> *"There followeth after me today,*
> *A youth whose feet must pass this way;*
> *This chasm that has naught to me*
> *To that fair-haired youth may a pitfall be:*
> *He, too, must cross in the twilight dim -*
> *Good friend, I am building this bridge for him."*

The Apostle Paul taught that *"charity never faileth"* (1 Corinthians 13). The reason charity never fails and the reason charity is greater than even the most significant acts of goodness he cited is that charity is not an *act*. It is a *condition* or state of being. Charity is attained through a succession of acts that result in a conversion. Charity is something one becomes.

Challenge

Because charity is a gift of the Spirit, it is something we can pray for. As you offer your prayers each day, I challenge you to ask for this gift to love others as Jesus Christ loves us. As you do, your heart will begin to change, and you will be filled with this love - a love that never fails.

Lesson 19: The Importance of Remembering

It had been at least a year since I sat down at the battered, out-of-tune piano that occupies my living room. It's the same piano I practiced through thirteen years of piano lessons – from the time I was 5 until I broke my arm in an auto accident at age 17.

Sitting in front of the chipped ivory keys was like sitting down to chat with an old friend who lets you pick up exactly where you left off years earlier. Opening a songbook, I selected one of my favorite songs. Much to my astonishment, my fingers still remembered the notes, and I was able to play a somewhat complicated piece without too many mistakes. Some things you never forget, I suspect.

Seconds barely passed before four little hands joined me. I'm positive my three-year-old daughter and one-year-old son were convinced that their accompaniment enhanced the melody to new heights. I couldn't help remembering my grandmother who let me strike the upper octave notes as she played *Red Wing*. At the age of four or five, I believed my contribution added such grandeur to the piece. Maybe that's because her praise and encouragement made me believe that it did. I realize now, of course, that all it really amounted to was a bunch of noise.

Song after song they pounded and sang along. Normally, this would have been extremely distracting, but I found that if I concentrated on the melody, I could tune out all the noise around me. I didn't notice their banging, their singing or even the TV in the next room. The melody went straight to my heart as I concentrated on the words of the song I played: 'I feel my Savior's love in all the world around me. His Spirit warms my soul through everything I see. He knows I will follow Him, Give all my life to Him. I feel my Savior's love – the love He freely gives me.'[1]

Anyone else entering the room would have thought it was the biggest bunch of noise they'd ever heard. But as I played and thought about the words, I felt the message of the song so intensely. It didn't matter that chaos surrounded me, the message and melody dominated my thoughts.

As I played it struck me that this is like our lives. The clutter and clamor of daily living can so easily drown out the Savior's love and His message if we let it. The only way we can stay trained on the melody and the message is by carefully listening for it and actively participating in the melody. Being a contributor to the melody makes it so much easier to distinguish it from all the distractions and busyness of life.

Discovering and fulfilling our compelling mission helps us remember to listen for the melody. But even then, we humans have a terrible tendency to forget.

It is so easy for us to forget the greatness of God. Moses continually told the Israelites to remember their bondage in Egypt and the Lord's deliverance. He said, *"Remember this day, in which ye came out from Egypt, out of the house of bondage; for by strength of hand the LORD brought you out from this place"* (Exodus 13:3). Why do you think it is so important to remember our past challenges and the Lord's deliverance from them? Judges 8:34 says, *"And the children of Israel **remembered not** the LORD their God, who had delivered them out of the hands of all their enemies on every side, and **they fell into iniquity**."*

> As our relationship with Heavenly Father and His Son Jesus Christ deepens, the understanding of who we are and who we can become expands. We begin to focus more on eternity than these fleeting moments of mortality. We see the big picture and our role in it. If we take our eyes off the Master and forget our Heavenly Father and Jesus Christ, the vision of our own possibilities dims and eventually our lives disappoint us.

How can we remember? It is the small and simple things that help us stay on track. Attending church, daily scripture study, daily prayers, and making and keeping covenants with the Lord all help us remember Him and what He's done for us.

As I've discussed before, inspirational music can help us remember the Lord and his blessings. In the Old Testament, Moses set the historical events of the Israelites' deliverance to music (Exodus 15). Moses knew that music touches the soul on a profoundly emotional level and that it would help the people remember the Lord and their deliverance. Make sure the music you listen to is clean and inspiring. Continue to collect music that will uplift your soul when you are struggling and help you remember all that God has done for you.

Challenge: Keep a Journal

Another tool in remembering is keeping a written record of your spiritual progress. A journal or even emails to a confidant can be used as a history of your spiritual progress. Today there are many ways to keep a journal - blogging, typing your journal on your computer, or an old-fashioned handwritten journal. If you decide to use a digital journal, be sure to back it up frequently and print a hard copy. Referring to these written records often helps you remember what the Lord has done and is doing in your life.

I challenge you to start keeping a journal - especially of your thoughts and feelings as you read your scriptures. Jot down notes of how what you have read applies to you. Write down the things for which you are praying, and document when those prayers are answered. Over time, you will collect a marvelous written record of the evidence of God's workings in your life. You will be able to see how He shaped your life. You'll become adept at recognizing when the Lord is trying to steer you in a new direction, helping you to develop a new talent or introducing you to someone you can serve or who will teach you valuable lessons. Without a written record, it is so easy to forget all the times that the Lord has blessed you. But with it, you will find courage when you are afraid and strength to continue when you are weak. You will know with a surety that all things do indeed work together for your good because you love Him and are called to fill a divine mission (Romans 8:28).

Resources

[1] Words by Ralph Rodgers, Jr. and Music by K. Newell Dayley, *I Feel My Savior's Love*, 1979.

Lesson 20: Seek Ye First the Kingdom of God

After telling His disciples to take no heed for material things, suggesting they consider the lilies of the field and the birds of the sky and how they are clothed and fed, Jesus said, *"Seek ye first the kingdom of God and all these things shall be added unto you"* (Matthew 6:33).

The key to decluttering our lives and finding peace amidst chaos is reordering our priorities so that the kingdom of God is in the number one spot. As we share what we learn with others, we remember where we've been and how far the Lord has brought us. Make it a daily part of your morning prayers to ask the Lord for ways that you can serve others and help to build His kingdom. In his little book, *The Prayer of Jabez*, Bruce Wilkinson uses the lesser-known Biblical hero, Jabez's prayer to illustrate how Jabez became *"more honorable than his brethren."* The prayer is found in 1 Chronicles 4:10,

> *"And Jabez called on the God of Israel, saying, Oh that thou wouldest bless me indeed, and enlarge my coast, and that thine hand might be with me, and that thou wouldest keep me from evil, that it may not grieve me! And God granted him that which he requested."*

The four elements of Jabez' prayer were the following:

1)   He asked the Lord to bless him.

2)   He asked the Lord to enlarge his coast, or in other words, enlarge his opportunities to influence and serve. He asked the Lord to make him more than he was before.

3)   He asked for the Lord's hand to be with him. In other words, he asked for the Lord's help and guidance and for His Spirit to be with him so he could handle the opportunities that flowed.

4)   He asked to be kept from evil. He asked for help in avoiding and sidestepping temptation. He didn't ask the Lord to help him *through* temptation, he asked the Lord to help him *stay away* from it completely.

The prayer of Jabez is a perfect model to help us remember the Lord and to remember who we are. It helps us remember our importance to God, and our God-ordained mission. By incorporating these elements into our daily prayers, we can't help but remember because

1) We will be asking for the Lord's blessings.

2) We will be asking each day that He give us opportunities to use our time, talents and abilities to serve Him and build His Kingdom.

3) We will be asking for His Spirit to be with us, or His "hand to be with us." In order to expect to have His Spirit to be with us, we know that we must remember Him and be living in a manner that pleases Him. Having His hand with us is critical when we have asked for opportunities to serve, because the opportunities that come are usually bigger than what we can handle on our own.

4) We will be consistently asking for help in sidestepping temptation and being kept from the evil influences of the world around us.

This formula works. I actually stumbled upon this combination a year or so before reading *The Prayer of Jabez*. All my life, I've been taught to pray to have His Spirit with me, to be able to keep His commandments, and to ask for His blessings. But not until 2001 did I actively start praying for the Lord to send me opportunities to serve Him. When I started praying for the Lord to send me people I could help and when I started letting Him know that I really wanted to be a part of building His Kingdom, I was amazed at the results. People started coming to me from everywhere. I could spend an entire day answering emails and teaching others what I'd learned. It was like a flood of opportunities and blessings poured out on my head.

A Warning

I must add a bit of a warning here. Don't make my mistake. The flood of people coming to me began to be a little bit overwhelming. I was extremely blessed in this, maybe I was too blessed? My home business grew by 50% even though I spent only a fraction of the time I used to spend on it and my family relationships improved. I think it became a little emotionally overwhelming to have so many people asking my advice, leaning on me for support or asking me to tell them about the gospel. It seemed bigger than I was, and it really was. But I knew that if I had the Spirit with me, I could handle it.

I'm not sure why, but I think it had to do with my business growth and learning that I was expecting my sixth baby that made me slow down the pace. I gradually began only asking the Lord to send me opportunities on the days that I didn't have a lot of other work to do. My logic was, "I've got some things of my own I need to do today, I'll just say a regular prayer today and not ask for the extra opportunities, because I don't have time for that today."

Some days I did better. I prayed, "Heavenly Father, help me accomplish this and that and then I'd be happy to use the rest of my time on whatever you need me to do." That worked. He always helped me accomplish what I needed to and still left time to do what He wanted me to do. I'm not sure why or when I stopped asking for the opportunities to serve above and beyond. Eventually, I reduced my asking to maybe once or twice a week. Then because I had fewer people's problems and challenges to research, I began reducing the time I spent really studying the scriptures like I should, and accordingly the opportunities diminished.

When I didn't ask, I didn't receive. What I learned from this is that **we control the flow of the Lord's opportunities and blessings**. We can run as fast as we want to. If we decide to slow down and walk, the Lord will let us slow down and walk. But nothing beats the exhilaration and the sheer joy of running with the wind. When we refuse to run, we miss out on abundant blessings.

The greatest danger in slowing down our pace is that it is so extremely easy to forget what it felt like to run. We get out of shape spiritually, and it becomes so much more difficult to remember how to run again. We become lazy and slothful and lax in our scripture study and prayers. It's so easy to slip back to where you started without constant vigilance.

As I desired to pick up the pace, I asked the Lord to help me set a pace that I could physically and emotionally handle – one that is suited to my time, abilities and family's needs. All things must be done in wisdom and in order. The Lord does not require us to run faster than we have strength. What is important is that we are diligently moving forward toward the prize. That diligence comes from continually studying our scriptures on a daily basis, offering consistent fervent prayers, and looking for opportunities to serve where we are able. Whatever you do, don't slacken your scripture study or prayers just to slow things down. Ask the Lord to give you what you can handle while hanging onto the lifelines of scriptures, journal keeping and prayer. Letting go is too dangerous because remembering becomes so difficult without them.

Marnie L. Pehrson

If you fail to remember and endure, you will start sliding back down the steps. The steps work in reverse too. If you fail to remember and endure, you'll start to lose your vision. If you lose your vision, you'll have a tougher time loving others with the pure love of Christ. If you slip further, you'll lose your change of heart and you'll lay aside Christ's yoke and take up your old one that you used to wear.

If you start having a tougher time loving others or if you start feeling discontent, depressed or that something is amiss, start remembering and enduring. Repent where necessary. Pull out your journal and recall how you used to be and how the Lord delivered you. Review your mission statement daily. Start praying earnestly for clarity of vision and immerse yourself in the Word of God. Remembering and enduring is critical. It's your maintenance plan that keeps you moving forward on the strait and narrow path toward your goal. And what is that goal? It's the very throne of God where He will say, *"Well done thou good and faithful servant. Thou hast been faithful over a few things. I will make thee ruler over many things: enter thou into the joy of thy Lord"* (Matthew 25:21,23).

Lesson 21: The Formula for Releasing Stress and Worry

When I was a small child, my father found a cat bird inside the house. It frantically flew about, bouncing into walls and windows until he finally caught it. He held it tightly. At first the bird struggled for freedom, squawking, scratching, clawing and crying to be released. The harder the bird struggled, the more my father held onto it, restricting its movements to keep it from injuring itself further.

My father didn't want to keep the bird tightly bound. He would rather let it move about freely. But for the safety of the bird, he needed to keep it confined within his hands. The bird struggled for some time and then finally began to sense that my father meant it no harm. When it quit struggling, he relaxed his hold on it. If it fought, his hands once again became confining. Eventually, the bird completely relaxed, and my father set it on the kitchen floor, and it toddled about. By the time the bird could be set free, they had become friends. They had come to trust one another.

My dad took the bird outside and held open his hand for it to go back to its natural habitat, but it wouldn't leave. Instead it waddled around in his hand, climbed up his arm and perched on my dad's shoulder. It didn't want to leave him! Finally my father set it on a porch railing. Reluctantly, after some time, the bird joined its friends in the trees. Even then it perched in a nearby tree and chirped merrily talking to my father for quite some time.

My father tells this story every now and then, and I've always felt it held some significance about life, about a principle of freedom and gaining trust. Most recently, I've come to see the symbolism of how our Heavenly Father deals with us. Like my father, our Heavenly Father is there to help and protect us. He too wants us free to fly and explore the full potential of our divine creation. But often we're like that injured bird, trapped inside a house. We squirm, fight, claw and squawk, but in our wounded condition, our Heavenly Father holds us tightly, restricting our movements.

Just as the bird fought to escape in the beginning, we too fight and claw to reach our goals and aspirations. Like the bird trapped in the house, inside our own limiting borders, our Heavenly Father knows it's not possible yet. It's neither the time nor the place. We must first learn to relax and fully trust Him. Only then, when He's confident that our mad scramble for control will not cause us to injure ourselves further, does He relax His grip.

Once we calm down and trust Him fully, He opens His palm and sets us free to explore a little. Interestingly enough, at this point, when we've come to love and trust the Father, our goals and aspirations don't seem so important anymore. But our Heavenly Father hasn't held us just so He can confine us. No! Now that we've learned how to trust, relax and communicate with Him, He wants us outside so we can fly! He wants us to fill the measure of our creation in a great big world that He created! Ultimate happiness and joy only come for us and Him as we learn to trust Him enough so He can completely liberate us from the confines of our own limiting beliefs and boundaries.

Christ is the Author and Finisher of Your Faith

In Hebrews 12:2, Christ is referred to as the "author and finisher of our faith." When we put ourselves in His care, His goal is to "finish" - "polish or perfect" our faith. His sole objective is to increase your faith to a level that you can return home to live with Him and your Father in heaven. When we are filled with this faith, we have no room for worry.

As a fiction author, I've gained new insight into the role of our Savior as the author and finisher of our faith. For example, a good author doesn't give you all the facts in the first chapter. He doesn't solve the mystery in chapter one or two. He weaves a tale, holding you in suspense, helping you learn and grow with the characters, come to love the hero or heroine, and then wows you in the end with a wonderful conclusion. He might foreshadow a bit, might give you a foretaste of how it's all going to work out, but He won't reveal the ending completely. That would ruin the story! You might even know how the story will most likely end (happily or with the hero reaching his goal) but you don't know HOW just yet. That's how life is. That's how God works

If we could relax and get to the point where we truly enjoyed the story (resisted flipping to the end to see how it's all going to work out) then we'd enjoy life a whole lot more. So how do you do that? How do you truly relax and live in the NOW? He's already promised us a happy ending if we trust Him in faithfulness! How do you come to truly believe in Him for a happy ending? How do you trust that not only will all things work together for your good, but also you're going to love where He takes you? (Romans 8:28)

I believe the answer lies in discovering the line between what we control and what God controls. Which part of the creative process is ours, and which is His? Every good author eventually addresses the following questions: Who? What? Why? When? Where? and How? In life, there are only two and a half of these questions you can control - part of the Who (yourself) and the What and the Why. The rest are all up to God. The sooner we release the following questions, the sooner Heavenly Father will open His grip – much like my father did with the bird:

· How is it going to happen?

· When will it occur?

· Who else will be involved in making it happen?

· Where is it going to happen?

Once you release these questions to His care, you'll trust your Heavenly Father, and He'll trust you. You'll have a relationship, and He'll help you fly to your fullest potential. But as long as you struggle and fight over things you can't control, you'll be limited in your sphere of influence and opportunity like a bird trapped in a house.

James Allen in *As a Man Thinketh* put it this way: "As the progressive and evolving being, man is where he is that he may learn that he may grow; and as he learns the spiritual lesson which any circumstance contains for him, it passes away and gives place to other circumstances."

Throughout the next few lessons, we'll take an in-depth look at the "Who? What? When? How? Why? and Where?" questions of life and how we can learn to release those elements we can't control and become an active participant in the ones we can. First we'll start with the part of the creation process that God controls. Then we'll examine the "What" and the "Why" questions in which we have a part to play.

Who? The Secret to Stress-Free Relationships

"Who?" is actually a question you can control to some degree. You can control yourself. Ultimately YOU are the only person you can control. You have no right to control anyone else.

Thus, for example, it's fruitless for me to try to manipulate you into accomplishing something that I want for you. I have no right to force my will upon you. Likewise, you only have control over yourself. To manipulate a spouse or a friend to get them to do what you want them to do is wrong, and quite frankly, rarely works. Who wants to be manipulated or forced? I don't! Do you? The only exception to this rule might be small children for whom you are responsible to teach and train. Like my father keeping the bird safe, small children do need to be protected. You wouldn't take the time to entice a small child out of the middle of the road. You'd run over there, scoop him up and use whatever force necessary to preserve his life. Yet, even with children in less dangerous circumstances, it's best to lead, guide, and persuade, while keeping force to a minimum.

At first glance you might say, "Well, I only want to control myself. I don't want to dominate or force other people into doing things." I've always said that about myself, yet, there have been times when in the name of "leading someone to the light" I've been tempted and even succumbed to using Satan's tactics. For example, Satan's methods include guilt tripping, pressuring, arguments, contention, sulking, pouting, power struggles, competition, jealousy, manipulation and force.

Let's take a look at several typical times when we're tempted to manipulate others and how we might better handle the situation.

Spiritual Relationships

Paul admonished *"Be not unequally yoked together with unbelievers: for what fellowship hath righteousness with unrighteousness? And what communion hath light with darkness?"* (2 Corinthians 6:14) Yet, there are many times in life where the ideal is simply not realistic. You could already be in a friendship or marriage relationship with an unbeliever before you become a believer yourself. Or you may have family who are not believers. Other times, you may have a spouse, friends, or family members who believe, but they aren't quite as consistently obedient as you, or perhaps they have slipped into complete rebellion. There are a myriad of reasons why in a day-to-day environment you will encounter those who may not be on the same spiritual plane as you.

We shouldn't shun others who do not believe as we do. Rather we should be there to lift, serve and love them. Inherent in these situations are times of frustration when the person you care for is not reaching their full potential. They aren't seeing the possibilities that you see for them.

Probably the hardest challenge in letting go is when our goals, plans, and dreams involve other people and their ability to grow on a spiritual level. When your future is tied to someone else, and he or she is unwilling or lacks the vision or courage to go where you want to go, what can you do? Do you halt your development and progression to wait on this other person to catch up? Do you run on and leave them behind? Or is there some other happy medium? You can't force someone else to see your vision, to follow your path. Arguing and pressuring only serve to drive them to dig in their heels, or worse, run in the opposite direction.

When we think of how God leads us in our lives, we find the answer. Firmness, not force is the key. God never gives in or wavers in His course, but He is longsuffering and ever-willing to take us back. We, as He, must be firm in our convictions, steadfast, focused and committed. Leading others up the path of truth requires love, patience, gentleness, diligence, meekness — and yes, time.

How many times have we messed up and Jesus is still there waiting and willing — standing at the door and knocking if we will but let Him in? He never beats the door down. He never even picks the lock and sneaks in through manipulation. He doesn't shout, belittle or guilt-trip us from the other side of the door. He simply patiently stands there and knocks until the time arrives that we have the ears to hear the knocking and the willingness and courage to open the door.

Jesus knows that force, manipulation, power games, and dominion will never lead someone else to the light. Love, service, patient teaching and a good example will do more to soften hearts and shape lives than any argument or debate. Do you have a loved one who is choosing the wrong paths? Are they digging in their heels when you would really like them to join you on your walk up the path of truth? Then, follow Christ's example. Be His partner in this endeavor. Be an instrument in His hands to help your friend or loved one hear the knocking. Take the time to teach them to listen and hear the tapping. When the time is right for them, take their hand and walk with them to open the door through which more joy and happiness than they ever dreamed possible exists.

The beautiful thing about this process is that as we strain to hear Christ at the door for our friend's sake, we hear Him ourselves. As we take our friend's hand to walk with them to the door, we can't help but arrive there ourselves. And when our friend opens the door, we will be there to feel the flood of joy and happiness that flows as Christ enters.

Romantic Relationships

The most common advice request that comes in through SheLovesGod.com is romantic in nature. Generally, the woman writing wants to get married, and she's set her heart on one man in particular. Often, she's prayed and feels as if she's received a confirmation that this man is "the one." Now, how to make him realize that? What if he never sees it for himself? What should she do now?

Let's go back to our rule: You cannot control anyone but yourself. Everyone else is beyond your control, and you have no right to manipulate them or force them to see or do things your way. You are free to love, lift, inspire and serve. These you may do freely. But when you seek to force your will upon another through manipulation, mind games, or force, you're stepping over the line. Cross the line, and you do so at your own peril! Frustration, anxiety and even a complete destruction of the relationship could result.

Rest assured that if this man is truly "the one," he will come to know it for himself. This kind of revelation comes in pairs. God will not reveal a marriage partnership to one person and deny it to the other, but the timing of that revelation is in God's hands. "When" is a question only God can control. If you are in such a situation, then remember what you can do – love, serve, lift and inspire. Most of all, be patient! But do it all purely and without ulterior motive. If you act out of manipulation or game playing, you're traveling a risky path.

Later in the chapter on "What?" I'll explain how to get clear on what you want through visualization, goal setting and gratitude. If you choose to use these tools in a romantic relationship – avoid putting a name or a face on the vision or goal. It is perfectly fine to say, "I am so happy and grateful that I am married to a man who is romantic, fun, communicative, loving and who encourages and allows me to reach my full potential." It is not okay to say, "I am so happy and grateful that I am married to Fred Jones because he is romantic, fun, communicative, etc."

Leave Fred Jones out of it. You have no right to make a WHO a WHAT. He has his own volition. He's not an object for you to obtain or manipulate! Trust the Lord that if Fred chooses not to be a part of your life that God will lead you to someone even more suitable.

Business Relationships

In business, you'll often need to form relationships or alliances with other people to reach your goals. For example, a network marketer needs people for his or her team who are self-motivated, hard working, visionary and coachable. Like the romantic example, you may set specific targets for the type of people you want on your team, but you have no right to make specific people the "What" of your goal.

For example, it is helpful to write, "I am so happy and grateful that self-motivated, hard-working, visionary and coachable individuals are continually brought to my business team, and together we achieve [specific goals here]."

It is not proper to write, "I am so happy and grateful that Sam Jones, Mary Smith and Frank Bennett are on my team and are reaching [specific levels] because they are self-motivated, hard-working, visionary and coachable."

Even if you feel it's in their best interest, you have no right to set goals for someone else. Let them do that for themselves! Also, you'll experience less stress if you'll keep any goal that involves relationships impersonal – whether they be romantic, business, spiritual, friendships, or familial. You'll be less likely to meddle in another person's affairs, less worried over their immediate progress, and free to find better relationships that are more ideally suited if need be.

When we let go of our need to control other people, we release an immense amount of frustration, and we liberate the other person to more easily reach their potential. I have one friend in particular who I worked with quite intensely for a couple years on a spiritual level. This person made great strides and learned many new and wonderful things, yet she was still unable to fully commit to a spiritual course. It became very frustrating for me because obviously she wanted to reach a certain spiritual destination, but she let fear stand in her way. There's nothing quite so heartbreaking as watching someone you love deny themselves blessings just because they're scared to take a leap of faith – a leap you've taken and discovered that, for you, it wasn't such a leap after all.

Unfortunately, I must admit that I used many of Satan's tactics – guilt trips, manipulation and pressure. I allowed myself to become frustrated and even angry at times. Did this do any good? Of course not! If anything, it slowed her progress because she sensed my frustration and anxiety. No one wants to be forced or pressured!

In this particular incident, the Lord gave me a very clear answer that He had my friend within His care, and that she would be all right. She would reach her desired destination eventually. But, it wasn't my job to meddle in how or when she reached it. All of that was between her and her Father in Heaven.

When I finally relinquished everything but the vision He'd given me – the assurance that He'd given me that all would be well in the end – an immense burden lifted from my shoulders. I then realized it was never my responsibility to figure out the right words to say or the correct things to do to convince my friend to take a leap of faith. My job was simply to love, lift, serve and believe in her!

An amazing thing happened when I let go of my need to control. She made such an amazing amount of progress without me bugging her! She and the Lord did just fine on their own. In this particular incident, the Lord had given me a vision of the Who and the What, but I had to relinquish the When and the How!

Points to Ponder

· How does it make you feel when people try to manipulate or control you? How do you react?

· How have you sought to control other people, even in small ways, in the past?

· How will you let go of your need to control, manipulate or force others in the future?

· What will you do when other people disappoint you or let you down?

Lesson 22: God's Perfect Timing

Time and again, the Lord has taught me that His timing is best. It may seem like things aren't going to work out in time or that things aren't going your way, but if you'll trust His perfect timing, it will all fall into place.

One example of this was when my husband and I needed to get a bigger house for our growing family. Pay close attention to this story as I share it, for it is a good example of which Who? What? When? Why? Where? And How? questions we can control.

From 1995 – 1996, my sister Karen, her husband Glenn, my parents, Greg and I decided we wanted to get a large parcel of property and build homes on it. We had very specific criteria for what we wanted. My dad wanted a water source – either a creek or a pond. My sister and I wanted to be close enough to civilization that we could access things we needed for our home businesses. Finally, we all wanted to be far enough from the city to be isolated and away from city lights and noisy neighbors.

We designated my sister Karen to look for the property. "Please help Aunt KK find our property" became a regular part of our family prayers. I can still hear my little ones praying this. By December of 1996, we still hadn't found anything. Greg and I now had four children in a 1,100 square foot house. We were anxious for something bigger!

I'm not one to read a newspaper. I don't even care to watch television news, but one Thursday in December as I passed a newspaper my husband left on the kitchen table, something told me to pick it up and look in the land section. I opened it and found that the 100 acre Battlefield Stables by the Chickamauga Battlefield in Georgia was to be auctioned off on Saturday.

I had a distinct feeling about this ad, that it could be what we were looking for. We knew we didn't have enough money for 100 acres. We were looking for something more along the lines of 25 acres, but something told me to check into it. I immediately called my father and spoke to him about it. I asked if he'd go with me to look at the property. He said he would, but recommended that I not get my hopes up. Odds were it would cost more than we could afford.

We drove to Georgia that afternoon. Interestingly enough, we'd never looked in Georgia for property. We thought we should stay in Tennessee. But back to the story… it had been raining and the weather was chilly. My father spoke to a man at the stables, got a map of the property and found that they were auctioning it off in tracts. We wouldn't be required to buy all of it. My dad looked at the map and decided he'd like to look at the back 24 acres. I had the baby with me, so I stayed in the car and waited for him to trek back there.

I still remember waiting with Jillian who was only a month old, hoping and praying that this would be the answer to our prayers. I felt hopeful, but even if my dad came back with a positive report, would we be able to win the auction?

When my dad returned to his station wagon, he was so excited. This was the place! It had a creek surrounding two sides of the property. It had a hill overlooking a beautiful open meadow. It was only 10 minutes away from major stores, only 20 minutes from Chattanooga, Tennessee, yet was completely isolated. It had everything we wanted!

We went back home and told Greg and my sister and brother-in-law about it. My brother-in-law, Glenn, was hesitant. He actually considered moving his family to Pennsylvania with his job and didn't think now would be the time to buy a piece of property. Neither he nor my sister was incredibly thrilled with the idea of moving to Georgia. With a little coaxing, Glenn, Karen, my dad, Greg and I attended the auction on Saturday morning. Before the auction, we walked back to the 24 acre plot. As we came into the clearing, there was an audible sigh from each of us. We looked toward the hill and could picture our houses there. We just knew that this was our property! It would require building a half-mile road to reach it, but my dad had a bulldozer and knew how to use it.

We agreed unanimously that we wanted it and went back to sit down in the folding chairs under the auction tent. We watched the other plots go for $5,000 an acre. We knew we couldn't afford $5,000 an acre for 24 acres! We weren't even sure where we'd get the money for it at a lower price. Greg and I had saved some money, but it wasn't enough. My dad said he could talk to my uncle about getting some cash for my part of the inheritance on my grandfather's estate that was still in probate. But we couldn't be certain we'd get it.

Whatever we bought that day would have to be paid in full within a week. My sister had more money saved than we did, so if we won the property she could put down the deposit.

We sat there in one of the back rows observing attentively as these plots went for twice what we could afford. We decided we could pay perhaps $2,500 per acre at most. We designated one of us as the bidder. When the plot came up for auction, I had nervous knots twirling in my stomach, and my heart thumped in anticipation.

We had a few people bid against us, but not as many as the other tracts – probably because this tract didn't touch the road and would require the expense of building our own. We ended up winning the auction for $2,400 per acre! We were so excited, but we still weren't sure how we'd come up with the money within a week. My dad talked with my uncle and got my share of the inheritance in cash whereas normally it would have taken years. My sister finagled her finances and got her part, and my Dad worked his magic to find his share. We bought the property, and my dad set to work building the road.

For us, it was nothing short of a miracle. Through this experience I learned three important lessons:

- Get a clear picture of what you want and ask specifically. We knew what we were looking for in our property, and we asked the Lord persistently for it.

- Don't worry about how it's going to happen. But most definitely, listen to the still small voice when it prompts you! If I hadn't picked up that newspaper, we wouldn't have found our property.

- When you find what you want, grab it and trust that the Lord will provide a way. We weren't sure how we would come up with the money. We just trusted that the Lord would open the door. He did!

I designed our house plan. We found a reasonable builder and started construction on our new home in September of 1997. Karen and Glenn started theirs about the same time. We made some repairs on our home and put it up for sale, but it didn't sell. Our new home was scheduled for completion, and we still didn't have a buyer by February. I started sweating bullets and checked into ways we could possibly rent our current house and live in the new one. Our credit was bad because of a debt consolidation we'd done in 1991, so we would need a FHA loan. Because FHA would only finance up to about $95,000, we'd have to come up with the rest in cash. How were we going to do that?

We had some money saved, but not the $21,000 we needed. Even with the sale of the old house, coming up with that much would have been extremely difficult. Finally when the realtor contract was up, our new home still wasn't done because of all the rains we'd had that winter. That bought us a little time. I went to the store and bought a kit on how to sell your own home. I found a local mortgage company who would finance our existing house for 100% financing for the new buyer and had them print a flyer for me on what the buyer would pay per month to live in the house.

Then I ran a "for sale by owner" ad in the local paper, and dropped the sale price down so that the realtor commission wasn't on it. It was a steal of a deal, and I gave anyone who came to look at the house the flyer from the mortgage company so they would know exactly what it would take to get into the home.

We had a buyer within a couple weeks. Because our new house wasn't done, we actually closed on the old house before the new one completed. Because of builder delays, we had to be out of the old house before the financing could be arranged on the new one. The builder let us move into the new house and pay him rent until the financing finalized. By the time we closed, two months later, our credit history had improved enough that we were able to get a regular loan. We weren't bound by the FHA limitation and were able to get into the house for the amount of money we had saved!

I learned from this experience that God's timing is perfect! He knows what He is doing. All the worrying and attempting to manipulate the situation to get the house to sell sooner – if it had worked – would not have been the best timing. We wouldn't have had enough money for the house. And the way it worked out, our old house was perfect for the nice young couple who purchased it.

"For the vision is yet for an appointed time, but at the end it shall speak,
and not lie: though it tarry, wait for it; because it will surely come, it will not be late."
(Habbakuk 2:3)

"Humble yourselves therefore under the mighty
hand of God, that He may exalt you in due time."
(1 Peter 5:6)
"I will therefore that men pray everywhere,
lifting up holy hands, without wrath and doubting."
(1 Timothy 2:8)

Challenge

In moments of your greatest "lack," when what you want or need most seems unobtainable, reframe the situation as an opportunity to prove to the Lord that you trust Him completely. Reframe that season of your life as the climax leading up to your miracle. Persist in faith, and believe that your miracle will come at the exact instant you need it. Listen for that still small voice, act courageously upon its directions, and your miracle will come in God's perfect time.

Lesson 23: But How?

I want to get out of debt, but how? I want a new car, but how will I afford it? I want to get married, but how am I going to meet the right person? I want a bigger home, but how will we obtain it? Do you find yourself asking questions like these? You know what you want, but you have no idea how you're going to achieve or obtain it.

When I think of the "How" question, I think of the parable of the acorn. Think about an acorn. Within it lies the blueprint for a full grown oak tree. But it isn't an oak yet. It's just the plan. It must be planted in the right type of soil, nourished and given time to grow into its ultimate creation.

Notice that the acorn only gathers what it needs as it needs it. It doesn't collect bark while it's sprouting from a seed, and it doesn't worry about going out and finding leaf elements while it's small. It has the vision or blueprint for its ultimate objective – an oak tree – but it doesn't know when or how the things it needs will come to it. It doesn't go out and fight and claw to get what it wants. It doesn't need to steal anything from anyone else. Everything it needs comes to it. We need to be like the acorn and trust the vision and take action on our current environment.

What if an acorn said, "Why try? I have no idea where I'm going to get that bark. Where am I going to get those leaves? I'm just a seed! I'm too small!" Yet, this is exactly how we're prone to think. "I can't make a big difference in the world; I'm just one little person with few talents or skills." Or "I want to write a book, but I'll probably never find a publisher, so why try?" Or "I have an idea for a revolutionary invention, but why make it when I can't afford to have it manufactured and marketed?"

When we think or say things like this, we're not taking into account that God will give us everything in our immediate environment that we need when we need it – just like He does for the acorn. *"Consider the lilies of the field, how they grow; they toil not, neither do they spin: And yet I say unto you, That even Solomon in all his glory was not arrayed like one of these"* (Matthew 6:28-29). If the things we need are not readily available, He'll bring them to us! If there is no way in sight, He'll open a way.

I cannot tell you how many times the Lord has brought someone into my life from clear across the country to bring me the skills or the resources I needed next. One instance in particular comes to mind.

There was a door that I'd been beating on for nearly a decade that refused to open for me. I wanted to write a book that would be sold on the shelves of one particular bookstore chain. Over the years, I've submitted manuscripts to this chain's publishing house, only to receive rejection letters. Then I self-published and sent my books to this company, but the door remained sealed.

Over a decade I continued to write on a consistent basis. When I couldn't find a publisher to take on my work, I learned how to do the technical part of publishing for myself. When the bookstores wouldn't give me shelf space, I used virtual shelf space on my own web sites, Amazon and the web sites of major bookstores. All the while I kept knocking on the door of this one particular bookstore chain.

Then in early 2003, a local friend introduced me to her sister whose books were carried in the bookstore chain that I'd been trying to get into for years. Her sister, who lived on the West coast, read my books and kindly gave them to her distributor with a personal recommendation. After several months of review, they agreed to distribute them and within a few months, the bookstore chain that I'd been pursuing for a decade purchased a batch of *Lord, Are You Sure?* to carry in their bookstores! Since that time, the same bookstore and many others have carried my various books.

When the time was right, it all flowed so effortlessly and the desires of my heart were granted. I never cease to marvel at how the Lord can use seemingly small and simple things to bring great things to pass. He knows the roads that will bring us to our desired destination. I didn't know that the bookstore chain I pursued only worked through specific distributors. I thought I could just keep sending books. But the Lord knew how the system worked.

I also believe that the Lord knew I wasn't ready ten years earlier. My talent needed polishing, and I needed experiences to teach me a message worth delivering. Had the Lord made this introduction three, five or ten years earlier, I would not have had the skill or the message. But when the skills and the message were available, the doors opened easily.

> Psalm 37:23 tells us that *"The steps of a good man are ordered by the Lord; and He delighteth in his way. Though he fall, he shall not be utterly cast down; for the Lord upholdeth him with His hand."*

It takes time to order our steps. Skills must be polished, knowledge attained, experience accumulated and relationship developed. While God can do all these instantaneously Himself – because He has all knowledge, we as human beings do not. Were He to pour the knowledge suddenly into our minds, it would not be the same as if we had worked, studied and attained it through experience.

Too many people give up when they initially meet failure. They put their desire on a shelf and assume that it is not meant to be. They don't realize that if you have the desire, then you have the power. An interesting byproduct of the relationships with my author friend and distributor is that they encouraged me to try my hand at fiction. As a young person in high school, I wanted to write fiction, but never thought I had what it took. I didn't think I could write the details. In the end, not only did I learn that I could do it, but I thoroughly enjoyed it! Writing fiction has become a wonderful blessing in my life – a treasure I never expected to find – an example of how the Lord doubles our talents when we use them.

If there is only one thing you learn from this story, let it be that if you have the desire, then you have the power - the greater the desire, the greater the power. Don't bury your righteous desires. Seek the Lord's guidance and direction as you study, learn and grow. Give Him time to order your steps as you hold onto your vision. Trust Him with the how and the when!

> "Delight thyself in the Lord; and he shall give thee the desires of thine heart. Commit thy way unto the Lord; trust also in him; and he shall bring it to pass... Those who wait upon the Lord, they shall inherit the earth."(Psalms 37:4-5, 9)

Another example of the way the Lord takes care of things when we release the "How" to His care is when I developed a clear mental image of some changes we wanted around our house and property. I wrote a detailed description of how I wanted our property to look with a fenced in area for horses, a barn, and places for chickens and goats.

In keeping with these principles, I quit focusing on "how" or "how much" all of this would cost, but I did spend hours envisioning it. I never told anyone else of my dream – not even my husband. Nothing really happened toward it that I could see for about a month. Then one day in October of 2004, my nephew (who lives next door) called me and said he had a friend who raised horses and needed somewhere to graze them. In order to let them graze their horses in our field, my nephew wanted to put up a fence *exactly* where I've been envisioning it. I was floored, because the way he described the fence was exactly as I pictured it.

I asked him if that much fence would be expensive, but he said that his friend had the posts and that they would build it. I wholeheartedly agreed to his plan and told him about my vision for a barn, goats and horses and offered our help in building the fence. He loved the idea and so it began there.

One Saturday afternoon a few weeks later I noticed that the gateposts along with several fence posts were in place. I took a walk to see where I'd like the barn to go and then sat down on a hay wagon facing the field. While I pictured it all in my mind, a car drove up and three people stepped out and started working on the fence. They were my nephew's friends who raise horses. I watched them drive several posts and reflected in wonder at the fact that all I had to do was envision it, and here it was being built right in front of my eyes - at absolutely no cost to me! Within another week, there were horses in our field!

I'll give you one more example. We have a half-mile driveway that cuts through a field and up a hill to our house. On the left of our dirt driveway is a sod farm and on the right is a field with horses. When I say dirt driveway, I mean dirt, mud, and lots and lots of potholes. My friend's kids like to come to our house just so their car can bounce through the potholes and get "Marnie mud" on it. It's that bad. Oh, we grade it, patch it, and try to keep it smooth, but the gravel we dumped on it several years earlier had long since washed away with time and flooding. Re-graveling it was out of the question. We were looking at $5,000-$6000 for the main stretch. We just hadn't been in a position to do that. It hadn't been a priority amidst other needs.

Yet, for the last couple years as I'd driven up and down our road, I'd envisioned it with a thick, lush layer of gravel. I imagined the crackle of it under my tires and felt gratitude for the smoothness of the ride. I never thought much past it than that. Just envisioning, feeling gratitude and then going about my way. I never stressed or strained to find a way to raise money to gravel the road, never checked on the best prices, never did anything. Just dreamed every now and then.

Then on September 26, 2006, I drove down to pick up the kids from the bus, and the curve of our road had gravel on it. I assumed the sod farmer did it. We let him use our road to access his field, and I figured he was trying to be nice and patched a troubled spot.

I drove back down to pick up the next group of kids and there was more gravel. It was as if it had dropped from heaven. I never saw a truck, never saw a road grader, never saw any sign of a workman. Then, the next morning when I drove the kids to school, almost the entire main stretch of driveway was graveled! I couldn't help but laugh. I laughed all the way down the driveway until my kids thought I'd lost my mind. It was as if little gravel elves scurried out in the night, did their work, and vanished. For me, it was a miracle, a sign that God lives, that He cares about little ol' me! The laws of the universe are still in motion. I learned later that our kind neighbor had done it. He was probably tired of driving his expensive heavy equipment up our pothole-laden road, but he will never understand the magnitude of what he did for my mindset, nor ever comprehend the sheer joy I experienced as I heard the thick gravel crunching beneath my tires!

To me, it was a very clear message. If God can make gravel appear on my driveway with no more than the little bit of imagery and gratitude I'd done, then anything is possible — I mean anything! So I witness to you today that God lives, He knows you and your needs. He will orchestrate whatever is necessary to bring to pass your worthy desires. It may seem to be taking forever, but in a heartbeat, it can all change. What a difference a day makes!

I learned an important lesson from these experiences and others like them. Sometimes we get too hung up on "how" we're going to make our dreams happen when really all we need to do is figure out "what" we want, ask the Lord for it, follow His promptings, and watch it unfold. Sometimes earning the money isn't even required. Normally, I would have tried to calculate costs, set up a plan to save for what I wanted and rounded up people to do the work. But in these circumstances, no effort on my part was even required. Each situation is different of course. Sometimes we must get out there and do the work. I'm certainly not advocating laziness. But sometimes, the Lord is willing to fight our battles for us, and all we need do is *"stand still and see the salvation of the Lord"* (Exodus 14:13)!

Points to Ponder

- What would you dare to dream or pray for if "how it would happen" was no longer an issue?

- List some times when you didn't know how it would all work out, but you put forth the necessary sacrifice, courage and faith to proceed anyway? How did it develop for your good?

- Search the scriptures for individuals who didn't know how they'd obey the Lord's commands, but faithfully moved forward anyway.

Lesson 24: From Whence Comes My Deliverance?

Earlier I shared the story of how we acquired our land on which to build. My family decided on a clear set of criteria for our property, and we began looking in Tennessee for it. We hadn't even considered Georgia. It wasn't that we felt anything extremely adverse to the state; we'd just always lived in Tennessee and loved it there. In the end, the Lord led us to a piece of property right across the border into Georgia that met our needs.

Ultimately, the move did more than give us the property we desired, it also put us in a position to make friends and associations that would greatly influence our lives and our children's lives in phenomenal ways. The Lord wanted us here for a reason – to serve and to be served.

Scripture is replete with examples of God making wonderful things happen in places one would never expect. Think about Joseph who was sold into Egypt. Who would think that the Lord could use him in prison? Yet, he did. Who would think an Israelite would be second in command only to Pharaoh over all of Egypt and help preserve that nation and Abraham's chosen family? Joseph's brothers certainly didn't!

Think of Moses who found his refuge in the house of Pharoah's daughter. Surely, Moses' mother never expected her son to find safety in the arms of the very family who set out to kill him! Certainly Israel never expected their deliverer to spring from the house of their enemy - Pharoah's own courts! Moses never expected to find God in the wilderness. Most of the Israelites never believed they could find healing by looking at a brass serpent on a pole, but those who had the faith to look lived while those who refused perished.

Ten of the twelve spies sent into Canaan didn't have faith to believe that God could give them a Promised Land inhabited by giants. The lad Samuel didn't expect to hear God's voice in the middle of the night. He came to Eli three times before he finally understood that God spoke to him and would call him as the next prophet in Israel.

When Samuel came to the house of Jesse in search of the next King of Israel, he expected to select one of Jesse's older strapping sons. But the Lord told Samuel, *"Look not on his countenance, or on the height of his stature; because I have refused him: for the Lord seeth not as man seeth; for man looketh on the outward appearance, but the Lord looketh on the heart."* Samuel asked if there were not another son, and Jesse told him of his youngest son David who tended the flocks. That day, God selected a mere lad, the youngest of Jesse's family as the next king of Israel. The Philistines never expected their hero Goliath to be slain by this same scrawny little Israelite youth.

Who would expect the King of Kings and Lord of Lords to be born in the obscure village of Bethlehem in a lowly stable? When Philip told Nathaneal, *"We have found him of whom Moses in the law and the prophets did write, Jesus of Nazareth, the son of Joseph,"* Nathaneal replied doubtfully, "Can there any good thing come out of Nazareth?"

Time and again the Lord has shown us that things are not always as they appear. Miracles rarely come from where we expect. *"God hath chosen the foolish things of the world to confound the wise; and God hath chosen the weak things of the world to confound the things which are mighty"* (1 Corinthians 1: 27).

When we relinquish our need to control and our expectations about from where our deliverance will come, we open ourselves up to a whole new world of possibilities.

A good example of getting a clear picture of what you want, but not limiting the Lord to where it comes from is something that happened to my second oldest sister. Lisa was about twenty six and unmarried, but she wanted very much to have a family of her own with a good faithful man. She had a clear idea of the type of man she wanted to marry. She wanted a man who belonged to her same denomination with similar beliefs and values as her own. Yet locally, she could not find anyone among those she dated who felt like the right match for her. She had several marriage proposals, but none felt right.

One weekend she and a friend drove all the way from Tennessee to Ohio to a single adult Church conference. During that weekend, she met a man who fit her criteria. But he lived in Chicago, and she lived in Tennessee! They didn't let this stand in their way, though. By the end of the conference, they both knew that they had met their future spouse. I remember my sister coming home from this weekend and telling me she'd met the man she would marry.

She did, and he's been a wonderful husband. They lived in Chicago for several years and then moved down to Tennessee where they built a home and are raising their two fine sons to love and serve the Lord.

If my sister had been too scared to travel outside her comfort zone, she never would have met her husband. She didn't limit the location from which God could deliver her miracle, and in the end she's been richly blessed.

Points to Ponder

· Search your memory for times when your blessings or answers came from a place you never expected. Document these in your journal.

· Search the scriptures and ponder upon those instances were deliverance came from an unusual place or source. For example, what lesson did Jonah learn about not misjudging a "place" or an entire city of people?

· How will you keep your options open in the future and look for deliverance and miracles to originate anywhere - perhaps even from your trials?

Lesson 25: What Are the Desires of Your Heart?

Thus far, we've talked a lot about the things we can't control. But there is one very important thing we can, and that is "What" we want. Jesus repeatedly told us to ask, knock, and seek.

Yet, of all the questions, I think it's ironic that most of us never get clear on "What" we want. Oh, we do in a few areas. We might want a bigger home, a better life, a spouse, etc. But few of us get specific about exactly what we want. We don't take the time to clearly envision the house or how we want our life to feel and look or what characteristics we want in a spouse.

Most of the time we just whine or complain about what we don't have, but we don't get a vivid picture of what we want it to be like. For example, I often griped about my old clunker van, but I didn't decide what I wanted instead. I was too afraid to ask for what I really wanted, too afraid of what it might cost or what debt might be incurred to obtain it. Not until I got very clear on the make, model, year, style and features did what we want become available to us.

Get Specific

A little incident happened to me in February of 2005 that taught me a lesson in asking with precision. My nephew composes songs, plays the guitar and sings. He's quite the talented young man, and we always enjoy listening to him at family gatherings. There are a couple old songs that he plays that I really enjoy. One is a haunting melody called *Long Black Veil* and the other is *Folsom Prison.*

Before my nephew left to serve a two-year mission in the Dominican Republic in February of 2005, I asked him to "record those songs you sing for me." He promised he would and true to his word, the day before he left, he locked himself in his room and recorded a tape for me. But when I received the tape that night, I found three newer songs that he'd written. I do enjoy them, but they aren't the songs I wanted. You see I didn't ask specifically. I didn't say, "Noah, please record *Long Black Veil* and *Folsom Prison* for me." I just said, "Noah, please record those songs you sing before you leave."

Like a loving nephew, he recorded songs he sings for me. He genuinely wanted to give me what I asked for, but I wasn't specific!

Sometimes in life we don't get specific about what we want, and we get something, but it may not be exactly what we wanted. We need to pinpoint what we want. How else will we recognize it when it arrives? The next time you set a goal, don't let it be a vague, misty concept but a clear, concise request! Then put it in writing. If you've put your objective in writing, when your prayer is answered, neither you nor anyone else can deny that the Lord brought it to pass.

Write It Down

When I was about seventeen or eighteen years old, a teacher at church suggested we make a list of the characteristics we wanted in a spouse. I itemized 100 very specific characteristics I wanted in a husband and kept it in my journal. When I had been dating Greg Pehrson for about five months, my college roommates and I were sitting around looking at my list. One of my friends suggested I run Greg down the list. As a lark, I did, and he met 96 out of 100 items. I was quite startled because up until this time, I didn't seriously consider him as a marriage possibility.

Another roommate said, "Wow, have you prayed about this?"

"No! And I'm not going to!" came my adamant retort. I didn't want to get married. I was a freshman in college with my heart set on a career.

Over the next few weeks the Lord made clear to me that I did need to pray about the matter. When I did, I received a clear, firm answer that Greg was the man I should marry. We were engaged within a week of my answer and married six months later. If I hadn't had a clear written picture of what I wanted in a husband, I don't know how long it would have taken, or even if I would have recognized him as the man God intended for me to marry.

Use Gratitude to Shift Your Attitude

Jesus taught, *"Ask, and it shall be given you; seek, and ye shall find; knock, and it shall be opened unto you: For every one that asketh receiveth; and he that seeketh findeth; and to him that knocketh it shall be opened. Or what man is there of you, whom if his son ask bread, will he give him a stone? Or if he ask a fish, will he give him a serpent?"* (Matthew 7:7-10)

Paul taught in Philippians 4:6 "Don't be unduly concerned about anything; but in every thing by prayer and supplication with thanksgiving let your requests be made known unto God."

Notice Paul told us to ASK with Thanksgiving and to let our requests be made known with THANKSGIVING. Think about that! How do you ask someone for something and thank them for it at the same time? The only way to do that is if you sincerely expect the person to answer. You have faith in them and their desire to help you.

God wants to give good things to his children, but nowhere does He say, "gripe and ye shall receive" or "whine and complain and it shall be opened unto you." He simply said to ask. Asking requires clarity about what you want. Once we've asked and we've received an answer or a feeling of peace, we should expect that what we've asked for will arrive in God's good time.

James 1:5-6 tells us to "ask in faith, nothing wavering." But sometimes we become discouraged, and we fall back into griping or doubting. It can be difficult to hold the right attitude – an attitude of faith and expectant hope - when circumstances appear as if you're standing still or moving in reverse.

Are you like me? Whenever I hit a problem or challenge, my initial human reaction is one of the following:

- get angry, upset or pout
- start to lose faith that things are going to work out
- blame myself or others for my misfortune
- give up hope
- assume God is giving me a "serpent" when I asked for a "fish."

None of these are productive or healthy. Each of these reactions slackens my hope, weakens my faith, and distances me from God and my worthwhile goals. For you see, all the promises are unto them who *believe*. None of these human reactions foster faith – none of them persuades one to *believe*. Without faith, nothing happens. I recommend reviewing Lessons 5-6 on Gratitude.

The Big Vision

Some people have difficulty deciding what they want. They're too afraid that they'll choose the wrong thing or that by making one choice they eliminate other choices. In the end, they choose inaction and their progression stalls. I've been like that to some degree. While I generally have no problem setting short term goals for things I want, I've had difficulty selecting a big vision – the dream I choose to work toward.

Using gratitude to set short term goals and work toward them helps you actively build your faith muscles. Instead of waiting for life to bring you trials and force you to grow, you take control of the day-to-day elements of your life and consciously choose where you want to go and let faith in God carry you to your desired destination.

While doing this, one should still have a big picture of how they want their life to look, feel and be. Without a clear destination, we tend to be like a mouse turning a wheel one more round, but going nowhere. That was my problem. I had been using these principles for two years before I finally realized that I had neglected to solidify the big picture for my life.

Greg and I had been struggling under a load of debt, and all I could focus on was getting rid of it. My mentor in the principles of abundant living, Leslie Householder, repeatedly advised me not to focus on the debt. She said I needed to focus on something positive. Focusing on the debt would only cause it to remain. Whatever we give our focus, feeling and energy to grows. It's a law of nature. Debt was the last place I should have been putting my focus and feeling!

In an effort to keep the word "debt" out of my goals, I began working toward short term goals – monthly amounts of money we should earn that would meet our obligations and whittle them down over time. I did this for nearly two years with very little, if any, significant progress in the reduction of our debts.

Then one Friday in September of 2004, Leslie and I spoke on the phone about how things were going for us, and she asked me what I really want from life. I admitted to her that while we were doing well, we weren't making a significant dent in our debts – which is really what I wanted to happen. She challenged me to dream big. Again, she reiterated that I needed to stop focusing on the debt and challenged me to picture my life after it was gone. Up until this time, I just couldn't think past the debt or picture what my life would be like without it.

One thing she suggested was that Greg and I pretend to shop at the mall, use fake checks and write them out and see if we could spend $50,000. Of course, we weren't to give the store owners the checks! It would be an exercise in dreaming and in expanding our minds to the possibilities. I told her it was depressing to window shop because we didn't have the money for things. She told me that it's good to get depressed sometimes because it makes you disgusted enough to take action to change your situation.

Later that day I spoke with a longtime friend, telling her what Leslie said. She suggested that perhaps I got my thrill in life from pulling myself out of a tight financial spot. I had grown accustomed to making up the difference… leaning on the Lord and using gratitude to help me out of a pinch. She suggested that it had become a thrill for me. To a degree it was! In essence, I had become addicted to leaning on the Lord to pull us out of a tight spot and then getting excited when once more He did it. She suggested that if I could find my thrill elsewhere, then I might be able to break the cycle.

At this point I realized that evidently something was wrong in my thinking. I knew the principles of abundant living. I practiced gratitude, I could draw on the powers of heaven, and the Lord would pull us through, but something still wasn't right. I began praying, "Please teach me how to think!" That prayer led to one of my greatest breakthroughs... not only did I need to get clear on "what" I wanted but "why" I wanted it!

"Commit thy works unto the LORD,
and thy thoughts shall be established."
Proverbs 16:3

Points to Ponder

· What do you want from life? What would your ideal life look like, feel like, be like? What would bring you the most joy and happiness?

· Have you taken the time to prayerfully seek a confirmation from the Lord that the things you want are the ones He wants for you?

· Try adding "please teach me how to think" to your daily prayers and see what happens!

Lesson 26: What's Your Why?

In the fall of 2004, we decided we should probably refinance our house to consolidate debts, but I didn't have much faith that it would appraise for what we needed because our six children had done some damage to the house over the years. For example, they'd busted a doorframe, colored and knocked holes in the walls, and broken a pedestal sink in my office bathroom. After the pedestal sink being broken for a year, I finally replaced it.

The Saturday after realizing that I'd been focusing on short-term fixes (See Lesson 25), I had a dream. I dreamed that our second oldest son Joshua held up our younger son Nate so he could stand on the pedestal sink, and they broke it. I woke up angry – the understanding dawning that my entire life was like that – I fix it, they break it, I pay the debt and the interest or a crisis keeps bringing it back. I was going nowhere! Maybe you know how this feels! A picture of a mouse on a treadmill came to mind – I constantly repaired, repaid and fixed something that re-broke or never went away. It depressed me so incredibly to finally realize that all the "progress" I thought I'd been making for the previous two years wasn't really progress. I wasn't going anywhere – wasn't making any headway in eliminating debt or getting anywhere.

I was a rat on a wheel!

That was the start of the most depressing week of my life. I felt as if everything I'd been learning/practicing for the previous two years was getting me nowhere. All it did was help me spin the wheel one more round. Later that afternoon I went to a leadership meeting for church and the instructor giving the lesson played a CD with a stirring rendition of the hymn, *Be Still My Soul*. I love that version of the song and something she said – which I can't even remember now - made me get the message.

"If you want to get off the treadmill – BE STILL!"

Of course, it made absolute perfect sense! In order to stop spinning, I had to stop and step off the wheel. But, how could I be still? I had to work and earn money and support our family and make up the difference. How could I just be still and do nothing?

Yet, I felt depressed enough to try anything! I took an entire week and didn't work other than what was necessary to maintain my Web sites. I spent all my time cleaning the house – it needed it badly and it was the only thing that felt right. I dove into housework and thought about what I wanted out of life. A friend helped me work through an important issue. I realized I already had everything I wanted – I just didn't want to owe anyone for it, and there were a few home improvements and additions we'd wanted to make to make our home more orderly, attractive and unifying. My friend suggested I visualize a mortgage burning party with all my friends there and the mortgage paid in full on our house. Now this I could get excited about! I had my "why!"

I started picturing a big brass platter with Greg holding our mortgage papers over it and me lighting a match beneath. All our friends and family gathered around and celebrated with us. The house and property looked just how I wanted it. I now had a vision that would motivate and propel me forward! Leslie Householder suggested I write this vision down in detail, then distill it into a paragraph I could put on a note card with a date at the top like a journal entry. I did that and soon it became a vision that I called to mind anytime I became discouraged.

The more I envisioned, the more I realized I had something I could get excited about! I could sink my teeth into a feeling of relaxed freedom! I could get motivated about opening up our home to friends and family and sharing the blessings God has given us with others. I could get excited about developing our property so that our children learned responsibility and how to appreciate the gifts of nature. I now had a whole list of "why's" that would inspire and motivate me.

During my week or so of 'being still' all I felt compelled to do was work on the house. It felt like the right time to refinance. My oldest son and I painted, weeded the yard, and patched holes. We hired someone to pressure wash the outside of the house. We did everything we could before the appraiser came. Yet, still there were things undone – things that it was just humanly impossible for me to tackle on my own. I said a prayer and put it into Heavenly Father's hands. If it was meant to be, it would be. In the end, it appraised for more than we needed. We consolidated the bulk of our debts into a payment less than our original house payment!

This left us with a car payment and a debt I owed a family member. I really wanted that family member paid back. It had been a burden on my mind for several years.

A few months later we decided to get an equity line on our house and pay everything else off. We had the application turned in when right in the middle of the approval process, my husband lost his job. There was a very real possibility the loan would be denied with him not having a job. This time I just let go of it. I didn't worry. I told the Lord if it was meant to be, it would be and it was in His hands. We ended up getting the loan. With that loan and my husband's severance, the mountain of debt moved in a matter of a few months from the time I finally started looking at the big picture instead of focusing on short term fixes.

You wouldn't think a vision of a mortgage burning party would lead to consolidating all your debts into a mortgage, but until this happened, we could never make any significant progress paying twenty-something percent interest. A single digit interest rate on our home loan would make all the difference. Now the money we've been applying toward debts is actually attacking the principle instead of simply covering the ever accruing interest!

Interestingly enough, even with my husband's job loss we didn't worry. We knew it was for a reason. I've spent the last 15 years getting to do what I love while my husband's been stuck in a job he hated. The Lord took those years to help me build a business that could sustain us. He moved our mountain of debt just in time to coincide with Greg's chance to follow his dream. Now my husband can enjoy his work and focus on doing what he wants to do – building his own personal chef business. Plus, with him being at home more our family life has improved. We have a more secure, consistent, and harmonious atmosphere. God's timing is always perfect and His ways are always the best!

It's All About Emotions

Over time, I refined my goal and looked past the event of a mortgage burning party to a general view of our lives, our home and the feelings we would experience when things were orderly, peaceful, secure, harmonious, abundant and unified. In time I learned a very important lesson. **We think we want "things" but in reality it's just a feeling we're after. When we discover that we can feel that feeling anytime we choose, the feeling puts us in harmony with the people, things, circumstances and events that enhance, amplify and draw toward us more of the same desired emotions.**

It wasn't things that I wanted – wasn't necessarily the barn or the fence, horses, hardwood floors or a pool. Those things would be nice, but it was more that they painted a picture in my mind of the feeling I wanted to create in my life. What is important for me is to know that I'm making a difference for good in the world. My heart's desire is a home and family life that conveys feelings of peace, security, abundance, plenty, order, harmony, gratitude, love, unity, cooperation, and joy. My root desire is a home in which the Spirit of the Lord can dwell.

Once I realized that the feelings were what I wanted, and not necessarily "things" or "money" or even my "debts paid off," I discovered that I could feel those feelings at any time. I already had the ability to feel them either in my mind or even in my existing world. They were already there if I chose to see them and foster them. But I had to get off the rat wheel and "be still" to do it.

As a husband and wife, we began working toward this atmosphere in our home. We began striving as a family to keep our home orderly, peaceful and harmonious. As we fostered these feelings, more good things came our way. Of course we struggle; things aren't perfect all of the time. Sometimes there are messes. Sometimes there are arguments. But we're working toward those feelings we've identified as the desires of our heart. As we do this, each piece to the picture starts falling into place. It has to, because we are now living in harmony with the things, people, circumstances and events that will amplify and enhance those positive and uplifting feelings.

What Is Your Why?

In the formula which says that your focus, faith and feeling bring miracles to pass, your feeling is your "why." Without a clear and compelling "why" for accomplishing what you want, you won't make significant progress.

You have to experience some strong emotion. For some, that's excitement over a goal. For others it's getting mad enough or disgusted enough with the way things are to do something about it. In my case, I had to get depressed enough to change the way I thought. I had to get upset enough to step off my treadmill and take a good hard look at my life. I had to get a clear picture of my goal and why I wanted it.

What is your why? What feelings do you want to experience in your life and why do you want them? You can control your why. It's very important that your why is one that resonates with your spirit and feels right. It is only between you and God. Bring Him into the discussion about your "why." For example, if I choose to be a best selling author because I want to be mega rich and have everyone fall all over me with praise and accolades, then I think God would consider that a waste of time and may decide it's not such an admirable goal for me. Then again, He could very well give it to me and teach me that it's not all it's cracked up to be.

But if I choose to be a best selling author so I can promote good in the world in an impactful way, because I want to teach truth and make a positive impact on a generation or even future generations by writing a classic, then perhaps He'd see that as something He could support. The accolades might even be there... but they aren't my objective.

A Caution on "Why"

While we can control "Why" we want what we want, we should avoid asking useless "Why" questions. For example, very little can come of the pity party questions: "Why me? Why now? Why us?" These are all useless questions. When you're prone to shake your fist at the heavens and ask why something has happened to you, replace the "Why" with a "What" question. For example, these types of questions will help you find answers:

- What can I learn from this?
- What will I do now that I wouldn't have done otherwise?
- What can I do for others because of this situation?
- What do I want to have happen?
- What would need to happen for me to feel comfortable with this situation?

Use these questions to help you decide what you want to have happen next so that you can intelligently and specifically approach the Lord and ask for a solution. Whining and crying "Why me? Why now? Why us?" will get you nowhere. Be proactive and decide what solution you want and then gratefully ask for it!

Marnie L. Pehrson

Points to Ponder

· Why do you want the things you want? What is the big, compelling reason that makes you work toward and patiently seek your dream(s)?

· Are you focusing on the big picture or are you getting lost in the details? Are you spinning your wheels or being still and trusting God?

· Have you gotten too caught up in wanting "things" rather than getting to the root feelings that bring you joy and happiness? How can you evaluate and if necessary change this?

· How can you open your mind to the possibility that your Heavenly Father could bring you the feelings and desires of your heart in a different way than the method or vehicle you expect? In other words, is it possible that He could fulfill the needs and desires of your heart through alternate means than you think? Are you open to this possibility?

· How can you release the useless "why" questions that only lead to whining and ingratitude?

Lesson 27: Focus, Faith and Feeling

The only reason we want things or events to happen in our lives is because we want the feelings associated with them. Think about it … we want to feel love, happiness, success, harmony, security, romance, excitement, pleasure, or some other emotion. In our minds, we've identified objects, people, relationships or ideas with these emotions. For example, we might want to feel loved and we equate that with a romantic relationship. Or we might wish to feel important, and we equate that with nice clothes or an expensive car. We might want to feel successful and we equate that with a fine home.

It's important to examine our desired emotions. Some emotions are more worthwhile than others. We should prayerfully identify and evaluate our root desires to determine which ones are worth pursuing and which are not. For example, is your desire for a fine home linked to a desire to feel superior to other people? Or is it because you equate a fine home with harmony? Everyone is "wired" differently. For example, I equate a nice orderly home with both financial prosperity and spiritual harmony. You may not see it that way at all.

Once you've identified your desired emotions and what they represent in the physical world, start opening up your mind to the possibility that you can feel those feelings without the physical counterparts. For example, it's possible to feel loved without having a spouse. It's possible to feel successful without living in a 4,500 square foot home. Open your heart and mind to the possibility that God could give you the desired feelings of your heart in a way you hadn't considered.

Start seeking to feel worthwhile feelings as much as you can in your present environment – even if you can only feel them on paper or in your imagination. As you do this, you will draw the people, events and things to you that promote those feelings.

Also, remember to take action on your external environment in ways that support your desired results. There is a distinct correlation between our outside environment and our internal mind and heart. For example, once I realized that I equated an orderly home with success and spiritual harmony, I was able to bring my home into order and thus create that sensation of success and spiritual harmony internally. As I did this, I began to see a significant improvement in our finances and in how our children behaved. In essence, my home told me, "We're prosperous. We take care of what God gives us, and we live in spiritual harmony." It verified what I'd been telling myself internally but hadn't quite believed until my eyes could see some "evidence."

Focus + Faith + Feeling = Results

Anything in life is drawn to you when you apply your focus, faith and feeling to it. Whether it's wanted or unwanted, if you're giving your focus, faith and feeling to it, you're drawing it into your life.

This is why it's so important to release the negative emotions of worry, fear and doubt. They feed what you don't want and actually draw it toward you. Surely no one wants to feel worried, fearful or in pain. So why do we focus on and create those emotions in our minds? By doing so, we only draw events, people or things to us that make us feel anxious, frightened or in pain!

Focus your emotions using faith, gratitude and a clear vision of what you desire and your purpose for achieving it. Then, you will be feeding the feelings you desire and drawing them into your life. Remember, your focus is deciding "what" you desire. Get specific. Get clear with details. Feel as if you're already in possession of it; be grateful for it ahead of time!

"Feeling" is deciding "why" you desire it – what feelings will you experience when you have what you desire? Feel those feelings now! Don't wait to experience them at some later date. Identify the emotions you desire in your life and pull them out of your existing environment, relationships and experiences. They are there. You may have to re-order things a bit like I did with my home. If you're not seeing them, perhaps you aren't "being still." Or if your circumstances are just so contrary to the feelings you want to experience, close your eyes and imagine what your life will be like and look like when you feel how you wish to feel. Seek out and feed anything in your present environment that fosters these positive emotions.

"Faith" is letting go of the remaining questions for God to handle. Faith is knowing that all things will work together for your good in the appointed time and way. You express your faith through deep and sincere gratitude for things as they are right now and as you know they will be.

The quicker we let go of the things that are out of our control, the sooner we'll relax and be free to fly. Listen to the Spirit. It is your guide and will prompt you in how to act and what to do. Trust the good desires of your heart. Anything that is virtuous, lovely, of good report or praiseworthy, anything that lifts, builds or makes the world a better place is a righteous desire. Those desires are planted in your heart by God. Don't bury them! Feed them! Get clear on what you desire and why. Then, give the details of how, when and where to your Heavenly Father.

As you consistently act immediately upon each and every prompting given to you by the Spirit - regardless of how afraid you may be to do it – your desires begin to take shape into physical realities. As you come to trust the Lord fully, you will find that "peace that passes all understanding," and your heart's desires will distill upon you as the dew from heaven. Worry will become a thing of the past because now you know how to ask intelligently and specifically. You have a clear distinction between what you control and what God controls. Most importantly, you know you are a child of God with a wonderful future and a divine plan that He desires to assist you in fulfilling.

Lesson 28: Identifying the Spirit

Perhaps there is no greater skill we can acquire in life than learning to identify and listen to the voice of the Spirit. God continually speaks to us; the pity is that so few of us hear Him. And the reason we don't hear Him is because we're either distracted or have never learned to distinguish the voice of the Spirit from our own imagination or the voices of the world. Think of all the sounds, images, and information that clutter our lives. For starters, there's television, music, newspapers, ringing phones, and the internet. There are the legitimate demands for our attention by our family, employment and friends.

One could feasibly go through his entire life and never learn to hear the still, small voice of the Spirit. Unfortunately, living without the Spirit leaves us to our own devices. Alone, we lack God's direction and end up making mistakes we could have avoided had we heard God's forewarning messages. When we go it alone, we deny ourselves the sweet peace that only the Comforter can bring.

In the last days of His mortal ministry, Jesus promised His disciples the companionship of the Holy Ghost, the third member of the Godhead. He said,

> *"If ye love me, keep my commandments. And I will pray the Father, and he shall give you another Comforter, that he may abide with you for ever; Even the Spirit of truth; whom the world cannot receive, because it seeth him not, neither knoweth him: but ye know him; for he dwelleth with you, and shall be in you. But the Comforter, which is the Holy Ghost, whom the Father will send in my name, he shall teach you all things, and bring all things to your remembrance, whatsoever I have said unto you. Peace I leave with you, my peace I give unto you: not as the world giveth, give I unto you. Let not your heart be troubled, neither let it be afraid"* (John 14:15-17,26-27).

Here's an analogy I use for our ability to listen to the Spirit. Imagine yourself as a radio with thousands of different channels to choose from, but one channel is precious and sometimes difficult to locate. It requires some effort on your part to reach, but it is worth the quest, for it broadcasts messages from God.

On this "channel" you can find inspiration, impressions, images, feelings, directions, sounds, and beautiful creativity beyond the finite human mind. But your radio has to be especially tuned to pick up communication from this divine channel. It's not an all-or-nothing reception either. You can pick it up in a fuzzy mode, or perhaps with other channels overlapping it. But honing in on it in its clearest form takes developing a "spiritual ear" and "spiritual eyes." It takes time and effort.

To the spiritually indifferent or untrained spiritual ear it may sound like static. This is why Jesus warned us not to be one of those *"who seeing, see not or hearing, hear not or whose heart had waxed gross, and their ears dull of hearing and their eyes … closed"* (Matthew 13:13-17). Jesus knew that the answers we seek are literally staring us right in the face, but we can be too blind or deaf to notice them.

It takes faith and "hungering" to learn the language of the Spirit, to tune into God's "channel of communication." In this lesson, I'm going to give you two hints for tuning into this divine station, and another tool for knowing when you've reached it.

Hint #1: God "piggy-backs" His messages to you on the Word of God.

Studying the Word of God is a wonderful way to learn the language of the Spirit. When God speaks, He so often piggy-backs His signal upon the Word of God. For example, have you ever had a question on your mind, started reading a passage that didn't even relate to your problem, but while you were reading, your answer came? You could even have been reading something you've read dozens of times before. But this time it told you what you needed to know today. Next year the same passage could carry a totally different message to your heart. Studying the scriptures puts you on the divine channel, so that you can hear what God wants you to hear.

Hint #2: Keeping the commandments increases our ability to hear the Spirit.

In the passage from John 14 that I quoted earlier, Jesus tells us, *"If ye love me, keep my commandments. And I will pray the Father and he shall give you another Comforter…"* This is basically two important if/then statements which reveal another way to fine-tune our reception to the Spirit.

1. If you love me, you'll keep my commandments.
2. If you keep my commandments, I will give you the Comforter.

Keeping the commandments increases our ability to hear the Spirit. Granted, none of us is perfect. We're all going to slip and disobey God's commandments. But as we strive toward obeying God, repent where necessary, and begin anew, we bring our receivers into alignment with God's broadcasting channel. As we continue to do our best, the voice of the Spirit becomes clearer like a radio zoning in on a station.

Bit by bit or as Isaiah would say "line upon line and precept upon precept... here a little and there a little" the truer our communication and the clearer the voice of the Spirit (Isaiah 28:10).

It's like someone scanning the AM band on a radio. At first the signal may be fuzzy, distorted or jumbled, but as you love God, immerse yourself in the scriptures, and strive to live as He would have you live, the closer you hone in on that broadcast channel until you're enjoying a flow of communication from God that will guide you throughout your life.

And what are the benefits of the Holy Spirit according to the Savior? John 14 tells us:

- He will teach you all things;
- He will bring all things to your remembrance, whatsoever I have said unto you;
- He will give you peace - such peace that you have no need for fear.

And so as we love God and strive to follow His teachings, we become more adept at hearing His voice. And what does His voice sound like? Or feel like? Paul answers that for us in Galatians 5:22-23: *"But the fruit of the Spirit is love, joy, peace, longsuffering, gentleness, goodness, faith, meekness, and temperance."*

Those are the feelings we experience when we're tuned into the Holy Spirit. Notice there is no mention of hate, fear, impatience, irritation, sin, discouragement, doubt or over-indulgence.

By becoming more adept at identifying our feelings, we'll learn to recognize the Spirit. Then, when we pray, face challenges, learn a new principle, or must make a decision we'll be able to distinguish between what God wants us to do and what He advises against.

The Spirit Is Agreeing with Your Decision, What You Have Learned, or Your Course of Action When You Feel...	The Spirit Is Warning You Against Your Decision, What You Have Learned or Your Course of Action When You Feel...
Love	Hate
Joy	Confusion
Peace	Fear
Patience	Impatience
Gentleness	Anger/Hostility
Goodness	Darkness
Faith	Doubt
Meekness (aka humility)	Pride/Arrogance
Temperance	Self-indulgence/Selfishness

Challenge

I challenge you as you go throughout this week, to take some time to immerse yourself in the scriptures - really study them, apply them to your life and see what messages God gives you. Then, start to look for and recognize the presence of the Spirit of God in your life. Notice those feelings of love, joy, peace, etc. Also begin to notice the situations or choices that take you away from the Spirit. Then, consciously choose those activities, places, and associations that bring you closer to the Spirit of God.

I promise you as you do this - as you develop your spiritual eyes and ears - you will experience peace and joy beyond your ability to express in words. And then you will know as I know that God lives, that He loves you and wants to speak to you today and every day.

Lesson 29: Decision Making with Confidence

I have a friend who was weighing a difficult business dilemma. She explained, "I have a tough time making decisions. I labor over them — weighing their pros and cons, but then I'm never really sure which one is right or whether the decision I finally make is the best one. Heck, I can't even select the toppings for my pizza!"

This is a common problem for many. Some people can make decisions quickly and move on, while others take a long time coming to a decision, and still aren't sure whether the choice they made was the right one. Does it really have to take this long? Do we have to walk blindly — never knowing if the choice we made was the best one?

No! We can make informed decisions and walk forward in faith that our course is the right one. But, we have to lean on the One who knows the end from the beginning. He knows which path is right. He knows which course will lead us to the most happiness. As Proverbs 3:4-6 advises:

> "Trust in the LORD with all thine heart; and lean not unto thine own understanding. In all thy ways acknowledge him, and he shall direct thy paths."

This is not to say that God is going to give you the answer for every frivolous decision in your life such as which outfit to wear today, or what topping to put on your pizza. But on important issues that affect your life, the Lord is willing and waiting for you to ask His opinion.

Yet, He isn't going to just give you the answer either. God gave us our minds for a reason. He wants us to use them. In Luke 14:28 - 30, Jesus suggests we weigh the consequences of our actions,

> "For which of you, intending to build a tower, sitteth not down first, and counteth the cost, whether he have sufficient to finish it? Lest haply, after he hath laid the foundation, and is not able to finish it, all that behold it begin to mock him, Saying, This man began to build, and was not able to finish."

Study the pros and cons of any question in your mind. Use your own logic; pay attention to any feelings or warning signals you may experience. It may help to write the pros and cons down on paper. Come to your own decision.

Then, go to the Lord in prayer and tell Him what you have decided to do, and ask Him if it is the right thing to do. Let Him know you're willing to abide by His will. James 1:5-8 admonishes:

> *"If any of you lack wisdom, let him ask of God, that giveth to all men liberally, and upbraideth not; and it shall be given him. But let him ask in faith, nothing wavering. For he that wavereth is like a wave of the sea driven with the wind and tossed. For let not that man think that he shall receive any thing of the Lord. A double minded man is unstable in all his ways."*

Notice that James teaches that God is willing to assist us with wisdom when we ask Him. But we have to ask in faith, nothing wavering. We can't be wish-washy, indecisive and tossed. Generally speaking, we should come to our own decision, then ask God if it is right. He doesn't like double-mindedness. It's easier for us to get a clear message from our prayers if we've put thought and study into the situation and then go to Him for a Yes or No answer. Ask God to give you a feeling of peace if it is correct or a bad feeling if it is the wrong choice.

After you pray, listen closely for any feelings you may have. If you have feelings of peace, positive excitement, happiness or joy afterwards, then you know you've made the correct decision. If you feel depressed, unsure, uneasy or disturbed, you know it's not the right decision. Go back to the drawing board and start again.

What Do You Do When No Answer Comes?

Sometimes you'll make a decision, pray about it, and feel nothing either way. You have a few options in this situation. First, give it some time, ponder on it some more, and an answer may come to you over the next days or weeks. If time is of the essence or if you have waited and still no answer is forthcoming, you could rethink the situation, search the scriptures, and see if you missed something. Try rephrasing your prayer or choosing another option and praying about it.

Sometimes an answer will come only after you've proven to the Lord that you're serious about wanting an answer. When my husband and I were considering getting a new van, we prayed about whether it was a wise decision since it would mean getting a car loan. I didn't want any more debt - not unless I was 100% sure the Lord wanted us to do it. My husband prayed about it and almost immediately felt it was a good decision. I felt okay about it, but I wasn't 100% certain. I knew myself well enough to know that should problems arise, and I were to lean on my husband's decision without getting my own witness I would regret it.

I prayed about it for almost two weeks without an answer. Finally I decided to fast for 24-hours to let the Lord know how important an answer was to me. No answer came immediately after fasting. But I did not feel bad about the decision either. So we found a new van that we liked on the Internet. We rented a car to drive a couple hours south to look at it. While I was driving back from the rental car place on the day we were to go look at the new van, the answer came so clear and certain that I could no more deny it than I could deny the sun shines on a hot summer afternoon. I knew that the Lord wanted us to have that van. I knew why He wanted us to have it and what He wanted us to do with it. God reminded me of Jesus telling Peter where to cast his net to catch the fish with the coin in its mouth so they could pay their taxes. The Lord assured me, that He would do the same for us.

The answer came with such force, that tears streamed down my cheeks on my drive home, and I am not the type of person to cry easily. There was no denying the answer. And there is no denying that the Lord kept His promise many times over. Within less than a year, that van was paid off, and we haven't had a car payment since.

So, if you've prayed and given it time, yet still no answer is apparent, go ahead and make your best choice. Take action toward it (like we did by shopping for the van, selecting one, and renting a car to go buy it). If you take a few action steps along your decided course, usually it will become apparent whether you've made the right decision. More often than not, you'll quickly know whether it's right or wrong. Things may start opening up for you and a positive feeling may come. Or, after you've moved forward, you may learn that it wasn't such a good idea after all, and you can turn back.

For whatever reason, the Lord sometimes delays His answer until you've taken a few steps into the unknown. It's sort of like walking down a long dark hallway, where the doors of opportunity don't open until you've stepped into the darkness.

Remember, the Lord is always there for you - in the darkness and the light. He's told us to ask and we shall receive, seek and we shall find, knock and it shall be opened unto us. Sometimes those answers come quickly, other times after some pondering. At other times, it may take a few action steps. But, I hope you will always ask God before you make important decisions. Don't lean on your own understanding when a confirmation of your decisions can be obtained. Ask God in faith, nothing wavering and you can go forward in confidence that your choices are right.

Lesson 30: Heavenly Father's Bread Trails

We've been discussing recognizing the Spirit, decision-making, and knowing when God is answering your prayers. In this lesson I'd like to talk with you about one of Heavenly Father's most common methods for imparting insights and understanding.

I tend to have an inquisitive mind. I like to ask deep questions that some would say "aren't necessary to our salvation." Some peole are happy to set those questions aside until they meet their Maker, and that's fine for them. But I'm not always satisfied with that. I want to know how God works, or as Einstein said, "I want to know God's thoughts."

Many times my prayers revolve around requests for this type of enlightenment. I want my Heavenly Father to teach me truth, His laws, and how He sees things. I've also asked Him for practical insights on how to operate my business, how to interact with the people in my life, or how to run our household. I've found that He's happy to share those insights with me.

In fact, that's how I've operated my business for 18 years. Once a gentleman examined my web sites and admired, "You have such an interesting business model. I don't believe I've ever seen another like it." I thought to myself, *"Business model? What business model? I just pray for help on what to do next and act on the inspiration I receive. If there's a business model, it's not one I envisioned, but one my Father in Heaven designed!"* As one of my friends says, "What God originates, He orchestrates."

Let me clarify one thing, though. Rarely do I kneel down to pray, ask for understanding, and arise with an immediate answer. Instead, one of three things happens:

1) An idea will come to mind and I will feel an excitement that propels me to rise to my feet and get to work. That action will lead me to greater understanding and open doors of opportunity.
2) I feel peaceful assurance that an answer is coming.
3) I don't feel anything in particular, but continue to expect an answer.

In the 2nd or 3rd situations, I proceed with my eyes and ears open, expecting God's answer to come. I know that the Lord will answer my prayers. It may take days, weeks or it may develop over the course of months. But, He has never failed me.

The most common method of "personal revelation" I receive, is via what I call Heavenly Father's bread trail. This is a method He uses to teach us over time in packets of inspiration that eventually build into a complete picture. It's like puzzle pieces He gives you as you go. For me, these pieces most often arrive while sitting in church or reading my scriptures. Or insights may come during conversations with a friend or while pondering on the subject. Other times pieces appear in the middle of the night or while washing dishes, walking, or working in the garden.

It comes down to praying for insight and then mulling upon the question in a relaxed, expectant way. When you do this, your eyes and ears are open for clues. Isaiah said it best:

> "But the word of the LORD was unto them precept upon precept, precept upon precept; line upon line, line upon line; here a little, and there a little" (Isaiah 28:13).

Heavenly Father likes to let us discover answers for ourselves. He knows that if we put work and effort into it, it will mean more to us. He knows this "discovery process" makes the answer a permanent part of us, whereas if He just said, "Here's the answer" it wouldn't be as powerful.

Another metaphor that I think fits is this one. Have you ever been awakened from a night's sleep by someone turning on a bright light over your head? How does that make your eyes feel? It's startling and blinding, isn't it? But what if the light is turned on gradually, allowing your eyes to adjust - like the sunrise that eventually reaches its zenith overhead? Your eyes are much better able to adapt. This is how Heavenly Father teaches us, gradually increasing the light until we go from complete darkness to the sun shining at noonday.

Challenge

The next time you need insights, don't be afraid to ask. And don't let anyone else tell you that your questions are foolish or don't need to be answered. You'll be surprised at the deep questions the Lord is willing to answer. Pray with expectancy and then keep a lookout for Heavenly Father's bread trail. Enjoy the journey as your life becomes an exciting treasure hunt. God's treasures are the eternal ones of wisdom, knowledge, people, understanding and truth.

It's my prayer that you may enjoy the journey and His riches in abundance!

Lesson 31: God's Angels on Earth

Continuing with our discussion on how Heavenly Father answers prayers, I would be remiss if I did not mention one of His greatest methods for answering them. That is through the existence, efforts, and kindness of others.

In 1 Corinthians 16:15-17, the Apostle Paul is closing up a letter to the Corinthian saints. He speaks of the house of Stephanas who were newer converts to Christianity. He says "they have addicted themselves to the ministry of the saints." I love that word "addicted" in this context. He means devoted, but I like the term "addicted" because it truly is an addiction once we catch the spirit of it.

When we become converted, the desire of our heart is to "strengthen our brethren." That's what Jesus told Peter: "When thou art converted, strengthen thy brethren" (Luke 22:32). It's really not something you have to force. Once you're converted, you naturally reach out to others. You can't stand to watch them suffer or wander in darkness. You want to reach out and lift them on your shoulders.

Upon conversion, our desire to be like the Savior increases. We're filled with His love which makes us want to care for, teach and love those around us. It literally becomes a sweet addiction. The wonderful thing is that it is an addiction with no side-effects! Try finding that anywhere else in the modern world.

This kind of love not only enables us to help others in need, but it also allows us to let others shine. When filled with this love, we no longer feel less because someone else is more. We don't feel inferior if someone else is better than we are at something. Rather this type of Christ-centered love rejoices in the triumphs and talents of another.

I cannot begin to enumerate the number of people who have touched my life and answered my prayers. When I lacked knowledge, these people shared theirs. When I lacked vision, these people helped me see. When darkness engulfed me, these people brought understanding and enlightenment. When I needed help, they've been there.

I feel like Paul as he described his friends Stephanas, Fortunatus, and Achaicus when he said, *"for that which was lacking on your part they have supplied"* (1 Corinthians 15:17).

Where we're weak, others are strong. And where we're strong, others may be weak. That is the beauty of God's creation. Like a symphony with a diversity of instruments,

God created us to harmonize and blend with each other - each playing our own unique part.

But, sometimes we refuse help from others. Why do we do that? It reminds me of the story of the man whose house was flooding and he prayed for help.

Someone passed by in an all-terrain vehicle and offered him a ride, but he said, "No thanks, the Lord is going to save me."

The water continued to rise until he had to go to the second story of his house. Someone in a rowboat came by and offered him help, but he said, "No thank you, God is going to save me."

The person in the rowboat went on. The water rose even higher until the man had to climb to his roof. At this point a helicopter came and offered him help.

Again he said, "No thanks, God will save me." The floods rose. He drowned and went before the Lord. Upset, he cried, "Lord, I had faith. Why didn't you save me?"

To which God replied, "What more did you expect? I sent you an all-terrain vehicle, a rowboat and a helicopter!"

It's crucial that we do not become so proud or arrogant that we will not accept help from others. Just because you need help from someone else, doesn't mean you're inferior or that you're not doing your duty. It doesn't make you less of a man to ask for directions. It doesn't make you any less of a woman to let a friend clean your house when you're sick.

Other people can literally be the answer to our prayers, but we have to allow them to do it! I often refer to Heavenly Father as the "Master Matchmaker" because not only do other people have the answers to our prayers, but simultaneously we are usually the answer to theirs.

When I think about the most influential people in my life - the ones I cherish most - they are the people who have helped me learn something new. While they've taught me, I've been able to share my talents with them. We've been equally blessed by the exchange. Heavenly Father never helps just one person. While He's answering your prayer, he's answering other people's as well.

When we share what we know and have with others, all are blessed. I firmly believe that a great percentage of the time other people have our answers. They are in our lives to teach us something, to support us in what we've already been taught, or even to test our knowledge of what we've learned up until now.

In this light, even those who treat us unjustly are in our lives for a reason. They are there to help us prove our knowledge or to improve it. When we look at others from this perspective, we begin to see that those who are drawn into our lives are there for a reason. How can we hate them without hating a part of ourselves? How can we belittle them, without belittling a part of ourselves? For on a deep level, they are a part of us, and we have drawn them into our lives because we needed them there.

Challenge

Think about the five most influential people in your life. What have you learned from them? How have they made a difference in your life? Select one of these people and write them a note, or give them a call and thank them for the impact they have made. While you're at it, take some time to thank your Heavenly Father for these people who've been sent like angels to lighten your way.

Lesson 32: Let Go and Let God

In Lesson 30, we talked about Heavenly Father's bread trails. Now, I'd like to give you an illustration of one such bread trail I followed recently. I'm going to outline it below in the way I received it and then hopefully by the end, it will give you the enlightenment it gave me.

First, it started with a conversation with a friend who is experiencing some financial trouble. She had an overdue health insurance payment that needed to be paid since she has health problems. She contacted me for advice because she had her children's back-to-school expenses coming up the following week. If she paid her insurance, she wouldn't have enough left for the back-to-school expenses.

I advised her to pay the insurance payment since it was past due and trust that Heavenly Father would provide the needed funds for her children the following week. It's been my experience that when we release the needs of the future to God's care and do what we can about today's issues, He always provides. This was a scary prospect for my friend, but I stood firm in my suggestion. I told her not to take my word for it though. I suggested she pray and get a confirmation that what I was telling her to do was the right thing for her. She prayed about it and paid her insurance payment. The next week, another friend gave her the money to pay her children's back-to-school expenses - completely out of the blue.

The advice Jesus gave comes to mind, *"Take therefore no thought for the morrow: for the morrow shall take thought for the things of itself. Sufficient unto the day is the evil thereof"(Matthew 6:34)*. In other words, God will give you everything you need today to deal with the challenges of today. Don't start fretting over tomorrow... just do the best you can with today.

The second piece to the puzzle came when a single friend and I were having a discussion about "letting go." She very much wants to find her "soul mate" and be married, but for some reason this quest has eluded her for years. And I'm really not sure why. She's a wonderful, giving, kind-hearted person; and there's absolutely no reason she should have difficulty in this area that I can see. She's been trying to use God's universal laws in conjunction with prayer to ask for help in this area and then let go and give the situation to God. The problem is that about every two weeks or so she starts getting depressed and taking back her troubles.

She compares letting go and trusting in God's provisions to diving head first into a pool of water, something she never learned to do as a child — no matter how hard her father tried to teach her. I spoke to her at length about what "letting go" means to me. She said our conversation helped, but I'm not certain that I articulated clearly enough, or that I even can. It's one of those things you have to experience, I guess. Yet it got me thinking… "What does it mean to let go and let God… and how can you really explain that to someone?"

This brings me to today as I was sitting in church. Our bishop started the meeting by saying that he knew that a lot of people in our congregation where dealing with some serious challenges and adversities. He admonished us to keep the faith, keep reading our scriptures, keep paying our tithes, and keep going toward the light. "Faith precedes the miracle," he reminded.

His comment on adversity and faith made me think of my friends and their challenges, and also a few of my own. As I sat there thinking about what has helped me get through my own adversities, I pondered on the phrase, "Faith precedes the miracle." Faith truly is the way we endure challenges and activate God's miracles in our lives. Nothing happens without it. Yet, how do we develop it?

The story of the children of Israel wandering in the wilderness eating manna came to mind. Remember that story? Each day they were to gather enough manna (heavenly bread) for that day - no more, no less. If they gathered more, it would just get wormy and spoil. They were to leave what they didn't need on the ground, and the sun would evaporate it. Only on the day before the Sabbath could they gather enough for that day and the next so they could rest on the Sabbath. Interestingly enough, manna gathered on Friday managed to last an extra day without spoiling.

What brought the children of Israel to this wandering, surviving day-by-day situation? They hadn't had the faith to enter their promised land. They were afraid of the giants and didn't trust the Lord to deliver them. They couldn't "Let go, and let God." So, He put them in a training period in the wilderness and taught them how to let go. He taught them how to live in a state where they were entirely dependent upon Him for their survival. He tutored them in how to only trust in Him. Not idols, not their own industriousness, not their own ingenuity, or even their own preparedness. They had to live on what God saw fit to give them day-by-day, and learn to trust that tomorrow He'd help them like He did today.

The next example from scripture that came to mind was the rich young man who came to Jesus and asked Him how he might gain eternal life. Jesus told Him to keep the ten

Marnie L. Pehrson

commandments. The young man said he'd done so since His youth. *"Then Jesus beholding him loved him, and said unto him, One thing thou lackest: go thy way, sell whatsoever thou hast, and give to the poor, and thou shalt have treasure in heaven: and come, take up thy cross, and follow me."* (Mark 10:21). The young man was sad upon hearing this, and went away grieved because he had great possessions.

Some may think Jesus' advice extreme. But, where was the young man's trust? It was in his possessions. Jesus knew that until the young man experienced "lack" in the very thing in which he most trusted, he could never learn to live by faith. And faith is everything. After all... it is faith in the Lord Jesus Christ which leads to salvation!

What do the children of Israel and the rich young man have in common? Neither of them had the faith necessary to witness a miracle - not the miracle of acquiring a physical promised land or a spiritual one. But God did not give up on them. Instead, He schooled the children of Israel for forty years. While we don't know what happened with the rich young man, Mark tells us that "Jesus beholding him loved him." I have a feeling that if we knew the rest of the story, we'd see that God loved this young man enough to patiently tutor him in faith as well. I like to think he too eventually entered his spiritual Promised Land.

God tutors us just as assuredly as He tutored those of old. When we experience lack . . . when we're wandering around in our own wildernesses, God is trying to teach us to trust. He hasn't forgotten us. He hasn't left us alone. And He's not trying to punish us either. I believe that He is trying to teach us how to trust in Him - how to let go and let Him take control. Only in a state of what we perceive as "lack" do we learn to trust Him to take care of our "uncertain" tomorrows.

Challenge

Think about your own struggles. How many of them relate to worrying about tomorrow's issues? Are you worried about next week's house payment? Are you worried about next month's school exams? Or perhaps it's next week's employee evaluation that has your stomach in nervous knots. Maybe you're worried you'll end up with cancer like a family member, or that the dentist will say you need a root canal. Maybe you're worried you'll always be single or that you'll never be able to have children. Maybe you have a serious illness and you're afraid you won't have the strength to endure it.

All of these worries are worries over possible problems of tomorrow. Now, I'm not advising you to be unprepared. I'm not saying to squander your money and to just trust that God will bail you out tomorrow. I'm also not saying to eat junk food and trust God will always keep you healthy. God wants you to do the best with what you have today. Be a good steward. Take care of the resources He's given you. But leave tomorrow's troubles for tomorrow. With God's help, **take action** where you can today and leave tomorrow to Him. As you continually take these leaps of faith, you'll exhibit miracle-producing faith - faith necessary to enter the Promised Land you seek!

> *"Trust in the LORD, and do good; so shalt thou dwell in the land, and verily thou shalt be fed. Delight thyself also in the LORD; and he shall give thee the desires of thine heart. Commit thy way unto the LORD; trust also in him; and he shall bring it to pass"* (Psalms 37:3-5).

Lesson 33: Tapping a Power That Makes You Extraordinary

You are not alone. No matter how imperfect, weak, or untalented you think you may be, you can still do amazing things. There is a power that you can tap into that enables ordinary people to do extraordinary things. It's a power I access whenever I've done all I know to do, and it's still not good enough. It's the power by which anything remarkable in my life is accomplished. It's not me - it's this power that works through me. I'm just an ordinary person like anyone else.

"What is this enabling power?" you ask. It's called grace. Why do you have access to it? Because God is your Father. The riches of eternity are in His hands and are His to give. His sole objective and desire is to endow you with all that He has.

Here's the rub . . . your attaining these riches is contingent upon obedience to eternal laws - laws that God obeys and that He's trying to teach you to obey so you can obtain all that He has. Each law has consequences for living in harmony with it or in violation of it. Every blessing we receive is because we've obeyed a corresponding law. On the opposite end of the spectrum, there is a negative consequence associated with the violation of each law.

Some of these laws we know - like gravity or centrifugal force. Others we may not be familiar with, but that doesn't keep them from having an effect on us any more than a baby not understanding gravity would keep it from falling off a couch.

Because we are imperfect humans, we can't constantly live in compliance with every eternal law. Many of us don't even know what those laws are! Unfortunately, there's a penalty associated with every violated law - whether we understand that law or not. But all isn't lost. That's where mercy and grace come in. God's Son Jesus Christ paid the price associated with our disobedience and bridges the gap between what we are able to do and what is necessary to attain all that the Father has.

The distance between our best efforts and ultimate compliance is bridged only by GRACE (God's Riches At Christ's Expense). This grace is more than a last saving act that "gets us into heaven." It is a day-to-day enabling power that we can tap into, if we will only do it. It's the power to excel, to be remarkable, and to achieve far beyond our natural abilities. It requires a partnership with Christ to use it, for He is the source of this grace.

The concept of grace is outlined in Ephesians 2:8-10:

> *"For by grace are ye saved through faith; and that not of yourselves: it is the gift of God: Not of works, lest any man should boast. For we are his workmanship, created in Christ Jesus unto good works, which God hath before ordained that we should walk in them."*

Because on our own we fall miserably short, our works cannot save us; but the purpose of God's grace is to recreate us in Christ so that we can walk in good works. It is important to note that God gives us grace so that we can do His works and build His kingdom. A natural outflow of being in a state of grace is an abundance of good works (also referred to as "bearing fruit"). If you're connected to the vine (Jesus Christ) then you'll produce fruit (good works).

> Jesus said, *"Abide in me, and I in you. As the branch cannot bear fruit of itself except it abide in the vine; no more can ye, except ye abide in me. I am the vine, ye are the branches: He that abideth in me, and I in him, the same bringeth forth much fruit; for without me ye can do nothing"* (See John 15:1-7).

Activating God's Grace

So how do we activate this grace? Here are 5 simple steps.

Step 1: Humility. Acknowledging your weakness, your dependence upon God, and your need for a Savior is the first step to accessing grace. You must realize that you need Him to make up the difference between where you are and where you want to be. Without Him, you're nothing.

Step 2: Ask God for Help. Jesus repeatedly admonished us to ask and you shall receive, knock and it shall be opened unto you. Ask the Father in the name of the Son for the help you need. Be specific. Don't whine or gripe; ask specifically in positive terms for what you want.

Step 3: Receive. Expect an answer! Know that an answer will come. Keep your eyes open for it; seek it. Receiving is a verb and requires action on your part. You must **seek**, **feel gratitude** that an answer is coming, and **intend to act** upon the answer once it arrives.

Step 4: Act. Do all you can do - reach toward His reaching. Listen and act upon the feelings and promptings you receive from the Spirit. No matter how small or insignificant it might be, you must act. Sometimes what you feel prompted to do may seem like it isn't going to take you where you want to go or isn't big enough to make a difference. Do it anyway. Do all you can and doors will open.

Step 5: Continue in Gratitude. Keep being grateful for guidance you've received and guidance you haven't yet received. There is no greater exhibition of faith than to be grateful for things your spirit tells you are true, but which your natural eyes cannot yet see.

Anytime you've come to the end of what you know to do, anytime you're feeling down or lost, or anytime things are going just the way you want them to, use these 5 steps. You'll notice that acknowledgement and gratitude to God permeates this process. Without gratitude, you cannot activate or maintain a state of grace. With grace and gratitude, nothing is impossible.

Lesson 34: Each Life that Touches Ours for Good

One of my favorite hymns is called *"Each Life That Touches Ours for Good"*[1] It not only makes me think of people who have blessed my life, but also makes me want to be the type of person who makes a difference in other people's lives.

Each life that touches ours for good
Reflects thine own great mercy Lord.
Thou sendest blessings from above
Through words and deeds of those who love.

What sweeter gift dost thou bestow,
What greater goodness can we know
Than Christ-like friends whose gentle ways
Strengthen our faith, enrich our days?

My sister-in-law Deanna Rose is a talented pianist. She plays a beautiful rendition of this song in her *Beacon of Light* album. You can hear it at www.deannarosemusic.com

I think the reason I love this song so much is because when I think back on my life, the things I've learned and my happiest memories always go back to the people who have touched my life for good.

Every August I spend a week with one of these Christ-like friends whose gentle ways strengthen my faith and enrich my days. She's one of those rare individuals who people flock to. I always stand back in awe and watch her fun and joyful personality draw others to her. Both young and old gravitate to her, and I'm not sure they fully comprehend why, other than you just feel so wonderful around her.

This year as we were driving from our hotel to a bookseller's convention, I commented on how amazed I am by her ability to draw people to her. You can't be around her without feeling good about yourself. I don't care if you're a postal worker, a waitress at a restaurant, a friend, or a "fan" — you can't be around Marcia Lynn McClure[2] and not come away without saying, "Wow, that woman is fun! I felt wonderful when I was with her." It even comes through in her books, which is why she has so many devoted fans.

Marnie L. Pehrson

What is her secret? I'll paraphrase what she told me because I can't remember it verbatim:

> "People have so many difficult things happen in their lives. For example, customer service people have people griping at them. People have bad days. Each person has their own challenges. I want people to encounter at least one person who brightens their day and makes them feel special. I don't care how rich or poor you are, you're a child of God and that makes you special. I want people to know how special they are."

What an amazing gift! What a remarkable way to look at everyone you meet! Can you imagine what kind of world this would be if each one of us thought this about every person we met? Where would be war? Where would be crime? They would vanish from the earth!

As I've pondered my friend's words, I've thought of the Savior and how multitudes flocked to Him. He lived His life serving others - making them feel special. He never condemned, He never belittled. Rather, He healed, blessed, and loved. His knowledge that we are each children of God permeated every action. It emanated from His personality.

The only people He seemed to have any amount of irritation toward were the scribes and Pharisees who hypocritically set themselves up as "better" than their brothers and sisters. Interestingly, as I spent the week with my friend, I noticed this was her "pet peeve" as well. And I think that's only natural for someone who sees others through God's eyes - who looks with compassion even upon perishing souls.

Personally, I think this ability to make others feel special is a gift from God - a natural part of my friend's personality. But it's something we can all strive to emulate. It all begins at a thought level - how we think about others. It's a perfect example of how what we're thinking affects what we draw toward us, how others feel about us, and how they eventually end up treating us.

It's a gift we can each pray for - this charity or pure love of Christ that looks for the good in others. As the apostle Paul wrote in Corinthians 13:

> *Though I speak with the tongues of men and of angels, and have not charity, I am become as sounding brass, or a tinkling cymbal. And though I have the gift of prophecy, and understand all mysteries, and all knowledge; and though I have all faith, so that I could remove mountains, and have not charity, I am nothing.*

And though I bestow all my goods to feed the poor, and though I give my body to be burned, and have not charity, it profiteth me nothing. Charity suffereth long, and is kind; charity envieth not; charity vaunteth not itself, is not puffed up, doth not behave itself unseemly, seeketh not her own, is not easily provoked, thinketh no evil; Rejoiceth not in iniquity, but rejoiceth in the truth; Beareth all things, believeth all things, hopeth all things, endureth all things.

Charity never faileth: but whether there be prophecies, they shall fail; whether there be tongues, they shall cease; whether there be knowledge, it shall vanish away . . . And now abideth faith, hope, charity, these three; but the greatest of these is charity.

Challenge

Will you join me in this challenge to begin viewing every person you meet as a child of God who should be treated with respect, compassion and love? Will you endeavor to be one person in their lives who shows them Christ-like love and patience? Will you strive to understand that they may be having a bad day or may be struggling with unseen challenges? Will you be the person who makes them feel special today? I hope you will join me in this challenge. What an amazing rippling effect for good we can have together!

Note: As you strive to think this way, remember to be forgiving and patient with yourself as well. My friend's greatest lament at our recent event/book-signing was that she didn't have time to devote to every single person. She tends to forget the many she's influenced for good and only sees where she hasn't measured up to her own standards of perfection. Remember you're human and that you don't have infinite time to be all things to all people. Every little bit you can do counts! Remember to give the same compassion and patience to yourself!

Resources

[1] *Each Life That Touches Ours for Good*, Music by Laurence Lyon and lyrics by Karen Lynn Davidson.
[2] Visit Marcia Lynn McClure online at http://www.MarciaLynnMcClure.com

Lesson 35: Cast Not Away Thy Confidence

I once took on a new project which had all the earmarks of a prosperous venture. When the opportunity arose, it just felt so right. Everything seemed to fall into place and I knew I would be a fool to let it pass me by. I prayed about it and had a wonderful feeling that this was definitely a heaven-sent opportunity.

Once I committed to the project and began the training that was necessary to move forward, a feeling of panic seized me. Self-doubt and feelings of inadequacy and fear enveloped me. What in the world had I committed to? What made me think I could do this? People were counting on me, what if I let them down?

Had I not learned about what my friend Leslie Householder[1] calls, "the terror barrier" I probably would have backed out of a fabulous opportunity, retreated to the safety of the known, and forfeited the blessings that awaited me in the unknown. Anytime we take on something that causes us to venture outside our comfort zone, it is normal to experience feelings of fear, panic and dread. But if we have received a confirmation that our course is within God's will, we may know that if we forge ahead in faith — despite the odds — all things will work together for our good.

It is the first feeling that you must listen to when you pray about the matter. Was your initial feeling one of love, joy, peace? If so, you may know that you have made the right choice.

The Apostle Paul stated it this way, *"Cast not away therefore your confidence, which hath great recompence of reward. For ye have need of patience, that, after ye have done the will of God, ye might receive the promise"* (Hebrews 10:35-36).

I could not deny the initial confirmation of the Holy Ghost in this decision. So, I decided that if God brought me to this opportunity, then He would not leave me helpless. He would provide the talent, ability and resources to accomplish the task. Sure enough, as I proceeded forward and put my trust in God, everything fell into place. I was amazed at how easily things came for me and how incredibly blessed I've been. He provided patient coaches and all the resources I would ever need to accomplish my objective. Not only that, but I learned that I actually enjoyed what I once felt so fearful about doing. As I continued in the business endeavor I learned new things, met wonderful people and developed skills that I could use in every aspect of my life.

I am so grateful that the Lord has taught me this principle — that along with every golden opportunity, there is a natural tendency to feel fear and even terror. If you've received His confirmation that your course is correct, you can trust that He will provide everything you need to accomplish what He has put before you. Go forward in faith and trust Him. Thank Him in advance for what you know He will bring to pass. Your faith and gratitude will propel you beyond the terror barrier and into the blessings that await.

Challenge

Have you prayed about a course of action and received a feeling of peace only to find that you're hitting challenges or doubts? The next time you feel fear and doubt, look at it as a good thing - recognize that you are close - very close - to the blessings you seek.

Press forward with confidence and trust in the Lord that He will provide! Keep your eyes and ears open for the possibilities. Opportunities often come from unlikely places.

Resources

[1] Leslie Householder, www.ThoughtsAlive.com

Lesson 36: There Is a Time for Every Purpose and Every Work

"To everything there is a season and a time for every purpose under the heaven" says Ecclesiastes 3:1. While reading this chapter of Ecclesiastes, a portion of verse 17 stood out at me, *"There is a time for every purpose and for every work."*

Have you ever had a distinct impression that you should do something, but when you tryed to do it, you realized you were missing certain pieces and it just wouldn't work? Yet you were so certain when you prayed that this was something you should do. Why are you hitting a brick wall now? Why aren't things lining up immediately for you?

I've noticed that God sometimes gives us ideas whose time has not yet come. For example, many times ideas come to me with such force and in such a burst of light and knowledge that I know they didn't come from within me. There's no doubt that they came from God. I recognize these ideas because they fill me with joy and enlightenment. But often, I become so frustrated because at the time they come, I may not have the means or the knowledge to make them a reality. Reluctantly I file the idea back into a corner of my mind and eventually the time, season and purpose for that work presents itself.

If you'll indulge me, I'll share a personal example that is currently in progress. For years I've felt that I would someday be a speaker, that I would travel and talk to people about the things that God has allowed me to learn. That distinct impression came to me about seven years ago at a time when I was atop my own personal "spiritual mountain." But it just wasn't possible at the time. I had five children and was expecting a sixth. My husband worked a full time job and there was no one who could take care of my children while I went off gallivanting to teach what I was learning.

Yet, it was an idea that excited me. I really wanted to do it. I could hardly contain my enthusiasm for teaching the things I was learning. Because speaking face-to-face wasn't an option, I poured that enthusiasm into books, web sites and teleclasses. I waited . . . life went on and the Lord helped me build a business that is almost fully automated, that can support a family of eight. In time, my husband was able to stay home and work on a business that he enjoyed.

Eventually our sixth child started kindergarten, but just as we finally had all the children in school, other things took precedence. I'd all but forgotten my desire to speak. I'd gotten wrapped up in other projects and then an unexpectedly large tax bill arrived which sent my husband off to work a full time job.

In those months of my husband tied to crazy work hours, we couldn't plan anything because there was never enough notice from his employer. Being in this frustrating situation after enjoying so much freedom woke me up to what I had once had. I began to realize the opportunity we'd lost. Why hadn't we made more of the two years the Lord had given us? Why had I let those years slip through my fingers and not taken action on my bigger dreams?

The more my husband was gone, the more I realized that should he ever be given the gift of working from home again, I'd use it to do what I felt called to do seven years earlier. I'd get out and teach these things in a live setting.

Finally, in August, my husband's job became so unbearable, he decided to give a two week notice and rededicate himself to his personal chef business. He brainstormed marketing methods. He also committed to lightening my load around the house.

One day I finally approached him about my speaking idea and told him that it was something I felt led to do. Perhaps the time had arrived. My husband and I love to travel together, so I suggested we start in the Southeastern United States. I could arrange speaking engagements in cities like Atlanta, Ashville, Nashville, Knoxville, Huntsville Savannah, Destin, etc. Sometimes we could take the kids and make a little vacation out of it. Other times we might just take day trips or overnight trips. We have family members nearby who can stay with our children overnight.

Interestingly enough when I told my husband the idea, he got excited and said, "Every time I pray about what I should be doing the answer is always to help you with your business." When he's said that before, I thought I'd have to teach him how to design web sites. The thought didn't occur to me that what God was telling him was that he should be helping me get out and speak! I know… I know… I'm incredibly dense sometimes!

I'll be honest with you, I feel like I'm standing on a precipice where I'll need to take a leap of faith to step into the unknown. It's something I've long wanted to do, but have no idea how it's going to work. All the typical fears are there. Where will the people come from? What if no one shows up? Oddly it's not the public speaking that frightens me. The Lord has given me lots of opportunities to teach young people over the last three years; and believe me, you learn to lean on the Spirit when you're teaching teenagers! To me, this is just one more example of how God prepares us.

I keep thinking about the children of Israel who wandered for forty years in the wilderness. Finally, a more faithful generation, who had learned to trust the Lord for their day-to-day care, were willing to take a leap of faith. The priests bearing the Ark of the Covenant stepped into that swollen Jordan River. The waters were cut off and stood in a heap so that the children of Israel could cross. But it took that initial step of faith (Joshua 3 and 4).

From this experience and many others like it, I've learned that we need not question the inspiration we receive just because the way or means to accomplish it is not immediately available. Sometimes the Lord gives us this insight so we

1. Have a direction to pursue,
2. Can acclimate ourselves to the idea - especially if it seems like a daunting task,
3. Can accumulate the knowledge and experience the idea requires, and
4. Can be on the lookout for the opportunity when the perfect time arises – even when that opportunity is hidden within a crisis.

We need not be discouraged because we can't do everything we want to do right now. We can take comfort in knowing that the Lord has a time and a purpose for every righteous desire that He puts within our hearts. But when that door of opportunity opens, don't be afraid to leap.

The hard part for humans is having the patience to wait for God's perfect timing. We often try to force the issue. But our own efforts to manipulate a situation or to change the foreordained timing of events will only end in frustration. In God's timing, events just flow. **I can always recognize when the timing is off by when I'm having to work too hard to make things happen. That's a sure sign that God's telling me to wait for the right moment.**

Remember that the timing of inspiration and fruition don't always coincide. Console yourself in knowing that the inspiration and vision He showers your way today will eventually become a reality - even if it's in a distant tomorrow. Document enlightenment as it comes, and praise Him when its season arrives.

Lesson 37: The Law of Sacrifice

We've learned several of God's laws throughout this course, but there is one that you probably won't hear in worldly circles. Yet, I believe it is one of the most powerful — if not *the* most powerful of all laws. It rises above and compensates for our mistakes with the others. It is The Law of Sacrifice.

C.S. Lewis once wrote: "Christ says, 'Give me All. I don't want so much of your time and so much of your money and so much of your work: I want You. I have not come to torment your natural self, but to kill it. No half-measures are any good. I don't want to cut off a branch here and a branch there, I want to have the whole tree down. … Hand over the whole natural self, all the desires which you think innocent as well as the ones you think wicked — the whole outfit. I will give you a new self instead. In fact, I will give you Myself: my own will shall become yours.'"[1]

Wow! That's a lot to ask, isn't it? Or is it? Jesus said it this way, *"Every one that hath forsaken houses, or brethren, or sisters, or father, or mother, or wife, or children, or lands, for my name's sake, shall receive an hundredfold, and shall inherit everlasting life"* (Matthew 19:27, 29).

At the beginning of this course we talked about your mission or the righteous desires of your heart. Since then, we've been discussing ways to fulfill those righteous desires and how to become the person we envision. But along the way, let us get wisdom, and with all our getting let us get understanding (Proverbs 4:7). To become someone amazing requires sacrifice. In order to choose one path, you must sacrifice walking a dozen others. Granted, many times this may feel like no sacrifice at all. For example, I find it no sacrifice to get up each Sunday morning, dress my children and go to church. It's a wonderful blessing. While I'm there I feel the Spirit of God and learn wisdom and find treasures of knowledge and understanding. But for someone else, doing this may seem like a sacrifice. Sacrifice many times is all in our perspective.

Yet, other times God requires hefty sacrifices. The more valuable the prize, the more sacrifice is required. Sometimes we're required to make a succession of consistent sacrifices over time. For example, sacrificing a little time every day to pray and study God's Word pays dividends. Other times we might be required to make one big sacrifice. One of my favorite patriotic quotes from the American Revolution comes to mind:

Marnie L. Pehrson

"These are the times that try men's souls. The summer soldier and the sunshine patriot will in this crisis, shrink from the service of his country; but he that stands it now, deserves the love and thanks of man and woman. Tyranny, like hell, is not easily conquered; yet we have this consolation with us, that the harder the conflict, the more glorious the triumph. What we obtain too cheap, we esteem too lightly; 'tis dearness only that gives everything its value. Heaven knows how to put a proper price upon its goods; and it would be strange indeed, if so celestial an article as freedom should not be highly rated." [2]

Like freedom, there is a price attached to your mission. The greater the vision, the higher the price. Think back on your mission statement that you formulated at the beginning of this course. Does that mission get you excited? Does it stretch you? Does it perhaps even make you a little nervous as to whether you have what it takes? If it doesn't, then you aren't reaching high enough. But if it does stretch you, do you really think you can become that person without God? Did you know that your mission statement most likely only scratches the tip of the iceberg of what you can become with God's help?

"Yes, men and women who turn their lives over to God will discover that He can make a lot more out of their lives than they can. He will deepen their joys, expand their vision, quicken their minds, strengthen their muscles, lift their spirits, multiply their blessings, increase their opportunities, comfort their souls, raise up friends, and pour out peace. Whoever will lose his life in the service of God will find eternal life."[3]

Let me give you a scriptural example. As you may remember Abraham and Sarah were promised that they would have a son. When God changed Abram's name to Abraham (which literally means "father of many nations") he promised Abraham posterity as numberless as the sands of the sea and a promised land as well. Abraham and Sarah were a century old before they finally had their son Isaac. And just when things were going well, just when God promised that Abraham's seed would come through Isaac, God commanded Abraham to make a most peculiar sacrifice:

The Lord said to Abraham, "Take now thy son, thine only son Isaac, whom thou lovest, and get thee into the land of Moriah; and offer him there for a burnt offering upon one of the mountains which I will tell thee of."

Without questioning, Abraham rose up early in the morning, saddled his donkey, took two of his young men with him, and Isaac his son. They took wood for a burnt offering and went to the place God indicated.

Then on the third day Abraham lifted up his eyes, and saw the place afar off. And Abraham said unto his young men, "Abide ye here with the donkey; and I and the lad will go yonder and worship, and come again to you."

And Abraham took the wood of the burnt offering, and laid it upon Isaac his son; and he took the fire in his hand, and a knife; and they went both of them together. And Isaac spake unto Abraham his father, and said, "My father."

And Abraham said, "Here am I, my son."

And Isaac said, "Behold the fire and the wood: but where is the lamb for a burnt offering?"

And Abraham said, "My son, God will provide himself a lamb for a burnt offering." So they went both of them together. And they came to the place which God had told him of; and Abraham built an altar there, and laid the wood in order, and bound Isaac his son, and laid him on the altar upon the wood.

And Abraham stretched forth his hand, and took the knife to slay his son. And the angel of the Lord called unto him out of heaven, and said, "Abraham, Abraham."

And he said, "Here am I."

And the angel said, "Lay not thine hand upon the lad, neither do thou any thing unto him: for now I know that thou fearest God, seeing thou hast not withheld thy son, thine only son from me."

And Abraham lifted up his eyes, and looked, and behold behind him a ram caught in a thicket by his horns: and Abraham went and took the ram, and offered him up for a burnt offering in the stead of his son.

And the angel of the Lord called unto Abraham out of heaven the second time, And said, "By myself have I sworn, saith the Lord, for because thou hast done this thing, and hast not withheld thy son, thine only son: that in blessing I will bless thee, and in multiplying I will multiply thy seed as the stars of the heaven, and as the sand which is upon the sea shore; and thy seed shall possess the gate of his enemies; and in thy seed shall all the nations of the earth be blessed; because thou hast obeyed my voice" (Genesis 22:1-18).

There are several things that I'd like to point out about this story that we can apply to our own heart's desire. Abraham wanted to be a father of many nations. That was a desire of his heart. God promised him that he would have this righteous desire, specifically telling him that this posterity would come through his son Isaac. Then just when things started to look up, God asked Abraham to sacrifice the son through which the promise was made!

In Hebrews 11 we gain a little insight into what Abraham was thinking. *"By faith Abraham, when he was tried, offered up Isaac: and he that had received the promises offered up his only begotten son, of whom it was said, That in Isaac shall thy seed be called: Accounting that God was able to raise him up, even from the dead."* (Hebrews 11:17-19).

Abraham went to that mountain thinking, "The Lord said that Isaac is my promised son through whom my posterity will come. Now He's asking me to sacrifice Isaac on this altar. I don't know how He's going to do it, but if God has to, He can raise Isaac from the dead."

What faith! Do we have that kind of faith? When we ask the Lord for something and He gives us a promise — a confirmation of peace that our course is correct — what happens when things start to look grim? Do we doubt? Do we falter? Do we blame God and say He isn't keeping His promises?

I want you to know that when you have set upon a path that will do great good, when you've received a confirmation from God that your course is correct, you will most likely come to a point where you are asked to make a sacrifice. It will appear as if God is asking you to give up the very thing you desire. He may ask you to lay on the line the very thing He promised you. It may look as if it's being taken away from you. Or it may look as if the odds are stacked against you.

Why? There are several possible reasons:

1) God may be testing your faith;

2) God may want to see how much you love Him. Do you love Him even more than the desire of your heart?

3) Most likely, God may want you to learn something about yourself - about how much faith you have and how much you love the Lord.

I believe that Abraham learned something about Abraham on that mountain. He learned just how committed he was to the Lord and how much faith he had that God would still fulfill His promises - even if it meant raising Isaac from the dead!

I would be greatly remiss if I did not also point out the marvelous parallel between Abraham's sacrifice of Isaac and our Father in Heaven's sacrifice of "His son, His only son." That phrase runs like a refrain through Genesis 22, "thy son, thine only son." This sacrifice in Genesis 22 is a foreshadowing of the sacrifice of the Only Begotten of the Father. "For God so loved the world that He gave his only begotten son…" (John 3:16).

Like Isaac, Jesus carried the wood that would be used in his own sacrifice. Like Isaac, on a hilltop Jesus Christ willingly laid his life on the altar. Like Abraham our Heavenly Father loved His Son and offered Him as a sacrifice. But unlike Abraham and Isaac, there was no ram in the thicket provided for the son of God.

His ultimate sacrifice activates the power of grace in our lives. It makes the impossible possible. And because He was willing to do so much for us, shouldn't we be willing to sacrifice all that we have, all that we are, and all that we hope to be for Him? Only by doing so can we unlock our full potential.

> "Try as you may, you cannot put the Lord in your debt. For every time you try to do His will, He simply pours out more blessings upon you. Sometimes the blessings may seem to be a little slow in coming— perhaps this tests your faith—but come they will, and abundantly. It has been said, 'Cast your bread upon the waters and after a while it shall come back to you toasted and buttered.'"[4]
> - Ezra Taft Benson

Challenge

Life in many ways is a test to see if you will "seek first the kingdom of God" (Matthew 6:33) for only then can "all these things be added unto you." Examine your own life, and find one thing you can lay on the altar to more fully follow the Lord.

- Will you sacrifice a favorite sin?
- Will you sacrifice your time to serve others?
- Will you sacrifice your talents or your money to build the kingdom of God?
- Will you sacrifice something you own to bless another?

Take a hard look at your life and the desires of your heart. What, if anything, are you putting before God? How can you place it on the altar to show Him that you are choosing this day whom you will serve with all your might, mind and strength?

In doing so, you will unlock the treasures of heaven.

Resources

[1] C.S. Lewis, Mere Christianity, New York: Collier Books, 1960, p. 167.
[2] Thomas Paine, *The American Crisis*, no. 1, 1776
[3] Ezra Taft Benson, "Jesus Christ - Gifts and Expectations," *Ensign*, December 1988
[4] Ibid

Lesson 38: It All Boils Down to Trust

I once had a friend tell me that she would be more likely to take a leap of faith in being obedient to God if only she could trust where He was taking her was where she wanted to go. It was an honest statement - more honest than most of us would care to admit. But isn't it true? Examine your own heart. We discussed sacrificing our will to God's in the last lesson. Doesn't our lack of sacrifice come down to a lack of trust? We're not really sure if we can get by without this "thing" or this "desire" or this "way of life."

Think of the rich young man. Jesus asked him to sell all his worldly goods, give the money to the poor, and follow Him. What kind of trust would enable you to sell everything you had, give it to the poor, travel the country penniless and teach the gospel of Jesus Christ? What would make you lay it all on the line?

I've come to the conclusion that faith in Jesus Christ - the kind of faith that we're trying to develop in this course - is impossible without:

a.) knowing that God exists;

b.) possessing an understanding of His character, attributes and perfections; and

c.) knowing that the course we are traveling is according to God's will.

In previous lessons I've taught the importance of knowing that your course is in line with God's will. And, I think it's safe to assume you believe in God or you wouldn't be reading this book. But I do not believe I've given sufficient attention to "b" above.

Faith in God boils down first to trusting Him. But before you can trust anyone, you have to know them. You have to know they won't let you down, that they have your best interest at heart, that they aren't flaky or wishy-washy, and that you're going to like where they're taking you. You can't be expected to sacrifice your will to anyone without first knowing who they are and what they will do with you. You must know God's true character, attributes and perfections before you can have the kind of faith that leads to an abundant life in this world and in the eternities.

> C.S. Lewis used a perfect analogy: "You never know how much you really believe anything until its truth or falsehood becomes a matter of life or death to you. It is easy to say you believe a rope to be strong and sound as long as you are merely using it to cord a box. But suppose you had to hang by that rope over a precipice. Wouldn't you then first discover how much you really trusted it?"[1]

God, in essence, is asking you to hang by a rope over a precipice. Wouldn't a study of that rope — its character, attributes and perfections — make it easier for you to have faith in that rope?

> Proverbs 3:7 tells us to *"Trust in the Lord with all thine heart and lean not unto thine own understanding. In all thy ways acknowledge Him and He shall direct thy paths."*

I believe a great portion of why we are here on this earth is to learn to trust to the point where we're no longer leaning on our own ingenuity, knowledge, skill, or bank account. Through gradual and increasing "tests" we are asked to hang by that rope. Will you use it to strap a mattress on the back of your car? Will you use it to tie a valuable antique in a truck? Will you hang by it over a 5 foot drop? A 10 foot drop? A 2-story drop? Will you dangle your family from a skyscraper with it?

Through repeated and successive trials, tests and challenges, God teaches us to trust that rope. And perhaps I should use a capital letter on Rope, for Jesus Christ is that Rope. He is our Savior[2], our Anchor[3], and the True Vine[4].

But how can we know this for sure? It's a process that doesn't happen overnight. Head knowledge comes first, then heart knowledge. Start with a study of God's character. Listen to eye witnesses who can testify to his personality. The best place to start is in the Word of God. That's really what all those stories in the Old and New Testament are about. They are stories of people who had interactions with God and who could testify to how He responds in various circumstances.

- They instruct us in how He responds to our obedience and to our disobedience (Deuteronomy 8:20, Deuteronomy 7:2-5, Isaiah 1:19).

- They teach us how He acts toward the penitent and how He responds to the self-righteous or the hypocrite (John 8:3-11, Matthew 23: 13-15, 23, 25, 27, 29).

- They educate us about what happens to civilizations that are ripe in iniquity and what happens to nations whose God is the Lord (Psalm 33:10-12).

- They testify of His infinite love (John 3:16).

- They give eye witness accounts of His death and resurrection, verifying that He lives and that through Him we may too (1 Corinthians 15).

- They testify of His ability to bring order out of chaos {Genesis 1). Further they teach us that God is not the author of confusion but of peace and order (1 Corinthians 14: 33, James 3:16, Ephesians 4:5).

- They tell us what He wants most from us (Psalm 34:18).

- They testify of the miracles that are possible for the righteous who have faith in Him (Hebrews 11;32-35).

This is but the tip of the iceberg of God's character and attributes which you can learn from the scriptures. A thorough study of God's word will help you gain the "head knowledge" you need. Then, as you feel the Spirit testify to you that what you are reading is true, you gain the first stirrings of "heart knowledge." But, I believe true "heart knowledge" comes when we use what we've learned in real life. When we've dangled by that Rope over a cliff and lived to tell the tale, we absolutely know the strength of that Rope.

And once we've experienced it, it is our responsibility to testify as to the security of the Rope. As Jesus told Peter, *"Simon, Simon, behold, Satan hath desired to have you, that he may sift you as wheat: But I have prayed for thee, that thy faith fail not: and when thou art converted, strengthen thy brethren"* (Luke 22:31-32).

Satan desires to sift YOU as wheat as well. I pray that your faith will not fail. I pray that you will cling to the Rope, to Him who is the True Vine. Then, when you have come through safe and sound, it's your responsibility to stand up and testify to others that Jesus Christ carried you through. "Heart knowledge" isn't really yours until you've shared it.

I can tell you from my own experience that God lets you "wander in the wilderness" until you learn that you can trust Him. Each time you encounter a challenge you learn a little more about Him. You also learn something about yourself. Eventually, you'll learn that He will never fail you when you follow His teachings and put your trust in Him.

I leave my testimony with you that Jesus Christ is the living Son of the living God, and that He loves you and wants to bring you home. It is His work and His glory to bring to pass the immortality and eternal life of mankind. You are a child of God, and He created you to experience joy.

Marnie L. Pehrson

I testify that He has made my burdens light. Over the years the Lord has tutored me in trusting Him and He continues to do so. To the extent that I put my faith and trust in Him, I do not feel the burdens upon my back. He's taken the time to teach me that He will never fail me nor forsake me. I know now what is meant by a *"peace that passes all understanding"* (Philippians 4:67). You too can experience that peace if you take the time to know Him… and that's really what it's all about.

> *"And this is life eternal, that they might know thee the only true God, and Jesus Christ, whom thou hast sent"* (John 17: 3).

Challenge

Take some time to study the scripture references within this lesson. And then make it your quest to study the Word of God, looking for the attributes, character and perfections of the God you serve.

References

[1] *A Grief Observed, The Complete C.S. Lewis Signature Classics*, p 448
[2] John 4:42
[3] Hebrews 6:19
[4] John 15:1

Lesson 39: Open Palms

One of my favorite depictions of the Savior is the Christus by Danish sculptor Bertel Thorvaldsen. It's a snow white marble statue of the Savior with his arms outstretched, palms open, the tokens of the remarkable sacrifice He made for us engraven upon the palms of His hands (Isaiah 49:15-16). As I stand before this statue, it is as if He beckons me, *"Come unto me, all ye that labor and are heavy laden, and I will give you rest. Take my yoke upon you, and learn of me; for I am meek and lowly in heart: and ye shall find rest unto your souls"* (Matthew 11:28-30).

Besides the matchless gift those scars represent, His open palms symbolize all that He stands for, died for, everything He is, and everything He teaches and exemplifies. His hands are the opposite of the clenched fists so commonly found in this hardened world. His outstretched palms are the antithesis of tight-fisted greed, unforgiveness, self-centeredness or stinginess.

With Him there is an overflowing abundance of love, kindness, mercy, longsuffering, forgiveness, patience and a desire to lift, build and bless. Was there even once that He turned someone away for being too old, too young, too rich, or too poor? Did He ever command, "Go away, there's not enough for you here?" Did He ever say, "Oh, you're too far gone, there's nothing I can do for you now?" Never!

If only we could live as the Savior lives and love as He loves!

I believe happiness and peace only come to us in this troubled world when we strive to live as He lives. As we release our need for control, our desire to dominate, to be right, and to get the last word, we become a little more like our Savior. When we release our compulsion to tenaciously hang onto the things we possess, we open ourselves up to rich and abundant blessings.

> Jesus taught, *"But love ye your enemies, and do good, and lend, hoping for nothing again; and your reward shall be great, and ye shall be the children of the Highest: for he is kind unto the unthankful and to the evil."*
>
> *"Be ye therefore merciful, as your Father also is merciful. Judge not, and ye shall not be judged: condemn not, and ye shall not be condemned: forgive, and ye shall be forgiven: Give, and it shall be given unto you; good measure, pressed down, and shaken together, and running over, shall men give into your bosom. For with the same measure that ye mete withal it shall be measured to you again"* (Luke 6:35-38).

Marnie L. Pehrson

How easily we forget that every good thing we have comes from Him! Every gift, talent, and resource emanates from Him. It is only when we come to trust in His abundance - His boundless ability to forgive, to love, to bless and supply all our needs - that we relinquish our tight-fisted hold on the things of the world and experience the blessings only He can deliver. Jesus put it this way, *"For whosoever will save his life shall lose it: and whosoever will lose his life for my sake shall find it."* (Matthew 16:25).

It is said that faith precedes the miracle, but it is only through sacrifice that we build faith. What sacrifice are you willing to make to develop the faith necessary for your miracles?

- Will it be to give more generously to others?
- Will you release an old grudge?
- Will you let go of your need to control or manipulate another?
- Will you let go of your need for the last word?
- Will you relinquish your will to God's will in some area of your life?

I promise that as you make such a sacrifice upon the altar, blessings will flow to you. As they do, your faith will increase. With your strengthened faith, it will be a little easier to let another thing go and then another and another. Little by little, your faith will grow as you release one more thing that ties you to this tainted world, so that you may enjoy the blessings of His Kingdom.

It is my experience that He loves to bless us! He lives for it. It's why He came, why He died and why He rose again the third day and stands on the right hand of the Father (Acts 7:56). I bear my solemn witness that Jesus Christ lives, that He loves you, that He is our one and only advocate with the Father. He is our Redeemer, the very Lamb of God. With His sacrifice He purchased us, paid the unfathomable price that we may return to live with God again! (Ecclesiastes 12:7) But His work wasn't finished there! He still lives, answers prayers and desires to bless you on a daily basis. If you want to obtain those blessings, you must open your palms as He opens His. Sacrifice a piece of yourself: give, love, lift, bless and forgive and it will come back to you one-hundred fold! (Matthew 19:29)

Lesson 40: A Parable of Becoming

While studying Exodus through Joshua I've looked for patterns in how God deals with His children. If anyone had to spend a lot of time waiting for things, it was the children of Israel. I believe there's much we can learn from them about waiting, cycles and trust. Their journey is a powerful illustration of what it will take for you to become the faithful person that God knows you can become.

To recap their story in a nutshell, the children of Israel (aka Jacob) entered the land of Egypt during a famine. When they first got there, Jacob's favored son Joseph was Pharaoh's right-hand man. But time passed and Exodus 1:8 tells us that there arose a king who didn't remember Joseph. Because the children of Israel had grown so numerous, he decided to make them slaves to keep them under control.

They spent years in bondage until God spoke to Moses and delivered them. You've probably seen Cecil B. DeMille's *The Ten Commandments* and are familiar with their deliverance. After God parted the Red Sea and took them to the river Jordan where they were to cross into Canaan and take possession of their Promised Land, they became fearful. They wouldn't believe God could help them conquer the wicked giants of the land. They said the giants would eat their children for bread and that no matter how good the land was it wasn't worth getting killed over.

Because of their fear and lack of trust in God (who had shown them so many signs and wonders in Egypt and at the Red Sea) they were doomed to wander forty years in the wilderness until the older generation died out. God told them that their *"little ones, which they said should be a prey, them will I bring in, and they shall know the land which ye have despised."* (Numbers 14:31)

From the time the children of Israel left Egypt until they finally entered their promised land, there were seven incidents in which a segment of the population was destroyed. Rather than getting bogged down with the apparent strictness of God in the Old Testament, I'd like to make the analogy that Moses made and look at all of Israel as "one man" (Numbers 14:15). When we do, we see God's wisdom and mercy in what He did with the Israelite nation.

Jesus Christ used parables to teach on multiple levels, and I believe the story of the children of Israel is not only a history lesson but also one of God's most illustrative parables. It's a parable about how to gain amazing faith. It's an analogy about becoming the person God knows you can become. It's a story about how God teaches us to trust.

Marnie L. Pehrson

Instead of looking at those who were eliminated as groups of people let's look at them as personality traits. Here are the seven flawed personality traits or bad habits that God removed from the Israelite character in order that they could become "as their little children."

Had these flaws not been removed, the Israelites never would have had sufficient faith to receive their promised land:

1) **Idolatry.** Remember the golden calf incident while Moses was on Mount Sinai receiving the Ten Commandments? How are we idolatrous today? Do we put the workmanship of our own hands ahead of God? Our careers, our money, our time, our "things?"

2) **Lust.** They continually lusted after the things of Egypt (Numbers 11:34). How do we "lust" after the things of the world? Or the things we did before God delivered us?

3) **Fear and Faithlessness.** They believed the 10 spies and their evil report about the Promised Land (Numbers 14). Are we ever afraid to step out in faith? Do we ever let fear get the best of us?

4) **Pride and Arrogance.** After God told them they would have to wait 40 years, a portion of them tried to go ahead and fight the people of the land knowing they did not have God's assistance. Of course, they were slaughtered. Do we ever trust in our own ingenuity and resourcefulness? Do we ever try to force things that are not God's will or God's timing?

5) **Rebellious.** 14,700 died by the plague when they tried to usurp power and overthrow God's established leadership. Do we ever rebel against God by ignoring His teachings? Jesus said, *"If ye love me keep my commandments."* Do we ever try to set up our own rules and think God will continue to bless us when we have disobeyed His commandments? (John 14:15)

6) **Ingratitude.** The fiery serpents were sent when they continued to gripe and complain about the manna and quail the Lord sent to sustain them. (Numbers 17:5) How many times do we whine and complain that we only have enough to get by day-to-day? Or that God isn't giving us what we want fast enough?

7) **Whoredoms.** When they enjoined themselves to the people of the land and partook of their perversions, another plague was sent (Numbers 25). Are we lowering ourselves to the standards of the world and making excuses for it?

Through this succession of cleansing acts, God eliminated the traits that kept the children of Israel from trusting Him fully. In the end, they knew how to lean on Him. They were a faithful people who could access His power to enter the Promised Land, face the giants, and obtain their inheritance. Had any of these negative traits remained, it would have sabotaged their results.

Jesus said, *"Suffer the little children to come unto me, and forbid them not: for of such is the kingdom of God. Verily I say unto you, Whosoever shall not receive the kingdom of God as a little child, he shall not enter therein."* (Mark 10:14-15) Just as the Israelites had to become as their little children, we also must become as a little child if we're going to have the kind of faith and trust necessary to enter our own Promised Lands.

You see, God isn't punishing us when He gives us commandments. He's not trying to control or manipulate you. He's trying to teach you to trust Him. Until you trust Him and actually try to follow His commandments, you don't realize how much happier, easier and more fluid life can be. You'll notice that the Promised Land is described as a land "flowing with milk and honey." When you come to the point where your faith and trust is 100% devoted to God like a child's is to his father, things start to flow. I'm not saying that you don't have your challenges or trials, but there is such a difference in the level of peace that accompanies them when they do occur.

> 1 John 5:2-3 says, *"By this we know that we love the children of God, when we love God, and keep his commandments. For this is the love of God, that we keep his commandments: and his commandments are not grievous."*

God's commandments are NOT grievous. As the psalmist exclaimed, *"O how love I thy law! It is my meditation all the day"* (Psalms 119:97). God's laws are the plan of happiness. They are the pathway to peace. Jesus said, "I am the way, the truth and the life" (John 14:6). His way is the blessed way and the only way that leads to an abundant life!

Had God allowed the seven destructive character traits to remain, then Israel never could have become the nation he knew they could become. Similarly, God allows us to go through events, situations and waiting periods so that we can learn to give up our old ways and become the faithful person He knows we can become.

Just as He shaped a nation, He also shapes us. Throughout our lives He mercifully gives us opportunities to eliminate our idolatrous natures, our lust for the things of the world, our fear and faithlessness, our pride, rebellion, ingratitude and immorality. Why? Is it because we have to be perfect to obtain salvation? I think not. As far as I know there was only one Man who was perfect. But He did say He was the way. So I might ask you where in The Way was lust? Where in Him was idolatry, immorality, pride or rebellion? Where in Him was ingratitude, fear or faithlessness?

Challenge

Know that God has an inheritance for you. You are His child and as such He loves you enough to chasten you. As Paul put it:

> "For whom the Lord loveth he chasteneth, and scourgeth every son (or daughter) whom he receiveth. If ye endure chastening, God dealeth with you as with sons; for what son is he whom the father chasteneth not? But if ye be without chastisement, whereof all are partakers, then are ye bastards, and not sons" (Hebrews 12:6-8).

Examine your own life. Have you gone through some of these chastening experiences? What have you learned as a result? Are you currently going through a difficult time or a waiting period? What if you offered a broken heart and a contrite spirit? What if you willingly submitted as a child to your Heavenly Father? Might you more quickly learn the spiritual lesson from the experience and move on to a state of peace and abundance?

> *"If ye be willing and obedient, ye shall eat the good of the land."*
> Isaiah 1:19

Lesson 41: The Unifying Power of Service

Have you ever read the love story of Jacob and Rachel found in Genesis 29? It's a wonderful illustration of the power of love and service. Jacob, the grandson of Abraham, went to see a kinsman named Laban and immediately fell in love with his daughter Rachel.

So anxious was Jacob to gain Laban's permission to marry Rachel that he promised to serve seven years for her. Laban agreed. Verse 20 says, *"And Jacob served seven years for Rachel; and they seemed unto him but a few days, for the love he had for her."*

Have you ever experienced love like this? Has serving someone seemed to be no imposition, no hardship, but something you did gladly because you loved them that much?

Over the last couple months, I've witnessed this type of love shed forth in mass toward one of my best friends. It's been a wonderful thing to experience and behold. My friend Luanna is one of those rare individuals who genuinely connects with people - young people in particular. She leads and serves them with love. She's been a youth leader at church for several years now on multiple levels and has always given 110% to everything she does for and with young women.

In August 2007, Luanna learned that she had breast cancer. Within a few weeks she underwent a double mastectomy and is in the midst of a year-long treatment of chemo and radiation. Immediately an outpouring of love fell upon my friend. Her house was cleaned, her children kept, her lawn mowed, and meals made. One young woman and her sister bought Luanna a recliner so she could rest better after the mastectomy. Women brought hats, wigs and prayer blankets. What's more, people across north Georgia and Southestearn Tennessee have been fasting and praying for her.

As I sat with her the other evening, the women's leader from church informed Luanna that the young women across eleven congregations have united to see that her family has meals brought in during the extensive treatment period. On the days that she is too tired to feed her three children (ages nine and under) there will be meals in her freezer that she can pull out, warm, and serve so that she can conserve her strength.

With tears of gratitude in her big brown eyes, I listened to my friend testify to how her faith in the Lord Jesus Christ has grown through what many would consider a tragedy. She explains that her family is carefully protected inside a "prayer bubble" that she

Marnie L. Pehrson

can literally feel surrounding her. She finds herself comforting others and assuring, "Don't worry, it will be all right."

One of Luanna's young women who has now graduated from high school and is in college said it best, "Sometimes we get to see an angel formed before our very eyes."

As I watch my faithful friend endure this trial with grace and a peace that passes all understanding, I feel that I am watching an angel formed before my eyes. God is taking a remarkable woman and making her into a spiritual giant, and I feel honored to witness it. I feel honored to be of what small service I can be. For those of us who endeavor to serve her, I'm sure we will look back on this year and say it seemed but a few days for the love we have for her.

As members of our church rally around her, my brother-in-law observed that we may not be enduring the actual physical trial, but we are going through this with her. For Christ's followers what happens to one happens to all.

There are four things that I have learned from this experience. I'm sure there will be more along the way.

1. The beautiful thing about service is that it intensifies our love for others. Where love is not, service plants it. And where the bud of love exists, service makes it bloom.

2. Jesus meant it literally when he said, *"Come unto me, all ye that labor and are heavy laden, and I will give you rest. Take my yoke upon you, and learn of me; for I am meek and lowly in heart: and ye shall find rest unto your souls. For my yoke is easy, and my burden is light."* (Matthew 11:30)

3. Prayer works. God listens and answers prayers. While people aren't always immediately cured, they can still feel an overpowering strength and support from the prayers of others.

4. Serve others and in your hour of need you shall be served. *"Cast thy bread upon the waters: for thou shalt find it after many days."* (Ecclesiastes 11:1) I've watched my friend serve others in dozens of ways, most especially in helping young women come unto Christ and find the healing that only He can give. Because of her far reaching influence, those whose lives she's touched are now reciprocating in loving ways.

I love to sing the hymn, *"Have I Done Any Good in the World Today."*[1] It's a wonderful way to start a day.

Have I done any good in the world today?
Have I helped anyone in need?
Have I cheered up the sad and made someone feel glad?
If not, I have failed indeed.
Has anyone's burden been lighter today
Because I was willing to share?
Have the sick and the weary been helped on their way?
When they needed my help was I there?

[Chorus]
Then wake up and do something more
Than dream of your mansion above.
Doing good is a pleasure, a joy beyond measure,
A blessing of duty and love.
There are chances for work all around just now,
Opportunities right in our way.
Do not let them pass by, saying, "Sometime I'll try,"
But go and do something today.

'Tis noble of man to work and to give;
Love's labor has merit alone.
Only he who does something helps others to live.
To God each good work will be known.

If you know this song, why not sing it each morning as a reminder of what life is really all about?

Challenge

Is there a relationship in your life that is strained? If so, serve that individual. Be attentive to their needs, and cater your service to those needs. Don't ask what you can do to help, just do it. As you do so, your love for that person will increase. But remember, don't serve expecting them to return the favor. Our bread doesn't always return from the same people we cast it to, but return it shall in the very hour that you need it most.

Let us *"lift up the hands which hang down, and strengthen the feeble knees"* for as Jesus said, *"Inasmuch as ye have done it unto one of the least of these, ye have done it unto me."* (Hebrews 12:12, Matthew 25:40)

Resources

[1] *Have I Done Any Good in the World Today?* Text and music: Will L. Thompson, 1847–1909

Lesson 42: Let It Begin with Me

There's a beautiful Christmas song that begins, "Let there be peace on earth and let it begin with me." I think this motto would make all the difference in our families, in our friendships, in our nation, and in the world. If we remembered that "with God as our Father, brothers all are we," it would change the way we treated a stranger, a neighbor, and even the person who cuts us off in traffic.

Unfortunately, in today's society it's becoming increasingly popular to pick other people apart. Simply watch the trendy talent competitions on television for example. What do we see? Constant ridicule and criticism of people who are trying to do their best. Granted, competition does tend to breed quality and not everyone can win a competition. Yet, I've learned from parenting that if I want a higher quality of behavior or performance from my children, it will happen faster and more peacefully from a vantage point of cooperation and praise.

Let me explain...

When our oldest son was small, he often kept his room a mess. If I blew my stack and started yelling about what a pigsty his room was, he would literally freeze. He couldn't do a thing. The more I scolded, the more immobilized he became.

Eventually, I wised up and realized the poor child didn't know where to begin. It was all too overwhelming. So I got in the room with him, held up a plastic bag and said, "First let's pick up garbage." After the garbage was gone, we'd sort clothes. Next we'd pick up blocks, then find the action figures, and so forth. Not only did the room get cleaned faster, but also the process fostered a spirit of unity as we worked together on a task. Once the room was clean, we'd stand back together and bask in the cleanliness of the room and how much better it looked. We'd congratulate each other on a job well done and feel a measure of joy in having accomplished something significant together.

Now, as a young man of eighteen, my son and I still work together on projects. He's helped me patch water lines, herd goats, and repair things around the house. He's become quite a skilled worker, and there's a bond between us that is absolutely priceless to me.

It's scary to think what would have happened had I done nothing but criticize and scold. What if I had never praised him on his efforts? What if I had never fostered those talents in embryo that I could see in him? What if I'd never stepped in that room to work alongside him? Would he be the confident and talented young man he is today? Would he ever have learned how to break down overwhelming tasks? Would he have ever experienced the immense joy and satisfaction to be found in a job well done? Most of all, would we be as close as we are today?

I certainly don't claim to be an ideal mother, nor do I claim to always react in this way toward others. But "when I grow up" I'd really like to be a person who unfailingly builds others up, helping them become the best they can be.

As I see those rare individuals step out to try to make a difference for good in their own unique way, it breaks my heart when I hear naysayers belittling them from their idle couches. Critics may deride their diction, scoff at their hairstyle, or put down their lack of poise. Or they may simply say, "It's a good idea, but it will never work. They're wasting their time and money." Instead, let us be different. Let us say, "At least they are trying! At least they have the courage to step forward and try to make a difference for good." And then let us roll up our sleeves and get to work alongside them!

I would encourage you to take the gifts and talents God has given you and step courageously forward. You can make a difference in the world. There is power in one committed individual who stands on principle, unwavering and true. Let there be peace on earth and let it begin with you and me. And as we do this, let us block out the voices of the naysayers. Let us ignore the crowds with their bowls of popcorn perched on their laps ridiculing us for sport.

Instead, let us look at the opposition as a sign that we're on the right track. As Jesus said,

> *"Blessed are they which are persecuted for righteousness' sake: for theirs is the kingdom of heaven. Blessed are ye, when men shall revile you, and persecute you, and shall say all manner of evil against you falsely, for my sake. Rejoice, and be exceeding glad: for great is your reward in heaven: for so persecuted they the prophets which were before you…. But I say unto you, Love your enemies, bless them that curse you, do good to them that hate you, and pray for them which despitefully use you, and persecute you."* Matthew 5:10-12,44

Anyone who tries to make a difference will face opposition. But those who persist in a committed effort in spite of it will reap heaven's rewards.

> *"Let us not be weary in well doing: for in due season we shall reap, if we faint not."* Galatians 6:9

Lesson 43 - Are You Ready to Receive?

Each of us has felt like we were in bondage at one time or another. Some people are enslaved to addictions. (Don't put a plate of brownies near me!) Or maybe you've spent some time like I have, chained to a stack of bills. Perhaps your poor health (or that of a loved one) has made you unable to do what you wanted to do. For others, some of their relationships (or lack thereof) can make them feel trapped and unhappy.

Whatever the case may be, there is one important step that must not be overlooked if one expects to experience freedom. It's something the Lord emphasized with the children of Israel when they were about to be delivered from bondage. And it's something that became a yearly tradition - a graphic reminder of how important it is to be completely ready to receive deliverance.

In Exodus 12, the Lord tells Moses what they should do the evening of Passover - the night they are to be delivered from the bondage of Egypt. He tells them to prepare the sacrificial lamb, eat it all up that night, and burn any leftovers so they don't remain til morning. They are to make unleavened bread so it won't spoil on the trip. They're also to ask their neighboring Egyptians for gold, silver, jewelry and raiment. The Israelites found favor in the sight of the Egyptians and they actually gave them these things for their journey. (Remember, it never hurts to ask. Miracles do happen!) Then in verse 11 He says:

"And thus shall ye eat it; with your loins girded, your shoes on your feet, and your staff in your hand; and ye shall eat it in haste: it is the LORD's passover."

Can you picture this? Six hundred thousand people are totally dressed with shoes on their feet, their staff in hand. They've packed up their things; they've got unleavened bread for their journey and have lots of clothes and trinkets for trading along the way. They're grabbing this quick bite to eat before they leave because at any moment they've got to walk out the door. The minute Pharaoh says "go" they've got to "get while the getting's good." When the firstborn of Egypt are killed in the final plague, Pharaoh finally has enough. He doesn't even wait until morning. He calls for Moses in the middle of the night and tells him to take the Israelites and leave. Because they're completely ready, it's a quick exodus.

This reminds me of my children when I tell them they're going to stay at their Nana's house. Those munchkins dress down to their shoes and pack their little backpacks in a heartbeat. They're hovering in my office asking me every ten minutes when we're leaving and if it's time to go. They're ready dart out that door at any minute - even if I've told them it won't be for several hours. Try to get them moving like that before school and you'll see quite a different story. But when they're heading for Nana's, their desire propels them into action. They're ready to receive at a moments notice.

We need to be like the children of Israel and my little children. We need to have everything ready - have done everything we can do and just be waiting for the moment of God's deliverance.

What if you knew for a fact that tonight you would be delivered from your financial troubles, or from your loneliness, or whatever "bondage" you are experiencing? Would you act differently? What would you do to get ready? What if what you've been asking for and praying for happened tonight? Would you be completely ready to receive it?

Let me give you an example. If you're lonely and would like to have a husband or wife, what if that person walked into your life tomorrow? Would you be ready? Or would you say, "No, I'd like to lose some weight first." Or "I'd like to look my best when I meet him. I need a haircut and some new clothes. Oh, and my car is a mess. I'd need to clean it out. "

Whatever things come to mind that you'd need to do first are the things you should be doing NOW. In other words, you aren't ready for your deliverance if a list of things comes to mind that you'd need to do first. Get those things in order NOW. Live in a state of readiness.

Here's another example. Let's say your car is a clunker and you know you need a new one. What if someone handed you the money tonight, would you know the exact make, model and color you want? Have you studied consumer reports? Have you test driven cars and narrowed it down to the exact one you want? If you haven't then you're not ready to receive the new car. You're still in the nebulous "I wish" mode.

When you ask, get specific because not until you know what you're looking for will you recognize it. Once you're clear about exactly what you want so that you could identify it in a heartbeat, then do everything humanly possible to be ready to receive it.

What's more, what would your attitude be like if you knew that tonight you'd receive your answer? Wouldn't you be grateful and excited? Feel those feelings of expectant gratitude now!

Challenge

Think of your own life. Is there an area where you'd like to see improvement?

1. Get specific about what you'd like to see happen.

2. Ask your Heavenly Father specifically for what you want.

3. Assume He's going to answer your prayer right away. Make a list of everything you'd need to do to be ready to roll with it.

4. Do the things on your list. Be in a constant state of readiness.

5. Feel the feelings of expectant gratitude now. Be as excited as my children are before they go to Nana's house. Be as grateful and happy as the children of Israel must have been to finally be rid of their taskmasters.

Get ready to receive your miracle! It could be just around the corner!

Marnie L. Pehrson

Lesson 44 - Becoming an Instrument in God's Hands

Have you ever had a friend or loved one who was going through a difficult situation and you knew — you just KNEW — if they knew what you knew they could be happier? Perhaps they lack faith in God or an understanding of his great love for them. And you know if they knew God better, they could find happiness and peace.

But what if they aren't asking you questions? What if they avoid the subject of God? How do you help someone who doesn't seem to want your help? One of my children is facing such a situation. One of her best friends is going through a hard time and she wants so badly to help. She's prayed about it and feels that now is the time to do so, but she's scared. She's quite shy and doesn't know how to bring up the subject or how to begin. Yet, the answer to her prayer cannot be mistaken - she's in this person's life for a reason.

So, she asked my advice: How do you begin a conversation about God with someone who doesn't seem interested? Since my daughter has struggled with some of the same difficulties the friend is having, I suggested she begin there — with reflecting back on her own struggles and how the Lord has pulled her through. How has her relationship with Jesus Christ blessed her life and helped her deal with her challenges? In other words, share her testimony of the power of God and His love for each of us.

It's been my experience that no one can argue with your story. It's yours. You experienced it, and it's how you feel. They may not share your feelings or your beliefs, but they can't argue that you don't have them.

Her next questions were, but When? How? and Where? Do you recognize those questions from our earlier lessons? Those are the questions that God controls. I told her that Heavenly Father has revealed to her What her assignment is — it's to help her friend. He's given her the Who and He's given her the What. She knows the Why is because God loves and wants her friend to be happy.

The When, the How and the Where are within God's control. She doesn't need to worry about those. She just needs to trust the assignment and know that God will provide a way. Heavenly Father never gives us an assignment without providing a way.

The Cookie Principle

So what's the next step? I call it the "cookie principle." As you know, my husband and I have six children. And those six children love cookies. If I tell them I'm going to make cookies, but I start cleaning the kitchen first, sometimes they'll come to me and whine, "You said you were gonna make cookies? Why aren't you making cookies?" The more they whine, the more annoyed I become. After all, I said I was going to make cookies, don't they believe me? Don't they trust me? But if instead, they gratefully exclaim, "Mom's going to make cookies! We're going to have cookies!" I'll rush through the cleaning and get to baking faster.

My second son took this technique a step further. He used it to get me to make cookies when I hadn't originally planned to. With great excitement in his little voice he'd proclaim, "Mom, we could make cookies!" His sheer exuberance would propel me to my feet and I'd whip up an unplanned batch.

I think Heavenly Father appreciates a can-do and a grateful attitude. So, in my daughter's situation, I suggested she start thanking Heavenly Father that she's going to be able to help her friend. Acknowledge this assignment with gratitude and then pray that she'll be able to recognize the When, How and Where opportunities when the time comes. She can also pray that she'll know what to say and do and have the courage to act accordingly.

Why do I share this rather personal mother-daughter conversation with you? Because I believe this formula works in all our interactions with others. God put people in our lives to help them. He takes care of "who" we're to help by bringing people into our circle of influence.

God Never Wastes the Pain

Heavenly Father also allows us to go through difficult situations so that when we see others going through those same challenges, we can say, "Look, I've been there, done that, and God helped me through it." As we pray about how we can help others, God helps us feel a portion of His love for them. As my daughter says, "I just hate to see him suffer when he could be happy now." The love of God makes us compassionate. It makes us never want to see another person suffer.

Marnie L. Pehrson

The Formula for Being an Instrument

Combine this type of Christ-like love with your own personal challenges and then add the testimony you've gained through them, and you have everything you need to be an instrument in God's hands to bless someone else. Remember this formula:

Personal challenges + Testimony + Christ-like Love = Instrument of God

Once we've acknowledged what we're here to do, the next thing we should do is gratefully accept the assignment and make ourselves available to help. God will take care of the when, where and the how.

The Longsuffering of God

The last piece of advice I gave my daughter, I give to you as well. Our Heavenly Father is extremely patient with people. He's willing to work with them until they're ready to hear and understand. And we should be too. There are people in my life I've known for 5, 10 or 15 years who still haven't completely come around to understanding the infinite love and blessings God wants to give them. But God hasn't given up on them and neither have I.

It's been said that "constant dripping will wear away the hardest stone." We "drip" on others by sharing our own experiences of how God has blessed us through our struggles. As we "drip" we create a space for truth. Bit-by-bit, hearts soften. Line upon line and precept upon precept, we come to learn that God really will lighten our burdens and bring us to a place of infinite joy.

As I told my daughter, it's taken me about 40 years to come to the place where I feel comfortable in my own skin and where I trust the Lord isn't going to drop me. He's so longsuffering, so merciful and patient. When we seek to be a blessing to others, we need to be a mirror of His merciful and patient nature.

That's sometimes hard to do because when we feel the love that God has for others, we can't bear to watch them suffer. We want them to have happiness and truth now. God wants each of us to be happy now. But He's also patient enough not to force anyone's free will. Instead, like the constant dripping that can wear away the hardest stone, God puts people into our lives who "drip" on us until even the hardest heart is softened.

I am grateful for the angels God has sent to "drip" truth my way. I always say that Heavenly Father is the "Master Matchmaker." He always sends just the right people to give us the next piece to the puzzle. The beautiful thing about this is that while we're helping others, they always help us in return.

Challenge:

Who are the people who have impacted your life? Make a list of their names and what you've learned from them. Take time to thank God for them. Perhaps even take time to thank them for what they've done.

Now take an inventory of the people in your life and the challenges they're facing. Pray and ask Heavenly Father how you can help those within your sphere of influence. Is there someone who you should help? When you receive your answer, use the principles outlined in this lesson to step out and bless someone else's life in a way that only you can. After all, that's why you're there!

Lesson 45 - The Prophetic Power of Gratitude

Did you know that you just might have the gift of prophecy? Now I'm not saying you're a prophet, but I believe that to some degree you have the ability (with God's help) to predict your own future.

Don't believe me? Let me explain . . .

In the Bible the children of Israel made their escape from Egypt, crossed the Red Sea and then Moses stopped at that point while they were camping to write a song of praise to God. Exodus 15 is this song of praise that starts out with gratitude for the miracle of their deliverance. The song soon becomes a prophecy about their future.

Moses begins: *"The Lord is my strength and song, and he is become my salvation: he is my God, and will prepare him an habitation; my father's God, and I will exalt him."* (v2)

The next series of verses recount the Lord's miraculous parting of the Red Sea and the destruction of Pharaoh's army. After the story, he praises, *"Who is like unto thee, O Lord, among the gods? Who is like thee, glorious in holiness, fearful in praises, doing wonders."* (V12)

Then in verse 14 Moses begins to prophesy, *"The people shall hear, and be afraid: sorrow shall take hold on the inhabitants of Palestina. Then the dukes of Edom shall be amazed . . . all the inhabitants of Canaan shall melt away."* (V14-15)

Speaking of the future of the children of Israel he sings, *"Thou shalt bring them in, and plant them in the mountain of thine inheritance, in the place, O Lord, which thou has made for thee to dwell in, in the Sanctuary, O Lord which thy hands have established."* (V17)

Notice how Moses writes this song of gratitude to help the children of Israel not only remember the Lord's deliverance, but also to help them catch the vision of their glorious future. He's thanking God for what He's done and what He will yet do - with full confidence that it will come to pass.

We've discussed in previous lessons how to pray and know whether the desires of your heart are in alignment with God's will. Once you receive that feeling of peace and assurance that you are on the right path, it's time to start praising God. It's time to use the power of gratitude to help you increase your faith and maintain the vision of your promised future.

Of course the children of Israel didn't learn this lesson. Within three days of crossing the Red Sea (in the very same chapter as Moses' song) the people start murmuring about not having water to drink. Note that they don't ask for water... they murmur to Moses whining, "What shall we drink?" (v 24). There's a big difference between asking and murmuring.

What if they had said something like this instead? "Lord, we know that thou hast delivered us from Pharaoh and parted the Red Sea and have promised us a land flowing with milk and honey. We have every confidence that thou wilt give us water to drink. We ask that thou would bless us with water and we thank thee for hearing our prayers and providing for our needs."

Do you see the difference? Do you see the subtle prophetic power of gratitude? Do you think that if the children of Israel had always had an attitude of gratitude that they could have avoided the 40-year-wandering? I do!

Jesus, our great Exemplar, showed gratitude in all things and praised the Father ahead of time. Before he fed the multitudes with the meager loaves and fishes, He gave thanks to His Father. Before He raised Lazarus from the dead, he said, *"Father I thank thee that thou hast heard me"* (John 11:41). He even found something to be grateful for when people rejected His message. *"Jesus rejoiced in spirit, and said, I thank thee, O Father, Lord of heaven and earth, that thou hast hid these things from the wise and prudent, and hast revealed them unto babes"* (Luke 10:21).

Challenge

Write your own song of gratitude for the Lord's deliverance, blessings and watchful care in your life. Enumerate the times that God has come to your aid. Then step forward in time to the end of your life and list the blessings that you hope to receive as if they have already come to pass. Add these to your song of gratitude.

I think you'll be amazed at the clarity and vision you'll receive about what is truly important in life, who you want to be, and the things that matter most. Most of all, your gratitude will draw you closer to your Father in Heaven. In so doing He will draw closer to you (James 4:8).

Marnie L. Pehrson

Lesson 46 - Getting Past Your Fears

Each of us face moments in our life when we hit a wall of fear or uncertainty. We may feel as if the Lord sent us in a certain direction, but when we get there, we encounter an impasse. An example of this is the children of Israel arriving at the Red Sea with Pharaoh's armies behind them, desert on every side, and the Red Sea looming before them. They began to fear at that point and accused Moses of bringing them out of Egypt to die.

They did have the option of turning around and surrendering to Pharaoh. They could have thrown up the white flag and gone back to the "devil they knew." But God told Moses to tell the people to "go forward" … to face their fears. Moses then stretched forth his rod and the Red Sea parted, allowing the children of Israel to pass through on dry ground.

Moments like this could be called "terror barriers" and they come around quite frequently in life - anytime we're stepping out into the unknown and doing something that puts us outside our comfort zone.

This moment of fear isn't a sign from God that you're supposed to go back. It's just a signal that you are so close — so very close — to busting through to freedom. When you face these moments, there are five tools you can use to overcome your fears.

1. **Ask specifically** for what you want - don't whine and gripe like the children of Israel were so prone to do. Instead get specific about exactly what you want the outcome to be and ask God for it in humble prayer.

2. **Get a confirmation** that your path is correct. Present your decision to the Lord and ask God if it's right. If it is, you will feel the fruit of the Spirit (love, joy, peace, patience Galatians 5:22). By the Spirit's confirmation, you may know your course is correct and in line with God's will. If an answer doesn't come immediately, be persistent and allow time for the answer.

3. **Be grateful** for what is coming. Once the Lord has promised you the desires of your heart, start thanking him for what is on its way to you.

4. **Envision** - Keep a picture in your mind of where you're headed and the vision of what God has promised you.

5. **Act immediately** on any inspiration you receive. Listen to your strokes of inspiration. Trust them and act immediately upon them. Sometimes you may even need to take action before you receive your confirmation. For example, the children of Israel had to step forward BEFORE the water parted.

Lesson 47 - What Seeds Are You Sowing?

"He that soweth sparingly shall reap also sparingly, and he which soweth bountifully shall reap bountifully" 2 Corinthians 9:6.

Every seed must spend some time in the dirt . . . in those cold recesses of the earth where all seems dark, damp and bleak. Without this period of darkness, it cannot sprout or grow. Similarly, we may be called upon to go through some dark times where the light seems far away. It is in these moments that we gain the strength to stretch and fight for what we desire. As we exert our faith, we break free of our confining shell and stretch toward the light.

In life we plant many seeds. Seeds can be lots of things. They can be our thoughts, words, actions or our very lives. Whatever we hope to reap, we must first sow. Whatever we hope to harvest must first be sacrificed. If we want to grow corn, we must sacrifice a portion of that corn (which could have been eaten) to the earth. If we want to harvest beans, we must plant some of our beans in the earth.

All around us God shows us what it takes to reap bountifully. As far as I know there is no seed that reproduces in a one-to-one ratio. One bean seed produces a plant bearing many beans. One kernel of corn bears a stalk that produces many more ears of corn. Abundance is the natural order of things. Yet sacrifice is required to reap that abundance.

We must sacrifice some of our "instant gratification" for the things that last. If we eat our seed corn, from whence will tomorrow's harvest come? It takes faith to plant a seed. Every time I plant a garden I marvel as the seeds sprout and bear fruit. It truly is a miracle. By watching my earthly garden grow, I come to have faith that the spiritual seeds I plant will yield as great a bounty.

The law of the harvest is real. It is a true principle. Anytime we sacrifice something to God, He always pays back in a multiplied way. *"God is able to make all grace abound toward you that you always having all sufficiency in all things, may abound to ever good work"* (2 Corinthians 9:8). If we want this type of bountiful harvest, the verses preceding verse 8 tell us that we must sow bountifully and we must do so cheerfully. *"For God loveth a cheerful giver"* (2 Corinthians 9:7).

Jesus said that *"every one that forsakes houses, or brethren or sisters, or father, or mother, or wife, or children, or lands, for my name's sake, shall receive an hundredfold, and shall inherit everlasting life"* Matthew 19:29. He also said that *"whosoever will save his life shall lose it; and whosoever will lose his life for my sake shall find it"* (Matthew 16:25).

Whether we sacrifice our money, time, talents, resources or our very lives to God, He always pays us back many times over.

Whatever you want more of, "plant" some of it. Sacrifice a portion of what you have as the seed. You can't give the Lord a crust of bread without receiving a loaf in return. If you want more money, pay your tithes and offerings. If you want more time, sacrifice some of your time in His service. If you're lonely, reach out to someone else who is lonely. If you're depressed, ease the suffering of someone who is in similar or worse conditions. If you need a friend, be a friend.

Remember that seeds have different germination periods. Some seeds stay under the ground a long time before you ever see a sprout break through the soil. Dispute not because you see not. We don't ever know what's happening just beneath the earth's surface. Keep planting, keep nourishing, and keep giving. *"In the morning sow thy seed and in the evening withhold not thine hand for thou knowest not whether shall prosper, either this or that or whether they both shall be alike good"* (Ecclesiastes 11:6).

Happy is the person who is consistently sowing good seeds for he will reap an abundant harvest. Those who constantly observe the wind will not sow and those that regard the clouds will not reap (Ecclesiastes 11:4), but the person who sows anyway – even when conditions appear adverse will reap a bountiful harvest. *"Cast your bread upon the waters and you shall find it after many days"* (Ecclesiastes 11:1).

The greatest sacrifice we can make to God is our wills. When all is said and done, everything else is already His, and we're just giving Him back some of His own. The only thing that is uniquely ours to give is our will. This is why when ancient Israel made sacrifices to God there was a two-part sacrifice. In Exodus 29 the priest first made a sacrifice of a bullock as a "sin offering." It was burnt upon the altar and completely consumed. This bullock represented the bullish part of us – the natural man that is an enemy to God. It represented our bull-headed nature, our stiff-necked pride. The priest first placed his hands on the bull's head – transferring symbolically the sins to the bull and then sacrificing it on the altar. In essence by sacrificing the bull, the person making the sacrifice was saying to God, "I will give away all my sins to know Thee. My life is Yours. Not my will, but Thine be done."

Marnie L. Pehrson

The sacrifice of the bull, representing our sacrifice to God, was followed by the sacrifice of a ram (a male lamb) without blemish. This ram represented the sacrifice of the Only Begotten Son. While we do not sacrifice animals anymore, the atonement still has these two parts – the sacrifice of our will to God and Jesus Christ's infinite and eternal sacrifice in our behalf.

When we sacrifice a broken heart and a contrite spirit to God – when we plant that seed – we reap an infinite and eternal harvest. We reap happiness in this life and eternal life with our Father in Heaven. We become joint heirs with Christ; and all that the Father has He shares with us. For we are his children, *"and if children, then heirs, heirs of God, and joint-heirs with Christ"* (Romans 8:17).

So, I ask you, what seeds are you planting? In what areas of your life do you suffer lack? Identify those areas and make sacrifices there. If you need money, give money to God. If you need time, sacrifice your time. If you need love, then love others. If you want more happiness, bring more happiness to others. And most of all, if you want eternal life, give your life to God. If you want more freedom, give your will to God. As you do so, the bountiful and glorious law of the harvest will be activated in your behalf, and you will reap a hundredfold.

Lesson 48 - Are You Rejoicing Yet?

I am going to be brutally honest with you. Even though I set out at the beginning of 2007 to "Rejoice" I must admit I had a rough year. It seemed as if Satan and his pinched little minions determined to do whatever it took to hedge up the way and prevent me from "rejoicing." There were relationship issues, family dramas, financial crunches, my mother's heart attack, and a best friend's breast cancer diagnosis — to name a few.

On top of these there were times I felt so spiritually empty that I wondered what in the world I was thinking attempting to lead over a thousand people through a year-long spiritual mentoring.

Then in August, I met a woman who had been reading these lessons — not as a "subscribed" member, but through another woman who printed them out each week and took them to her. She spoke of the impact they made on her life. Her friend who was giving her the lessons went on and on about the dramatic improvement in this woman's life. The change in her attitude was like turning night to day. As I sat there listening to these two friends, and observing the glow in this lady whose life had made such a transformation - I knew - absolutely KNEW without a doubt that it was not me.

It couldn't have been me. Through a significant chunk of 2007 I'd felt as if I was just getting by, many weeks really having to stretch myself and seek extra spiritual guidance to put these lessons together because I'd promised to do so. I know I didn't (and still don't) have it in me to make the change in this woman. God took my feeble efforts and spoke what He wanted spoken to this sweet lady's heart.

I've pondered a lot about this experience, and I've gleaned a few truths that I'd like to pass along to you.

Our Actions Have Ripple Effects

We never know what impact a small and simple thing we choose to do can make on other people's lives. We may never know the full influence of what happens as one positive action inspires someone who then helps another and then another.

God Can Work Miracles with Consistent Positive Action

If I'd known that this woman (and perhaps others) would be so affected by what I'd chosen to do, I think I would have been terrified. I would have said, "I can't possibly

---

Marnie L. Pehrson

write or say anything that could help someone that significantly." And I would have been right - because it wasn't me! God takes our consistent actions - however small or feeble and transforms them into miraculous results.

God Loves Individuals

If this one woman was all who was helped in 2007, then it was worth it to me. Meeting her made my year. I am convinced that our Heavenly Father knows us individually, and He knows what we need. He can translate what one person says to be what another person needs to hear.

Sometimes God Gives Us Glimpses of Encouragement

This face-to-face meeting recharged my batteries. It took me from January to August to finally catch the vision of what God was doing with this program. But once I saw it, things started to change. I had my own spiritual reawakening, and I took on the challenge with renewed determination. I started to see all the setbacks of 2007 as the adversary's way of trying to thwart what God wanted to have happen. Of course, I couldn't let him win!

This led me to a lot of prayer and pondering about what God wanted me to do and what He wanted me to learn from my own challenges. I think it finally gelled for me in September on the lesson about the Law of Sacrifice. I remember taking my morning walk and just feeling on fire with enthusiasm for this work ... for the vision of what God can do in people's lives and my small role in it. All I wanted to do was spend 100% of my day doing whatever God wanted me to do. Everything else seemed trivial and silly.

I stepped in the door from my walk, entered the kitchen, and told my husband, "I'm back! I'm finally back!" He knew what I meant because we'd discussed my efforts to reach a spiritual mountain I'd been to before, but couldn't seem to rediscover. I felt as if I were standing at the zenith with God's marvelous possibilities spread before me in a breathtaking view. I knew where He was going, where I fit in, and what we could do together. I get excited just thinking about it. It's a joy that can't be expressed in words.

Of course, I had to ask myself what made the difference. What kept me in the valley, away from that spiritual mountaintop for so long? And why had I reached it again?

The answer was simple. I had let the cares of the world occupy my mind. I had let other things take first precedence — not overtly — but ever so subtly. At the moment that I surrendered all that I have, all that I am, and all that I hope to be to His care, everything changed. The pivotal moment came when I said and honestly meant, "My first objective is to help bring Your children home, to help people follow Jesus Christ more fully. Please help me see how I can do that." When I really gave Him back my whole heart and soul and said "Not my will but thine," everything changed. Everything.

For probably the first time in 3-4 years, I remembered what it meant and what it felt like to truly rejoice and keep on rejoicing day by day.

So, I ask you to think back through your life. Have you experienced those spiritual mountaintops when your heart thrilled to sing the song of redeeming love? Can you remember a time when you experienced a change of heart that filled you from head to toe with the love of God, a desire to serve Him, and an overflowing love for His children? Can you remember a time when you had absolutely no disposition to do evil, but to do good continually?

I would ask you, if you have experienced this change of heart, and if you have felt to sing the song of redeeming love, can you feel so now? If not (or if you never have) then ask your Heavenly Father to lead you to this place where you're willing to give all that you have and all that you are to Him. Ask Him to take you to a place where your primary heart's desire is to build His kingdom in the unique way that only you can.

Only here … at this place… will you be able to fully rejoice. You'll sing as I'm singing and you'll know as I know that He loves you more than words could ever express. You'll sing His praises, and you'll catch the vision of who He is, who you are as His child, and the miraculous things you can do together!

Lesson 49: Enjoy the Journey

"For I have learned, in whatsoever state I am, therewith to be content. I know both how to be abased, and I know how to abound: everywhere and in all things I am instructed both to be full and to be hungry, both to abound and to suffer need."

- Philippians 4:11-12

I think one of the hardest things in life is to strike a balance between striving for something greater and yet being grateful for the moment in which you reside. It takes courage and hope to recognize where you're suffering lack and yet be immensely grateful for what you do have. Whether you're reaching for greater spiritual awareness, financial freedom, a healthier lifestyle, or better relationships, it's important to see the perfection in where you are at this moment. When I say perfection, I don't mean flawlessness or that there's no room for improvement, I'm speaking of an awareness and acceptance that this point where you are now is where you have to be in order to get to where you want to go. NOW is part of your progression.

If you're miserable, then this moment is perfect if it leads you to dig deep, pray earnestly, and to be open to solutions. Sometimes you have to get depressed, angry or afraid enough to do something about a situation. So in that respect, even misery and depression are "perfect" if they make you seek God's guidance.

I think sometimes, I show greater faithfulness during great trials than I do in everyday life. It's hard to see the perfection in the mundane moments that aren't miserable but still fall short of the ideal. For example, you might be going along and things are okay, but you still feel dissatisfied because it's not where you ultimately want to be.

Personally, this is one of my greatest challenges. I have this picture in my mind of who I want to be, what I want to accomplish, and how I want my life to look. Instead of being grateful for the elements that are falling into place, I have a tendency to bog down mourning over the pieces that haven't arrived yet.

I can often be like a sapling who knows it's supposed to become a mighty oak, but gets frustrated because it's so small and insignificant now. I ask myself, "Where am I supposed to get all that bark and those leaves? How will I ever grow that tall and strong? Why is it taking so long? Shouldn't I be there already? Am I doing it wrong?" The thing is, it takes time to become an oak!

I have a feeling you know what I mean. It's human nature to think we can't be happy until we "arrive." I can't speak for people in other countries, but for Americans it's all about the getting and the having and the arriving. We'll be happy when we're financially free. We'll be happy when we have the new house. We'll be happy when we get married.

But when we obtain those things, we soon see that the happiness of the "arrival moment" is fleeting. It doesn't last long before we're onto the next thing. I think the desire for progression and increase is actually a divine characteristic endowed by our Creator. The challenge is that there must be a balance between striving to reach higher and better while always acknowledging the successes, abundance and blessings of today.

If we lose our desire to strive, we become complacent like the salt that's lost its savor or the lukewarm water that is spewed out of the mouth (Revelation 3:16). On the other hand, if we become overly obsessed with future horizons, we become ungrateful in the moment. Ingratitude is a dangerous attitude because it cuts the wires that connect us to God. And He is the very Source of our hope for future improvement!

Another aspect of this balancing act is getting clear on where we expect to obtain our happiness. There is no happiness as fleeting as worldly accolades, the acquisition of things, or the quest for power. I remember the first book publishing contract I received. I was so excited — for about twenty minutes. Then I thought, "Is this it? Is this all the joy this moment has to offer?" Somehow I expected more. And then I was off to the next goal.

Have you experienced something like this? You work long and hard for a goal and when it arrives, it's just not all you had it cracked up to be. It didn't instantaneously fill you with the lasting happiness you thought it would. Why is that? Because happiness isn't found in the arrival point. It's found in the adventure of becoming who God wants you to be — in reaching out and serving others with the time, talents and resources He's given you. It's not about the destination. It's about the journey, and until we learn to find joy in the journey, we'll never know true happiness.

Isn't it time we recognized the insatiable hunger for "more and better" that we humans experience can't be filled by the honors or riches of the world? It's an insubstantial meal. It simply doesn't satisfy. There is only one type of "meal" that can fill our divinely endowed hunger to excel. That meal is found at the Lord's table.

I love the words of Isaiah 55:1-2, and I'll paraphrase them a bit here:

> *"Come, my brothers and sisters, every one that thirsteth, come ye to the waters; and he that hath no money, come buy and eat; yea, come buy wine and milk without money and without price.*
>
> *Do not spend your money for that which is of no worth, nor your labor for that which cannot satisfy. Hearken diligently unto me, and remember the words which I have spoken; and come unto the Holy One of Israel, and feast upon that which perisheth not, neither can be corrupted, and let your soul delight in fatness."*

In conclusion, when we put Him first — when we spend our time acquiring spiritual sustenance — we experience a genuine satisfaction that fills our souls in no other way. By gratefully using what we've been given to lift, build and bless, we experience a genuine "fullness" that fulfills the deepest cravings of our souls. A meal at the Lord's table always satisfies.

> *"And Jesus said unto them, I am the bread of life: he that cometh to me shall never hunger; and he that believeth on me shall never thirst"* (John 6:35).

> *"But whosoever drinketh of the water that I shall give him shall never thirst; but the water that I shall give him shall be in him a well of water springing up into everlasting life."* John 4:14

Lesson 50: The Master Matchmaker

In Deuteronomy chapter two there's an interesting story that illustrates how God brings people into our lives who then make an impact for good. The chapter starts off with Moses recounting the travels of the children of Israel in the wilderness. They camped around mount Seir for a time and then in verse 3 the Lord said, *"Ye have compassed this mountain long enough; turn you northward."*

Next, God commanded them to go and trade with the descendants of Esau and the descendants of Lot (the Moabites). He strictly forbade their going to war with these people or trying to take their lands. Each group had their own inheritance from God that the Israelites were not to disturb. Each group had already driven out the wicked inhabitants and giants that once possessed their lands. They had inherited the promises given to their fathers. In other words, they'd already done what Israel needed to do.

We can draw a parallel to our own lives from this story. In life we have our own mountain experiences. A mountain for the ancients represented a place of communication with God, a temple-like location where man drew closer to the Lord, and God spoke to man. A mountain represents a place of revelation or an intensely spiritual experience. Often after we've had such a spiritual encounter, God leads us to interact with other people.

Let's say you're an Israelite. You know that God has promised you a special land flowing with milk and honey, but you also know that there are giants in the land and high walled cities that seem indestructible. Then the Lord sends you to go trade with the Moabites. You'll give them some of your gold and silver, and they'll provide you with raiment and food (something new to eat besides manna and quail).

Knowing that these Moabites have already conquered their giants and acquired their promised land, you probably have a lot of questions you'd like to ask them. You walk into the city, approach a merchant and strike up a conversation. The first thing you'll probably want to know (besides the price of the pomegranates) is, "How did you beat the giants? Was it scary? Tell me how you obtained your promised land." The merchant will then begin to share his story of how God delivered him and drove out the giants.

Two things happen from this experience. First, you gain greater insight into how God can help you obtain your promised land by seeing how He helped the Moabites. Your faith is strengthened by seeing living proof of what God has done for someone else.

Marnie L. Pehrson

Second, the Moabite is recalling his own deliverance and how God has blessed him. In sharing his experience with you, he remembers the goodness of God. He sees his blessings through your eyes and begins to comprehend just how fantastic they are. Then, as you share how the Lord delivered you from Egypt and parted the Red Sea, the Moabite merchant's faith is further strengthened and his heart draws closer to God.

This exchange of not only merchandise, but also spiritual experiences is pivotal for both of you. It strengthens faith and brings each person closer to the Lord. By the time you leave, you've made a new friend and a bond is forged between two people whose needs were met by each other.

I've had many such experiences… so many that I refer to my Heavenly Father as the "Master Matchmaker." When I think back upon the people who have made the greatest impact on my life over the last twenty years, I think of individuals who became my dearest friends as a result of this type of an exchange. Sometimes I was the Moabite - the person who'd "been there, done that" and knew something the other person needed to know. By sharing my experience my gratitude to God stretched to a higher level. I began to acknowledge the wonder of God's goodness in my life. I saw my blessings through someone else's eyes, and I rejoiced more fully than I ever had before.

Other times, I've been the Israelite trying to obtain a blessing, and God brought people into my life to teach me what I needed to know. These individuals were kind enough to share how they achieved what I wanted to accomplish. For example, I have a friend who taught me how to program web sites. This knowledge set me off on an incredible journey that led me to where I am today. Another friend taught me the laws of abundant living so I could overcome my financial challenges. Then there was the friend who helped me break into fiction writing by introducing me to her publisher and her entire fan base. Another friend spent a year tutoring me on how to write better fiction.

With each of these individuals, there's been a two-way exchange. I helped them with some aspect of what they wanted to do, and they were the perfect person to help me learn what I needed to know next.

It has been my experience that every major spiritual experience is followed by a new person who God brings into my life. This person is always someone with whom I can share what I've learned, and who will share vital knowledge and information with me.

There are times to be at the mountain: worshipping, studying, and learning. Then there are the times when you have to get out and share what you've learned and interact with other people. Through these types of interactions we solidify our faith and gain knowledge and insights that could only be acquired from another one of God's children.

Challenge

The answer to your prayers could be sitting next to you at church. It could be the person you meet at a business function. It could be the customer who phones you with a question. It could be the sister of your employee or a person on an email discussion list. Keep your heart open and expect your Heavenly Father to bring the right people into your life. Be willing to share your journey with them. Learn from what they can teach you. Be willing to stretch and give of yourself. You'll be amazed at what comes back to you. Relationships are among the greatest blessings Heavenly Father has to give. It's my prayer that you'll open yourself up to those blessings by opening yourself up to His children.

Lesson 51: Annihilating the Giants

Just before the Children of Israel were to cross into their Promised Land, God promised to help them drive out the nations of giants that possessed the land. These nations were wicked and involved in many types of depravity including human sacrifices. They had altars and graven images and special groves where they performed their rituals.

God told the Israelites to *"destroy their altars, break their images, and cut down their groves; for thou shalt worship no other god . . . Lest thou make a covenant with the inhabitants of the land"* and start going after their gods. (Exodus 34:11-15)

There is an important principle being taught in these verses. Whenever you want to make improvements in your life, don't leave yourself a doorway back to your old ways. In several of the stories in the book of Joshua you'll see that the Lord told them to get rid of every last trace of these wicked civilizations. One man was even put to death because he violated God's command and held on to some items he found among the wicked inhabitants.

Why is it so important to get rid of every last reminder of our old ways? Let me tell you a story about a lady I know. She is quite a heavy smoker. One day I was visiting with her and she said, "God helped me quit smoking several years back. I quit for four years. It was very easy to do. I would just dust around the pack of cigarettes on my coffee table without any problem. I'd move and clean around them. Then one day, I smoked one and I haven't been able to quit since."

I wondered to myself, "Why in the world did you keep them? Why not throw them away?" Had she thrown them away, she may never have taken up the habit again. Now with Parkinson's and Alzheimer's she's a fire hazard waiting to happen. If God gives you the power to overcome something, don't keep a souvenir hanging around to tempt you.

A recovering alcoholic should know better than to hang out at the bar. A person with a shopping addiction would do well to tear up her credit cards. Even keeping one card for "emergency purposes" is unwise. Whatever old habit you're trying to overcome, remove from your life all temptations and shut all doors to your old ways. Paul assured us that *"There hath no temptation taken you but such as is common to man: but God is faithful, who will not suffer you to be tempted above that ye are able; but will with the temptation also make a way to escape, that ye may be able to bear it"* (1 Corinthians 10:13).

God will help you overcome your weaknesses, but just because He promises to make a way of escape, doesn't mean you can deliberately expose yourself to temptation and not succumb. You've got to do your best and then let God make up the rest. What did Joseph who was sold into Egypt do when Potiphar's wife tempted him? He RAN! He didn't hang around and flirt, hoping God would make a way of escape after he'd pushed the limits.

The Importance of Replacing Old Habits

Jesus warned in Luke 11:24-26:

> *"When the unclean spirit is gone out of a man, he walketh through dry places, seeking rest; and finding none, he saith, I will return unto my house whence I came out. And when he cometh, he findeth it swept and garnished. Then goeth he, and taketh to him seven other spirits more wicked than himself; and they enter in, and dwell there: and the last state of that man is worse than the first."*

It's important to replace old habits with good ones. If you don't you'll create a vacuum and leave a doorway for old habits to return. And your last state will be worse than the first. If your old ways of entertaining yourself don't serve you anymore, find new ones that are positive and constructive. Make them something you can get excited about — things that you would never give up in order to go back to the old ways. For example, if you've normally dealt with stress by heading for the shopping mall and spending more money than you have, then take up some other hobby to alleviate your stress — like a favorite sport or walking or going to the library and selecting some enjoyable books to read.

Challenge

Prayerfully identify the activities and habits that aren't supporting your vision of the ideal you. Now come up with 2-3 enjoyable activities or hobbies you can pursue instead. Make sure they are ones that would bring you joy and have only positive side effects. Ask God to help you select one of the bad habits you'd like to change. Be tough with yourself and eliminate all souvenirs or temptations related to that habit. It's human nature to be afraid to go "cold turkey" but if you take that leap of faith to do so, you'll activate God's grace in your behalf. Don't forget to replace the old habit with the new enjoyable activities. Once you've mastered one new habit, move on to the next. You'll be amazed at how liberated you feel!

Lesson 52: Acknowledge the Gifts Around You

As I've scurried around this Christmas gathering presents for our children, I've spent a lot of time in the car driving back and forth to the store. After shopping one typically gray winter afternoon, I turned down the road that leads to our house. Suddenly before my eyes was the most breathtaking haze of red in the west. Ever so subtly the light behind the clouds was evident, not shining through, but creating this burst of color.

While I could not see the sun, I knew that it existed... that just on the other side of those clouds it shined brightly. Just because I couldn't see it, didn't mean that it wasn't there. I thought to myself, isn't this a wonderful gift? This canvas of sky upon which God paints his masterpiece -- this beautiful burst of red hovering in the clouds proves to me that the sun still shines — the Son still shines.

Have you ever considered the infinite gifts God has given us? Freely these gifts are given and yet we do not fully appreciate their magnitude. At Christmas I think we become a little more aware, a little more grateful. It's as if we shed a few scales from our eyes and start to see these gifts in a way that we might otherwise ignore.

Gift #1: The World

Have you ever considered the gifts that surround you constantly in this world - gifts you don't have to "own" to enjoy — the sunrise, the sunset, horses in a field, the mountains in the distance, or the ocean's shore? One of my favorite gifts in winter is the green grass on my neighbor's sod farm. That carpet of green that stays through the harshness of winter is a constant reminder that spring will come again, that life doesn't end.

Gift #2: The Light

At this season, our hearts turn to Jesus Christ more than at any other time of year. It seems as if Christmas makes everything softer, kinder and brighter. There is even a spirit of brotherhood amidst those who do not know God on a personal level. Christmas is a testament to the fact that the Spirit of Christ is given to every man that they may know good from evil. As John testified, Jesus is "the true Light, which lighteth every man that cometh into the world" (John 1:9).

At Christmas it is almost as if the Light cannot be darkened by the world. Like the burst of red I saw hovering in the clouds, juxtaposed against the dark, cold days of winter, the beauty of His Light cannot be missed. It's as if the Light shines brighter, and in its glow, the light within each of us warms and brightens in response. But is His Light really shining brighter? Or is it that suddenly we have eyes to see?

The light of Christmas works upon our consciences and rekindles those eternal truths of love, unity, peace, goodness, and truth. It fans the flame of what some would call conscience. This ability to discern truth from error and good from evil is a gift God freely gives to each person who enters this world. In a way it is one of our very first gifts in mortality.

Like every gift from God, it is of little value when ignored. Those who listen to their consciences and follow the Light are led to more light, for all truth leads to the Author of Truth. Others ignore the light until they no longer perceive it. This is why the light can shine "in darkness, but the darkness comprehends it not" (John 1:5).

Gift #3: Our Lives

"In the beginning was the Word, and the Word was with God, and the Word was God. The same was in the beginning with God. All things were made by him; and without him was not any thing made that was made. In him was life; and the life was the light of men." (John 1:1-5)

Jesus Christ not only is the Light of the Word, but also He is the Life of the World. As the Creator, He gave us our bodies. Our very existence is because of Him. Through His glorious resurrection He brings to pass the resurrection of each and every one of us. *"For as in Adam all die, even so in Christ shall all be made alive"* (1 Corinthians 15:11). Because of this great gift, each of us may exclaim as Job did, *"For I know that my Redeemer liveth, and that he shall stand at the latter day upon the earth: And though after skin worms destroy this body, yet in my flesh shall I see God: Whom I shall see for myself, and mine eyes shall behold, and not another…"* (Job 19:25-27).

Gift #4: The Atonement

Of course, the greatest gift so freely given by God to mankind is the gift of His Son. The anguish of Gethsemane, the relinquishing of Christ's will to the Father's, and taking upon Himself the sins of the world culminated on Calvary. His ultimate triumph occurred three days later with His resurrection.

Can there be a greater gift than someone else paying the penalty for all your sins? Than marking your debt paid in full? Is there any greater love than to conquer death and hell that we too may live eternally with our Father in Heaven? Is there any greater

---

Marnie L. Pehrson

sacrifice? Is there any more wondrous plan than this Plan of Happiness where Jesus Christ came into the world, set a perfect example, and then paid the ultimate price for our freedom?

I think sometimes we forget what this really means. Perhaps we could all do with a reminder. Revelations 21:4-7 describes our future better than I could ever convey:

> *"And God shall wipe away all tears from their eyes; and there shall be no more death, neither sorrow, nor crying, neither shall there be any more pain for the former things are passed away. And he that sat upon the throne said, Behold I make all things new. And he said unto me, Write for these words are true and faithful. And he said unto me, It is done. I am Alpha and Omega, the beginning and the end. I will give unto him that is athirst of the fountain of the water of life freely. He that overcometh shall inherit all things; and I will be his God, and he shall be my son."*

Challenge

I challenge you to look for these and other gifts in the world around you. Be one who has eyes to see and ears to hear. This type of gratitude for the gifts God freely gives will connect you to Him in a way that enhances your ability to hear His voice and have His Light present in your life.

Conclusion

We've covered so much in these lessons that it was a little overwhelming for me to think about writing a conclusion. Then I asked myself, "What do I want people to know more than anything?"

I hope that you have come away with a sure knowledge that Jesus Christ is the Savior of the world, the very son of God and our one and only advocate with the Father. Surely, He is the one and only Way, the Truth and the Light. He is the Gate by which we enter a joyous life here and eternal life beyond mortality.

You are here for a reason and that reason is to develop the faith necessary unto salvation (1 Peter 1:9). That level of faith comes from more than a casual acknowledgment that God exists. It comes through a genuine relationship with the Savior that can only be obtained by feasting upon the words of Christ, following in His footsteps, and becoming His partner in serving His children.

He has a very special plan for you that is uniquely suited to your individual personality, talents and life experiences. Even bad things you encounter will work together for your good when you love God and allow Him to use you (Romans 8:28). In fact, many people find that it is their trials that impact their life purpose most. My past financial challenges have enabled me to help others experiencing similar challenges. My friend who suffered in an abusive marriage now helps other women in abusive relationships. I see this happen over and over. You are here to use the talents, skills, knowledge and experiences of your life to serve other people. By doing so -- by allowing yourself to become an instrument in the hands of God, you develop faith.

As you take this purposeful journey, God will give you glimpses of what you are here to do. Your mission or theme for your life will become clearer as you study the scriptures, pray, and work to deepen your relationship with Him.

He wants you to succeed! No one on this planet was foreordained to fail, but you must choose His path. As you do so, always remember you are not alone. Don't let your fears, worries or insecurities stand in your way. You have access to unlimited power and unlimited possibilities through Christ's grace (**G**od's **R**iches **A**t **C**hrist's **E**xpense). This is the enabling power that makes the impossible possible and that transforms your best efforts into mighty words, deeds and actions that glorify God.

As you begin to live your mission, miracles will start to happen. Be aware of them. Document them. Be grateful for them. Gratitude unlocks the treasury of heaven. A lack of gratitude leads to pride. Once pride sets in, it doesn't take long before you'll be thinking it's you who's so wonderful instead of God. Ingratitude cuts the wires that connect you to Him. Surely the proverb is true, "pride goeth before a fall."

True and abiding faith -- a valiant faith -- can only be developed through sacrifice. The sooner you come to the point where you dedicate all you have, all you are, and all you hope to be to God, the sooner you can experience true joy and fulfillment. As we make ourselves available to God, we start to see around us people we can serve and individuals we can bless. By praying for and acting upon these opportunities, we are blessed with joy, happiness and success.

Remember... it's all about the people. I mentioned in the introduction to this book that it is helpful to encapsulate your mission statement into a short theme statement. If God has a theme statement, it would be, "to bring to pass the immortality and eternal life of man" (Romans 2:7, 2 Timothy 1:10). That is His mission, and to a great degree your mission is to assist Him in that work in the unique way that only you can.

If you've come this far in this course and still can't seem to put your finger on your purpose, adopt His for yourself. Commit yourself to assisting God in building His kingdom and bringing people to Christ. There is no greater joy. There is no way you can go wrong with this objective.

In fact, it may very well be the fast-track to discovering the unique value in your own life. As you serve others and bring them closer to Christ, He blesses you with skills, understanding, knowledge and talents that surpass your wildest dreams. I testify to you that He showers blessings upon your head. People will ask, "How do you do that? You're amazing!" You might say, "Thank you," but you'll know; and you'll tell all who will listen that it's not you. It's Him. It's His grace and His abundant blessings that make all the difference.

I bear you my solemn witness that Jesus Christ lives and He loves you more than you will ever know. He wants you to be happy and fulfilled, and He has provided means for you to be so. I hope that within these pages you have been brought closer to Him, and that you will continue to build a vibrant faith that leads you along your glorious purpose.

About the Author

Manie Pehrson is a mother of six and the creator of nineteen web sites including the longest running article directory on the Web, IdeaMarketers.com. The site serves over 34,000 writers who submit over 15,000 articles in a typical month. She is also the author of nine fiction novels and ten nonfiction inspirational books.

Marnie has been highlighting truth and talent for nearly 20 years. Whether she's writing a novel that spotlights individuals who've made a difference in the world or helping a talented entrepreneur create a platform for his life's work, or giving a seminar on how to live by faith so you can let your own light shine, Marnie's life is about underscoring truth and talent in innovative and compelling ways.

Through IdeaMarketers.com she helps talented professionals deliver their message to the online world by creating a platform from which they can establish their expertise. Marnie's clients refer to her as their "secret weapon" because she delivers so much in so little time -- always under-promising and over-delivering. Marnie is about finding and highlighting the "Wow" in people. Through her CreateAWOW.com podcast she spotlights people who have done things that make you exclaim, "WOW! I wish I'd thought of that!"

Marnie is the founder of multi-denominational SheLovesGod.com which hosts the annual SheLovesGod Virtual Women's Conference the 3rd week of October each year. She has served in many capacities within her church in presidencies of the women's and children's organizations, as a Sunday school teacher, seminary teacher, and pianist.

In 2007 Marnie led approximately 1,300 Christians through a weekly study course called Rejoice In 2007. She continues to help Christians find joy in life through her site www.IAmJoyful.com. You may reach Marnie and her various projects at www.pwgroup.com or by email at marnie@pwgroup.com.

Other Books by Marnie Pehrson

You Can't Fly If You're Still Clutching the Dirt:
How to Stop Worrying and Achieve Your God-given Potential
Inspirational Nonfiction, 148 pages, Paperback, ISBN 0-9729750-8-X
Deep down, you know God created you for a reason. He's told you that you're a child of God. You're made in His image, and He has a plan for you. You sense in your heart of hearts that you have wings to fly, but worries, fears, and insecurities drag you down to earth, preventing you from spreading your wings and taking flight.

This book will teach you how to quit worrying and trust God; easily distinguish between what you control and what God controls; find freedom to focus on the two decisions that are yours to make – What you want and Why you want it. Find deliverance from the worry-inducing questions of Who? When? How? and Where?

Lord, Are You Sure?
Inspirational, 152 pages, Paperback, ISBN 0-9729750-0-4
A roadmap for understanding how Heavenly Father works in your life, helping you understand why certain problems keep repeating themselves, how to break the cycle and unlock the mystery of why you encounter challenges and roadblocks on roads you felt inspired to travel.

10 Steps to Fulfilling Your Divine Destiny:
A Christian Woman's Guide to Learning & Living God's Plan for Her
Inspirational, 124 pages, Paperback, ISBN 0-9676162-1-2
Have you ever said to yourself, "I'd love to do great things with my life, but I'm just too busy, too untalented, too ordinary, too afraid, too anything but extraordinary"? Inside this book you'll learn how to reach your full God-given potential.

A Closer Walk with Him
SheLovesGod Study Lessons Volume 1
Inspiraitonal, 212 pages, paperback, ISBN 0-9729750-3-9
A collection of insights and ponderings on the scriptures and how we can apply them to our everyday lives. Great for the faith-lift you need in the morning, just before bed, or whenever you need a quick boost of inspiration. Each lesson is self-contained and independent. Read them in any order the Spirit moves you or read the 52 lessons in order as a yearly study guide - it's up to you.

Angel and the Enemy

Historical fiction, 288 pages, paperback, ISBN 0-9729750-9-8

The War between the States is raging and Angelina Stone's world is falling apart. Her beloved father lies rotting in a Union prison and when her Georgia home is invaded by Yankee officers, Angelina knows she will never be the same again.

Will Angelina be able to overcome her fears, lay prejudice aside, and learn to trust? When the stakes are high, will she risk losing everything? Only by doing so can she face the demons of her past and win the battle that rages in her own heart - a heart that is eternally tethered to . . . the enemy.

The Patriot Wore Petticoats

Historical fiction, 224 pages, paperback, ISBN: 0-9729750-4-7

Daring "Dicey" Langston, the bold and reckless rider and expert shot, saves her family and an entire village during the American Revolution. Having faced British soldiers, rushing swollen rivers, the "Bloody Scouts," and the barrel of a loaded pistol, nothing had quite prepared this valiant heroine for the heart-pounding exhilaration she'd find in the arms of one brave Patriot. Based on a true story about the author's fourth great-grandmother. Learn more at www.DiceyLangston.com

Beyond the Waterfall

Historical Fiction, 136 pages, paperback, ISBN: 0-9729750-7-1

Jillian's feet were precariously planted in two worlds: the Cherokee nation on the brink of extermination, and the world where Jesse Whitmore belonged. On her first meeting with him, the charming and handsome merchant had set her young heart ablaze. Yet, could she trust him? Or was he just like all the other white men she'd encountered? Would he stand beside her while she witnessed her nation ripped apart, or would he join the ranks of the powerful greedy to betray her? Based on family history and local legend.

Hannah's Heart

Historical Fiction, 162 pages, paperback,

ISBN: 1-59936-012-8, Granite Publishing & Distribution

Hannah Jamison is ready to give her heart away. Unfortunately, the man she's falling for shows no indication of ever reciprocating her feelings. When Mother Nature intervenes in her behalf, all Hannah's dreams seem to be coming true . . . until she discovers that following her heart means losing the ones she loves. Is Hannah willing to pay the price?

Savannah Nights
Modern Mystery, 140 pages, paperback
ISBN: 1-59936-025-6, Granite Publishing & Distribution
Samantha Reynolds set off for college, leaving her best friend Sean Cooper behind just when their friendship had started to blossom into something more. Sean leaves on a basketball scholarship at a major university while Samantha sets her sails for culinary school in Atlanta.

Over the years they lose touch until ten years later when Samantha is a prominent chef in an Atlanta restaurant. When her mother's untimely death shocks her world, Samantha heads home to Savannah, Georgia where she hopes to lead a calmer life. Instead, she ends up entangled in a mystery her mother was trying to solve. In order to piece together the puzzle Marjorie Reynolds left behind, Samantha turns to her old friend Sean, now a city alderman in whom her mother confided. Together they must learn what Marjorie discovered before Samantha ends up sharing her mother's fate.

Rebecca's Reveries
Historical Fiction, 224 pages, paperback,
ISBN: 0-9729750-2-0
Rebecca Marchant had led a sheltered life until she found herself inexplicably drawn to the home of her father's youth. Surrounded by the historical landscape of the Chickamauga Battlefield in Georgia, Rebecca finds herself plagued by haunting dreams and vivid visions of Civil War events. As Rebecca walks a mile in another girl's moccasins through her visions and dreams she learns about compassion, forgiveness, temptation and the power of true love.

To order call 800-524-2307 or visit www.MarniePehrson.com

www.ingramcontent.com/pod-product-compliance
Lightning Source LLC
Chambersburg PA
CBHW080659110426

42739CB00034B/3338